KINDLING

Daily Devotions for Busy Couples

B

KINDLING
Daily Devotions
for Busy Couples

PAT & JILL WILLIAMS
with Jerry B. Jenkins

THOMAS NELSON PUBLISHERS
Nashville

Published in Nashville, Tennessee, by Thomas
Nelson, Inc., and distributed in Canada by
Lawson Falle, Ltd., Cambridge, Ontario.

Printed in the United States of America.

Scripture quotations are from THE NEW KING
JAMES VERSION of the Bible. Copyright © 1979,
1980, 1982, Thomas Nelson, Inc., Publishers.

Library of Congress Cataloging-in-Publication Data

Williams, Pat, 1940-
  Kindling.

  1. Married people—Prayer-books and devotions—
English.   2. Devotional calendars.   I. Williams, Jill
(Jill M. P.)   II. Title.
BV4596.M3W55   1987   242′.2   87-20357
ISBN 0-8407-7606-3

1 2 3 4 5 6 7 8-92 91 90 89 88 87

To the hundreds of husbands and wives
who have written, called, or shared in person
what our written, spoken, or musical ministries
have meant to you.
Your encouragement has been
a treasure beyond words.

Acknowledgments

We never could have completed this book without the many hours of typing, photocopying, and mailing work of Delores Olson.

We also extend our gratitude to the ministry of Holt International Children's Services in Eugene, Oregon. If you desire more information about how you can help homeless children through the sponsorship program, the "Special Friends" medical support program, or special-needs adoptions, we encourage you to contact Susan Cox of Holt's national staff:

> Holt International Children's Services
> P.O. Box 2880
> Eugene, Oregon 97402
> (503) 687-2202

Pat and Jill Williams

Pat was for twelve years the general manager of the Philadelphia 76ers basketball team and is now the president and general manager of the Orlando Magic professional basketball club. He is a humorist and public speaker who appears several hundred times a year.

Jill is a former runner-up to Miss Illinois, a singer, violinist, and speaker. She has recorded three albums: "Beyond Imagination," "Completely Yours," and "Unsinkable."

Pat and Jill are the parents of eight children.

Other books by Pat include *The Gingerbread Man* and *The Power Within You* (both with Jerry Jenkins), *We Owed You One* (with Bill Lyon), and *Nothing But Winners* (with Ken Hussar).

Other books by Pat and Jill include *Rekindled* and *Keep the Fire Glowing* (both with Jerry Jenkins).

HOW TO USE THIS DEVOTIONAL

What an exciting commitment you've made, to spend a few moments together each day in devotion to Christ!

If this is new for you, or if it's something you practiced once and always intended to get back to, we have a few hints. First, carve out a few minutes each day to share the devotional. Experts tell us that if we do something daily for just six weeks, it becomes a habit, part of our lifestyle. We feel empty without it.

But you'll probably skip some days for one reason or another. It's important then not to despair, not to give up, and not to try to cover three days' worth of devotionals to make up for lost time. Simply pick up on the next appropriate date. Too many couples feel all is lost if they get off the track for a day or two, as if the point is never missing a day rather than enjoying those times when they *can* do this together.

Second, try a little variety. The husband may read the thoughts aloud one day, the wife the next. You might read them privately and then discuss them. If you're ambitious, memorize the key verse each day, or pick one each week. We list verses and longer portions by reference instead of writing them out for two reasons: (1) to leave more room for the brief devotional thoughts for the day and (2) to allow you to read the passages in the Bible version you prefer. Where we do quote verses within the devotional text, the verses are from the New King James Version.

Third, be flexible. If you have a half-hour, carefully read the Scripture, and use a commentary to help you understand each word. You might even start a notebook of what you learn. But if you have only five minutes, just read the devotional for the day, pray, and read the Scripture privately later when you have more time.

Fourth, remember that this is just a guide, a framework. Add whatever customs or routines you want to personalize this time for you and your spouse. You might add singing together or to each other, maintaining a prayer list, trading off leading in prayer, praying conversationally, or corresponding with missionaries.

Finally, this is no substitute for a more in-depth devotional life. Over the past several years, Pat has dug deeply into Bible commentaries on a daily basis, painstakingly moving through the Bible word by word and verse by verse, reading what the scholars have to say about the text and taking notes.

That should be the goal of anyone who can make the time to do it. Meanwhile, we offer *Kindling* as a way to keep your marriage spiritually warm. We want you to imagine that you and the Williamses are together each day for a brief Bible study. We will apply the spiritual truths of the Bible to the events of our everyday lives so we can make decisions according to God's Word.

We have deliberately taken a serendipitous approach, mostly keeping each devotional independent of the others. That way if you miss a day or two here and there, in most cases you will not have lost the flow. However, every once in a while we will spend an entire week on one topic. Sometimes this is because we are relating a vital occurrence in our lives, which cannot be shared with you in the short space of one devotional. Other times the topic dealt with was so important to the renewal of our own marriage that we want to give you an opportunity to walk through the steps in the process.

Certain themes and emphases—mostly on the home, marriage, and family—recur throughout the year, and we recognize the traditional holidays. Where does our material come from? From experiences in our lives and the lives of our eight children. From sources we trust. From Scripture. From godly authors. From every source of Christian reading material we can find.

More than anything else, we are readers. Our house is full of so many thousands of books that a few years ago we had to have someone come in and catalog them by the Dewey decimal system. It seems we spend every spare moment with our noses in books. For instance, you'll never catch us standing in line or waiting anywhere without a good book to redeem the time. Much of the material here has been gleaned from those sources, and we gratefully acknowledge all the helpful writers whose ideas have spawned these devotionals.

The story of our marriage, our crisis, and our marital rebirth is told in *Rekindled*. We have received hundreds of letters from couples whose marriages were rescued, due in part to that book. Yet we have received many other letters from heartbroken individuals for whom the message came too late.

Our prayer is that you will build hedges against the enemies of your marriage, and that each day's thoughts will serve as kindling for the campfire of your love and spiritual union.

KINDLING
Daily Devotions for Busy Couples

JANUARY 1

READ: Matthew 21:12–17
KEY VERSE: Matthew 21:16

Pat spoke recently in Elkhart, Indiana, and afterward a young married couple in matching outfits approached him.

The couple had gone through many of the same trials we had gone through in our marriage, but instead of having a big confrontation followed by weeks of turmoil, as we had experienced, this woman took her two young daughters and left her husband.

Thinking she was in love with another man, she saw him regularly. One time, after he had left the house, her four-year-old daughter said simply, "Mommy, you're naughty."

The words cut deeply. The woman examined herself to see why she was living so far from the principles she knew and believed (and which she had apparently taught her daughter).

Trying to re-establish the relationship with her daughter and—she thought—to help the little girl cope with a one-parent home, she told her, "From now on it'll just be you and Mommy, and we'll be best friends."

"Oh, no, we won't," the little girl said. "I'm not gonna be your friend until you're Daddy's friend."

Not let off the hook by her own preschooler, she sought help and found some in *Rekindled* (our book about the renewal of our marriage) and elsewhere, and the marriage has been reunited.

JANUARY 2

READ: Micah 6:6–8
KEY VERSE: Micah 6:8

Julius Erving, "Dr. J." to basketball fans, retired in 1987. He left a legacy to professional basketball that far exceeded his incredible skills. He was truly a man of humility, a soft-spoken giant among giants who outshined nearly everybody in performance, yet who said little in the way of self-promotion.

We were privileged to know him, for he played eleven years with the Philadelphia 76ers while Pat was general manager. When Dr. J. retired, sportswriters from all over the country called Pat for memories of the superstar Pat worked to acquire in 1976.

Pat's favorite Dr. J. story takes place in China, where several NBA players and executives and their wives were invited to teach clinics on basketball to the Chinese. The conditions were primitive almost everywhere, but no matter where we went, there was always one especially comfortable room. And it was always reserved for Julius and Turquoise Erving.

Finally, in the ancient capital city of Xian, Julius admitted to the entire group his deep embarrassment over the preferential treatment and said he hoped everyone understood that he neither asked for it nor was comfortable with it. In fact, he offered to give it up.

Rookie Gene Banks spoke for everyone: "Julius, we're just honored to have you on this trip. No room is too good for you."

JANUARY 3

READ: Philippians 3:7–14
KEY VERSE: Philippians 3:13

When you forget a name or your keys or an appointment, something has simply slipped your mind. But "forgetting those things which are behind" is an act of the will. While you're listing your resolutions for this new year—"reaching forward to those things which are ahead"— why not write down a few things from the past year you'd like to forget?

This activity might involve your entire family, just you and your spouse, or just you. (At the First Baptist Church, Orlando, we did this as a congregation.) List a secret sin, a major error, or anything you deeply regret. First, of course, deal with it before the Lord. He promises to forgive and forget, which is something we finite beings find very hard to do, especially the "forgetting" part.

If you do this activity as a family, the father should gather the lists, promising not to read them, and take them to a safe place (perhaps an empty garbage can) to burn them. When the ashes have cooled, he will bring them back to display to the family. Next time those sins are remembered, they should be thought of as ashes, for God sees them as even less than that.

A friend of Clara Barton, founder of the American Red Cross, asked her if she remembered a wrong done to her some years earlier. "No," replied Miss Barton. "I distinctly remember forgetting that." She had the right idea.

JANUARY 4

READ: Psalm 116:12–15
KEY VERSE: Psalm 116:15

What a sad day it was in our home when the call came. Mr. R. E. Littlejohn, one of Pat's dearest friends in the world, had died.

Mr. R. E., as everyone—including his wife—called him, had been the owner of the Spartanburg Phillies, a minor-league baseball club in South Carolina, when Pat was just getting started as a general manager. He was a quiet, godly man with a magnificent reputation and a shining testimony for Christ. When Pat knew he needed to receive Christ as his Savior, he went straight to Mr. R. E.

During Pat's few years in Spartanburg, he learned his craft, became a professional, and saw Mr. R. E. help smooth out Pat's rough edges. They kept in touch frequently over the years.

Mr. R. E. had a list of sixteen rules for success in the marketplace, which Pat memorized and practices to this day. Here are two highlights:

3. Never give the other fellow the impression that you think you know more than he does. You will destroy your influence with him and lose your ability to communicate properly.

11. A man must learn to handle his personal affairs before anyone will trust him with operating the affairs of a business.

JANUARY 5

READ: Ephesians 5:22–24
KEY VERSE: Ephesians 5:23

We had been married less than eight weeks when our first mini-crisis hit in 1972. It's a day we often chuckle about. If we had only known the real crises that were ahead because of the excess baggage we brought into our marriage, we might not have found it so amusing.

Jill came from a family where Dad was home every night at five-thirty. He never had evening meetings, never went out of town on business, and never worked weekends. It was a rude awakening for her to marry a sports executive who negotiated when the negotiatees wanted to, hosted every game (mostly at night), and traveled the country to scout other players.

She responded then, as later, by pouting. She took it personally every time Pat had to leave town. There were tears and fights, and Pat ran from them.

Then one morning, he received this notice:

"I, Jill P. Williams, do hereby solemnly swear, that from this day forward, I will not argue, fight, or pout to get my own way. My husband is the head of our home, and I will be submissive to his wishes."

It was signed in red ink, and the official seal was a Cheerio taped to the sheet. It became known as the Cheerios Pact.

JANUARY 6

READ: Genesis 12:1–8
KEY VERSE: Genesis 12:3

In her book *What Is a Family?* Edith Schaeffer gives a most picturesque answer to the question in the title. She thinks of a family as a living mobile, made up of human personalities. It is a work of art that takes years to produce but is never finished.

You've seen mobiles. Probably the most common are those that hang over a baby's crib. Various objects, held by strings, float in relationship to each other, yet independent of each other. Together, they make the whole.

The unit we call a family provides our anchor. The family has movement. It's constantly in motion. There are freedom and independence within limits, yet the individuals are part of the whole.

There never comes a day when two people in the family are at the same point in their individual growth. Each is developing independently in social, intellectual, physical, and spiritual areas.

Author and pastor Dr. John A. Huffman, Jr., says that every person in the family has an effect upon the others in all those areas. "Over a period of years, these fragile strings strengthen into strong, invisible steel which holds great weight, but is also capable of enormous freedom."

We want our family to be bound together by invisible steel.

JANUARY 7

READ: Titus 3:1–7
KEY VERSE: Titus 3:2

Since we've moved to Florida, we've seen how the sports seasons can overlap in a warm-weather climate. Basketball overlaps with soccer, which runs into baseball. Gymnastics spans all three.

Pat was running our private car-pool recently, trying to get Karyn from gymnastics to soccer, Bobby to and from baseball, and Jim to soccer. With Jim in the car, Pat found Bobby still in the middle of baseball practice, so he went to get Karyn.

That put Jim and Karyn together in the car with no other kids around—a rare occurrence in a family of eight children. Karyn chattered away at her big brother while he sat munching a high-carbohydrate snack his coach had recommended. It was developed during World War II as an easy-to-store, nutritious food for the troops.

With nothing to distract him, Jim maintained eye contact with his little sister and nodded and uh-huhed as she talked excitedly about her gymnastics training, her coach, and her teammates.

Suddenly, Karyn looked up, leaned forward to pull herself closer to Pat, and exulted, "Dad! I really like it when Jimmy eats this war food. It makes him so nice to me. He's listening to me and really paying attention. I wish he'd eat more of it!"

A little attention and a little humility are all it takes to make someone's day. You don't even have to invest in war food!

JANUARY 8

READ: Mark 10:1–12
KEY VERSE: Mark 10:9

When Dr. John A. Huffman, Jr. (pastor and author) was in college, he took a course on the sociology of the family and learned about several types of persons who should not get married. Believe it or not, careerists (those who put their jobs above all else) were listed along with criminal psychopaths and homosexuals.

"As the professor described that personality type, I flushed with embarrassment. I could see myself. It seemed so unfair that I should never marry. I set about to modify my careerist bent, and God has divinely ordered my priorities exactly the opposite of how I would have been inclined to design them.

"My subsequent exposure to Senate Chaplain Dr. Richard C. Halverson confronted me with how important it is for every human being to put God first, one's marriage partner second, one's children third, one's brothers and sisters in Christ fourth, and one's work fifth.

"To make my work number five in priority makes me better at it than if I allow it to be number one. [My wife] Anne made an interesting observation. She said, 'That symmetry does make sense. After all, John, you have God for eternity, me until death, our daughters until they come of age, and brothers and sisters in Christ as long as we are in some kind of proximity to each other. And your job? Well, thus far it's been as short as three years and as long as eight.'"

JANUARY 9

READ: Ephesians 5:15–17
KEY VERSE: Ephesians 5:16

Were your New Year's resolutions frivolous this time around? Is it too early to ask if any remain unbroken? If they centered on such things as swearing off chocolate or not yelling at the kids, you may already be on thin ice.

Better our resolutions should emulate those of the Great Awakening preacher, Jonathan Edwards:

Resolved, to live with all my might while I do live.

Resolved, never to lose one moment of time, to improve it in the most profitable way I possibly can.

Resolved, never to do anything which I should despise or think meanly of in another.

Resolved, never to do anything out of revenge.

Resolved, never to do anything which I should be afraid to do if it were the last hour of my life.

Pat, as an obsessive-compulsive, type-A personality, has learned to reset his priorities over the years, putting wife and family ahead of all other pursuits except the pursuit of God. But still his basic plan is the same: to redeem the time.

Whether improving his physical condition, eating right, reading, studying, working, speaking, ministering, parenting, husbanding, administrating, promoting, or selling, his heart's desire is to do it as if it were the last hour of his life.

JANUARY 10

READ: Psalm 5:1–8
KEY VERSE: Psalm 5:8

Why is adoption still so controversial? We suppose people who have a lot of their own children get some teasing and questions, too, but having several adoptees *really* brings out the comments. Reactions to our two adoption experiences (two kids each time) have been interesting, occasionally bordering on offensive.

"Why do you people want more kids?"

"You must have a screw loose."

Well, maybe we do. The fact is, we love children. And when our doctor advised us not to have any more homegrown ones, we assumed it was of God. There is a great need for adoptive parents, we felt blessed and able, and so we made the decision.

Jill always felt that way. Pat came to the realization slowly. In fact, when she first mentioned it, years ago, he wouldn't even discuss it. When she pressed him on it, he said, "How could I love a child that wasn't even mine?"

It was a frightening, intimidating concept to him, and it became a major bone of contention in the marriage, along with many other things. But when Pat asked God to guide his life as David does in this psalm, Pat became more sensitive to Jill's needs. He was soon obsessed with her desire to adopt a Korean orphan.

We'd like to tell you the whole story.

JANUARY 11

READ: Psalm 69:5–18
KEY VERSE: Psalm 69:17

After years of either ignoring or arguing with Jill whenever she brought up her dream to adopt a foreign baby, Pat finally saw the light. In working on the things he felt God had pointed out to him as weaknesses in his role as a husband, he felt compelled to add to the list his insensitivity to one of Jill's lifetime dreams.

Three children had already blessed the home, and his feeling had been, "If you want more, let's have more—of our own." Jill felt frustrated, stifled in her heartfelt longing. She knew down deep that if it was of God, Pat would have to be excited about it. Meanwhile, what

7

was she supposed to do with the inner voice that told her she would mother adopted children someday?

If Pat's lack of enthusiasm was a message from God, she wondered if she could trust the still, small voice that piqued her anticipation. But during the marriage crisis, Pat put her desire on his list, not knowing how he would accomplish meeting it. He was dealing with several other pressing problems in the relationship that just had to be resolved, but the orphan issue was forced upon him in a way he couldn't ignore. In fact, being in the middle of the darkest days of the marriage, he hadn't expected to be emotionally moved by anything but his suffering wife.

JANUARY 12

READ: Psalm 121:1–8
KEY VERSE: Psalm 121:8

Pat was standing in line at a farm, waiting for a fresh Christmas turkey—of all things—when he became aware of the couple in front of him. Their baby was Asian, but they were clearly Anglo-Saxon. He wondered. He asked.

Sure enough, the baby was Korean. The couple must have thought him strange, a grown man, well dressed and clearly an individual of responsibility, breaking down before them. He fought for enough composure to ask more and more questions.

How had they decided to do this? How did one go about it? How was it working out? He was convinced God had put him in that line at that time for that purpose.

Pat asked if he could have their address and phone number, but they were reluctant to share that information. Somehow, he convinced them that he was legitimate, that his wife had always wanted to adopt a Korean orphan, and that he would love to have her meet them and let her and the children see the baby.

That very evening, the family visited the couple and their baby. As it turned out, they lived just a few blocks away in Moorestown, N.J. Jill was still suffering severe depression over the state of the marriage. She had lost all feeling for Pat, yet she had to endure this social situation. Did she really want to adopt, when she wasn't even sure about what kind of marriage she had?

JANUARY 13

READ: Psalm 55:1–17
KEY VERSE: Psalm 55:16

In January of 1983, Pat called all over the country, finally reaching the Holt International Children's Services in Eugene, Oregon. They sent a detailed application to consider.

We held a family meeting to see how the children felt about it and what they would want, a brother or a sister. They were thrilled with the idea, but Karyn wanted a sister and the boys wanted a brother.

Jill, still not sure where the marriage was heading, looked to Pat. He naively thought that adoption would help solve some problems, and he said, "Why not?" February 1 was the date on our application for two children, a boy and a girl, brother and sister. One of the rules of the agency was that the children had to be related to each other.

Jill's fear deepened. Pat was trying everything he knew to salvage the marriage, but she didn't want to adopt children—even though it had been her lifelong dream—unless she and Pat were on solid footing. She hoped and prayed that her feelings would change before bringing needy children into that environment.

Jill's excitement about the adoption grew with Pat's determination to rejuvenate the marriage. Had things moved more swiftly with the adoptees, would she have backed out and not accepted them?

JANUARY 14

READ: Revelation 22:1–9
KEY VERSE: Revelation 22:5

An apple grower was asked what he thought heaven would be like. He said, "I sure hope I find trees. I don't want golden streets where the sun never sets. I want sunsets, October frosts, and January icicles— with a few March gales thrown in for good measure. It takes all those to give an apple the right flavor."

Well, that's a nice sentiment and told with delicious descriptions of earthly beauties, but the fact is, there will be no sunsets in heaven, for there will be no sun. Today's key verse is clear that there will be no need for "lamp nor light of the sun, for the Lord God gives them light."

It's hard for children—and sometimes for adults—to envision what heaven will be like. To the uninitiated, it may sound boring. According to the views of the secular world, we'll be wearing white robes, floating on clouds, and eternally playing harps.

Scripture paints an entirely different picture. Our friends from Walk Through the Bible Ministries point out at least seven things we will do in heaven. We will rest (Rev. 14:13), fellowship (Heb. 12:23; Rev. 19:7–9; 22:14), know God perfectly (Rev. 21:3; 22:4), worship (Rev. 19:1–8; 22:8–9), enjoy God and our new home (Rev. 19:7; 22:14), serve God (Rev. 22:3), and reign with God (Matt. 25:21, 23; Rev. 22:5).

We're ready. Are you?

JANUARY 15

READ: Colossians 3:18–21
KEY VERSE: Colossians 3:20

Jill remembers well the first time she got Karyn ready for the photographer. Just a few months old, plump and rosy-cheeked Karyn had a tiny turned-up nose and very little hair. "I literally had to tape the pink bow to the top of her head. Still, to me she looked like an angel."

All parents think their little kids are angels, but the angelic moments become less frequent as the children grow older. Only as we teach them to know and love the Father can we help them acquire celestial traits.

We want our kids to learn to do God's will. For them, while growing up, that generally means obeying their parents, plain and simple. The Scriptures tell us that we have been put in charge of them and that they are to obey us in the Lord, "for this is well pleasing to the Lord."

In a way, that can be a security blanket for children. God has ordained parents, so if children obey their parents, they'll be obeying God.

Pat, in his wise and uniquely nonyelling manner, asks the kids, "Who wants to be blessed of God?" As they all raise their hands—Michael imitating rather than understanding—Pat says, "The way for you to be blessed of God is to obey Mommy and me."

Simple to understand; not so easy to do.

JANUARY 16

READ: Colossians 3:20–25
KEY VERSE: Colossians 3:20

Of course we think all of our kids are the cutest, most lovable ever produced. Don't you think the same of yours? But apparently our oldest, Jim, has moved out of the cute kid stage and is emerging into what one of our adult friends refers to as "an absolute doll."

Still, we weren't prepared for the barrage of phone calls that started with his seventh-grade school year in a new town. When we got five in one day, a couple from girls Jim hadn't even heard of, Jill had had enough.

She began to tell the girls that he couldn't come to the phone just then. (He couldn't come to the phone because he didn't know it was for him, and he didn't know it was for him because she wasn't about to tell him until later.) She does deliver all his messages, to save face on both ends.

Are we old-fashioned to think it's tacky for girls to call boys? If we are, we're old-fashioned in other ways, too. We think kids want rules and limits. We think they need the security of knowing we won't be pushovers every time they complain.

We limit time on the phone, assign chores to each child, make reading a priority, and are crazy enough to believe that if we keep our kids busy, they won't have time to get into big trouble. Are you old-fashioned, too? Hang in there.

JANUARY 17

READ: 1 Peter 3:8–10
KEY VERSE: 1 Peter 3:9

For the next four days, we want to run through the basics of Dr. Ed Wheat's B-E-S-T system, as outlined in his *Love Life for Every Married Couple*. His principles of Blessing, Edifying, Sharing, and Touching literally rekindled our love and rescued our marriage in 1983.

Blessing simply means speaking well of your spouse and responding with good words. Silence can be a blessing sometimes, too, according to Ephesians 4:29: "Let no corrupt communication proceed out of your mouth, but what is good for necessary edification, that it may impart grace to the hearers." Beware of the tongue. It is generally wet and liable to slip.

We try to bless each other simply by doing kind things for each other. We try to remember to show thankfulness and appreciation orally. That is not always easy for Pat, and as Jill points out the need to do that in social situations, Pat remembers to practice the principle at home as well. Also, we pray for each other's good and for the highest blessing of God in each other's life.

An important key, according to Dr. Wheat, is that no matter how you are treated by your partner, blessing should always be your response. It sounds simple, and in a way it is. Commit yourself to doing kind things in order to live in peace and treat your spouse as you would treat a guest in your home.

JANUARY 18

READ: Proverbs 24:3–4
KEY VERSE: Proverbs 24:3

This is day two in our treatment of Dr. Ed Wheat's B-E-S-T system for happy marriages.

Edifying means building up your spouse. There are three basic ways to do this:

1. *Personal encouragement.* Verbal praise and frequent genuine compliments leave no room for criticism. Men are more used to taking criticism than women are as a rule, but neither marriage partner is built up by it. Leave teasing alone. Tyron Edwards wrote, "A deserved and discriminating compliment is often one of the strongest encouragements and incentives to the diffident and self-distrustful." We believe that encouragement is as vital to the soul as oxygen is to the body.

2. *Inner strengthening.* You can edify with a word fitly spoken (see Prov. 25:11).

3. *The establishment of peace and harmony by studying your spouse.* Learn likes and dislikes. Discover inner needs, desires, and strengths. Be interested. Care to know. Pay the compliment of becoming the world's greatest expert on your partner.

Pat has learned that Jill loves surprises. She loves to be dated, to get cards, to receive flowers, and to be romanced. She maintains that courting was fun, and there's no reason it shouldn't still be. She likes for Pat to use on her some of those creative juices he uses to promote professional basketball.

JANUARY 19

READ: Genesis 2:21–24
KEY VERSE: Genesis 2:24

Day three of Dr. Wheat's B-E-S-T system for happy marriages:

Sharing means just what it says, and nothing is left out. Though it's often difficult for a man to open up, both partners must share their time, activities, interests, concerns, ideas, innermost thoughts, spiritual walks, family objectives, and goals.

One of the major changes in our relationship since the crisis we wrote about in *Rekindled* involves our going to bed and getting up at the same time. We've found that many couples whose marriages are in trouble report their bedtimes have changed for some reason.

The problem began with Pat having to attend 76er games and Jill only going occasionally. Later, with the advent of cable television, Pat found he could watch basketball games almost around the clock. He was late to bed; then he rose early to study the Bible, and go to work. Jill was asleep when Pat went to bed and still asleep when he got up. After a while, it was as if two people simply boarded in the same house together.

It's crucial to develop a sensitive awareness between you and to follow the biblical principle of becoming one flesh.

JANUARY 20

READ: Mark 10:13–16
KEY VERSE: Mark 10:13

The last day in our four-day explanation of Dr. Ed Wheat's B-E-S-T system for happy marriages:

Touching is a cornerstone for the whole program. Without touching, the rest won't make for a long-term, happy relationship. Dr. Wheat says, "A tender touch tells us we are cared for. It calms our fears, soothes pain, brings comfort, and gives emotional security. We have a deep, unsatisfied need for the warmth, reassurance, and intimacy of nonsexual touching."

There are only three accepted ways in our society for men to touch: a handshake, contact sports, and sex. The problem is that men usually use touch only as a sex signal. A woman's need for affection is as great as a man's need for sex.

When he was in high school, Pat knew his buddies would snicker and make fun of him if he held a girl's hand. "It's almost as if you think that no matter where you are or how old you are, one of your old friends is sure to jump out from behind a tree and make fun of you if you hold your wife's hand."

On the bus to and from the victory parade for the 76ers when they won the 1983 NBA championship, Pat held Jill's hand. Sure enough, the next day, the owner of the club teased him about it. But he'd made the commitment and didn't care what anyone thought, not even his boss.

JANUARY 21

READ: Proverbs 31:30–31
KEY VERSE: Proverbs 31:30

Today is Jill's birthday, and while Pat will undoubtedly try to make it a special day for her, in many ways he will treat her as he has ever since he recommitted himself to the marriage more than five years ago.

It's standard operating procedure for Pat to encourage Jill just as much as she encourages him. She is encouraged to buy orchestra tickets and take a friend or have a date with son Jim or Bob for dinner at a nice restaurant. Jill has also had Pat's permission and enthusiastic encouragement to take Jim to Germany, then four years later to Israel. She took Karyn to Scotland last year.

He urged her to follow her dream and take flying lessons, to record solo vocal albums, and to write her own songs. Jill feels she has been given every opportunity to grow and be all she has wanted to be without Pat's feeling or acting threatened if she learns something about which he is not knowledgeable.

This concept seems foreign to some couples we have known. The husband seems to try everything in his power to keep his wife from learning or doing anything without him. Then he doesn't think she's very interesting because she doesn't have anything to talk about. We do plenty together, but it's the encouragement to act independently sometimes that makes Jill feel special.

JANUARY 22

READ: Proverbs 4:1–9
KEY VERSE: Proverbs 4:1

Jim is our quiet one. But Bob is the type who will call his dad to make sure he will be at Little League practice: "And what time will you be there?" Jim doesn't say much. Yet we know he has the same need of attention and approval from his father.

When Jim's current favorite seventh-grade girl had a birthday, Pat and Jim went to look for a card. Pat tried to offer a little advice, but Jim wanted to handle it himself. Pat teased him, "Listen, you live with two of the greatest experts on what makes a relationship fun and exciting. If you listen to Mom and Dad, you'll be awesome with the girls!"

"Ah, Dad. You guys only know what worked in 1970."

The olden days.

Not even our youngest takes counsel from oldsters. Once Michael, our two-year-old, was visiting Grandma and Grandpa Paige in Chicago, and he slept in a room right next to theirs. Every time he moved in the night, he hit the wall and woke up Grandpa.

Seeking a solution, Grandpa had a suggestion the next day. "You might get hurt banging against the wall in the night, Michael. Why don't you put your stuffed Shamu whale next to the wall?"

"Because then Shamu will get hurt, Grandpa!"

JANUARY 23

READ: Joel 1:1–7
KEY VERSE: Joel 1:5

The government reports that the demand for beer and wine is falling in America. Such statistics and reports jump out at Pat, because alcohol was a factor in his father's life.

It's encouraging to know that alcohol consumption is going down, but Health Secretary Otis Bowen released figures—as part of the *Sixth Special Report to Congress on Alcohol and Health*—showing that 18 million Americans have alcohol-related problems. Of those, 10.6 million are alcoholics.

James Williams wasn't an alcoholic, but he couldn't handle liquor. Pat remembers the almost-comical results of his father trying to carve a roast in front of guests after having drunk too much.

New Year's mornings were reruns every year as the family had to tiptoe past the couch where Pat's father slept off the effects of the all-night party.

When Pat was a sophomore in high school, he was called into the house to hear the news that his father, under the influence, had driven his Volkswagen under a parked truck and nearly killed himself. After that, Mr. Williams simply quit drinking.

His father's resolve, combined with the scares and scars of those past scenes, made Pat decide never to take the first drink. And he never has.

JANUARY 24

READ: Matthew 19:13–15
KEY VERSE: Matthew 19:14

That Jesus loved and revered children is as clear as anything in the New Testament. Yet one of Jill's pet peeves concerns adults treating children as less than human beings.

Sometimes adults refer to children who are present at a gathering as if they can't hear or speak for themselves. Often adults listen but don't hear.

Karyn went one day with Jill to the Bible study she teaches. During the opening prayer request time, when the women were to ask for prayer for themselves or for a friend in trouble, seven-year-old Karyn mentioned her teacher, who had undergone surgery.

Later, on the way home, Jill asked a very quiet Karyn what she was thinking about. Very disappointed, Karyn said, "No one prayed for my teacher."

Jill was chagrined to realize that even she had forgotten Karyn's prayer request. How important it is to think of children as full-fledged human beings with a right to be heard.

That wasn't the first lesson Jill has learned from Karyn. Once, after Jill and Karyn had sung before fifteen hundred people at a prayer breakfast and Karyn had received many compliments, Jill added her praise on the way home. Wistfully, Karyn observed, "You were the last one to tell me."

JANUARY 25

READ: Psalm 30
KEY VERSE: Psalm 30:6

By the time June rolled around in 1983, God had put the marriage back together. Pat had zeroed in on the areas where God had showed him he'd been insensitive over the years, plus he started applying the B-E-S-T principles from Dr. Ed Wheat's *Love Life for Every Married Couple.*

Meanwhile, though it had been painful and slow, Jill saw her emotions return. She went from having no feeling about anything or anyone to missing Pat when he was away. She eventually dared to believe that this wasn't just a temporary turning over of a new leaf on his part. He was sincere, and even if he failed, there was no question he had changed, and he loved her.

It would be many, many months before she could let her guard down and allow herself to trust that the marriage wouldn't fall apart. But she became convinced that the family and the marriage had been reborn and that she was ready to bring another child into it. Even two adoptees from across the ocean.

That summer, the social worker called. "I don't have a brother-sister combination, but I do have two little sisters. And boy, are they cute!" We couldn't wait until she arrived with the tiny black-and-white photographs. The kids were ecstatic. Pat worried about the hatchet job the orphanage had done on one girl's hair. Jill just knew, *These are our girls.*

JANUARY 26

READ: Psalm 56:3–13
KEY VERSES: Psalm 56:3–4

God's timing is always perfect. We didn't know how long it would take to get the girls, but He did. And in the meantime, our marriage was reborn. It was better than ever. The B-E-S-T principles were rubbing off on the kids, and we were one big happy family, about to get bigger.

We had copies of the pictures made and sent to Jill's parents and Pat's mother. The Paiges were reserved but happy for us. They had long known of the strain in the marriage, and then they learned of the crisis, so they were naturally concerned that Jill's life needed no more current complications.

Mrs. Williams was reserved, too, but both she and the Paiges would quickly warm up to the new grandchildren.

It was late August, and we were waiting, eager and anxious. We probably drove the poor social worker crazy. She kept telling us she'd call when she had any news, but we checked frequently anyway. "Any word? Any idea? Any guesses? When?"

We spent a few days at our retreat in Eagles' Mere, Pennsylvania, and took a call there about possible flights the kids could be on. It was like going through a pregnancy for Jill. The waiting, the tension, the longing.

Then the news. A Korean Air jet, Flight 007, had been blown out of the sky by the Russians. Panic and disbelief.

JANUARY 27

READ: Psalm 46
KEY VERSE: Psalm 46:10

Our girls had not been on Flight 007. But what if they had been? What if there was retaliation? What if another Korean jet was fired upon? We were scared to death, and all we could do was trust in God. Without our faith in Him, worry would have destroyed us. Finally, we went back home to wait. And wait.

Jill had already been through all of Karyn's clothes. She had moved furniture into the girls' room, stenciled the room with Victorian hearts, and bought teddy bears.

By September, we were still waiting. All three kids were in school, coming home every day expectant, wanting to know what we'd heard, when their sisters would arrive.

On Tuesday, September 13, Pat called Jill. He told her to sit down. "They'll be here tomorrow night on Northwest Flight 008. The nearness of the number to the ill-fated 007 is chilling, but we're trusting the Lord."

It was impossible to sleep, so Jill stayed up till the wee hours putting the finishing touches on the furnishings and the room. The next morning she sent three apprehensive kids off to school. In the afternoon, while washing her hair, she wondered if they'd like it. Her hair. She felt silly. Never mind how they'd like America or their new family, what about Jill's hair?

JANUARY 28

READ: Psalm 116:1–7
KEY VERSE: Psalm 116:2

The kids came home from school wired. They couldn't sit still. No one ate much dinner. Jill tried on four different outfits before finally getting dressed. She called two favorite baby sitters and the housekeeper, a Puerto Rican grandmother who had lived with us and cared for the three kids, and invited them to go to the airport. Jill's best friend, Betsey, also agreed to go.

At the airport, the parking lots were full. Pat told a policeman of our predicament and why we were there. He let us park near the door and pledged there would be no ticket.

Though we were two hours early, it seemed as if we were the last ones at the gate. It was bursting with people who had heard what we were up to. Three local TV stations were there with cameras rolling. The print media had photographers and reporters. They all wanted to interview us, but mostly they wanted to talk to Jim, Bob, and Karyn.

After a final briefing by the social worker, we watched the planes come in, wondering if each was the one. Not long ago we heard the famous storyteller Garrison Keillor tell of a family in Minnesota who went to the airport (early) to pick up their Korean baby. It was us all over. Jill willed each plane safely down the runway, hoping, wishing, praying. Finally, the announcement came. Flight 008 was on the ground.

JANUARY 29

READ: Luke 1:26–38
KEY VERSE: Luke 1:37

We watched the jet taxi to the gate, but the crowd was so thick, the first passengers disembarking could hardly get through. When they saw the TV cameras, they craned their necks to see what was the big deal. We didn't know that adopted babies were always the last to deplane. That knowledge would have made us a little less tense.

Our kids' faces were glued to the ramp, and they clutched the teddies, ready to give them to the girls. Finally, after everyone else was off the plane, a lady carrying two bedraggled little girls appeared. Seeing her carry them up the ramp was like seeing them born into our family.

Jill froze as if unable to move. The children were hers just as sure as if they had come from her womb. As she worked her way through the crowd and the glaring, flashing lights, the woman spoke and Jill read her lips. "Where's the mommy?"

The mommy, Jill thought. *That's me.* No question, no hesitation, no second thoughts. *These girls are looking for their new mommy, and I'm it.*

The woman was directed to Jill, who seemed to shift into slow motion. She felt herself numbly reaching out to Yoo Jin, now Sarah. The housekeeper reached for Yoo Jung, now Andrea, but a cameraman called out, "No! Let her dad hold her."

JANUARY 30

READ: Luke 1:39–56
KEY VERSE: Luke 1:49

We caught a glimpse of each other's eyes over the crush of people as we stood there holding our two Oriental dolls. We wept. They didn't look much like dolls just then. They were scared, pale, and exhausted. Their escort, Sally, encouraged us to sit down.

Jim, Bob, and Karyn pressed the teddy bears upon them and wanted to hug them. Sally gave us one bag, had us sign some papers, and told us the girls hadn't slept for twenty-seven hours. She briefed us on what they'd eaten, left a letter with us, introduced us to Grandma Holt, and headed for her return flight to Minneapolis.

It was a thrill to meet Grandma Holt, the woman behind the largest Christian adoption agency in the world. They say she's grandmother to more than fifty thousand Korean children. She had come just for the delivery of Sarah and Andrea.

After yet another final briefing by the social worker, we headed home. Our new family totaled seven, and with two baby sitters and the housekeeper, there were ten of us in the van. Sarah fell asleep on Jill's shoulder, and Bob and Andrea fell asleep on the way home. We wondered if the girls would sleep through the night. They awoke at home, and Karyn helped get them ready for bed. Then we all watched ourselves on the news. After that, we hoped for a good night's sleep. Ha!

JANUARY 31

READ: Psalm 126
KEY VERSE: Psalm 126:5

The girls were so fatigued they could hardly keep their eyes open. They didn't understand television, and it was evident they had no idea what they were looking at, even when we tried to point them out on the screen.

Around midnight, we put everyone to bed. We thought. Jim and Bob and Karyn dropped off immediately, having been up so far past their bedtimes. But they were in their own beds in their own rooms in their own house with their own family. So were Sarah and Andrea, but they didn't know or understand that yet.

Suddenly, in their weariness, they began crying uncontrollably, wailing mournfully for Ommah (mama), someone from the orphanage in Korea. It broke our hearts, even though we had been coached to expect it. We had read years ago of the famous former big-league pitcher, Jim Lonborg, who had endured for days the plaintive sobbing of his adopted Korean child.

Jet lag, confusion, exhaustion, hunger, and homesickness combined to make a miserable night. Jill took the girls to the master bedroom and held them, crying, until three A.M. Then it was down to the kitchen for crackers, bananas, and milk. When Jill found the words for these foods in the Korean-English dictionary and tried to say them, the black-haired sisters smiled through their tears.

FEBRUARY 1

READ: Psalm 128
KEY VERSE: Psalm 128:3

Following their after-midnight snack, the girls and Jill slept fitfully till six o'clock. The older children stayed home from school the next day to be with their new sisters. The first order of business was to bathe them and shampoo their hair. Then they were dressed up in new clothes and taken to the doctor for checkups.

They still seemed forlorn and lonely, and all they wanted to do was eat. They were both tiny, but could they ever pack away the food! They

21

had a big breakfast, but they wanted to carry bags of crackers with them everywhere. (Anything to keep them happy that first day!)

We had chicken soup and rice for lunch and chicken and rice for dinner. Just before dinner, a local television station called and asked to come by during the meal. Why not?

The cameras were rolling as Jill fed everyone rice, the Korean dictionary close at hand. Due to all the excitement and the lights, Karyn threw up on the table. Jill was mortified until the TV man said, "That'll be a great take." Everyone laughed, cleaned up, and kept shooting.

From that day on, the girls started adjusting. They became such outgoing, affectionate little things that they wanted to hug and kiss and be held by everyone they met.

FEBRUARY 2

READ: 1 Peter 3:1–7
KEY VERSE: 1 Peter 1:3

If today was Beautiful Women's Day, and we waited with bated breath while one of them looked for her shadow, we might wait a long time. Too many of them hate to even look in the mirror.

Research shows that 98 percent of American women are dissatisfied with their looks. You'll probably be as surprised as Pat was to learn that the 2 percent who *are* satisfied are not among the beauties. They are simply women who don't worry so much about themselves.

Jill wasn't surprised to find out that most beautiful women fall into the majority who don't like their looks. She was a multicontest beauty winner and first runner-up in the 1972 Miss Illinois contest, yet she still fights the same self-image battle.

It sounds strange—to men, at least—but she's in good company. Beautiful television actress Valerie Bertinelli has said, "I get these thoughts like *I used to be pretty; what's going on? I'm not aging well at all.*"

"Dallas" beauty Morgan Brittany says when she looks in the mirror, she sees "someone with features that are way too big—big eyes, big teeth, big smile, all on a very small face."

Strange as it may seem, a woman in your life today may need encouragement. And she may never tell you.

FEBRUARY 3

READ: Proverbs 1:1–9
KEY VERSE: Proverbs 1:8

Have you ever wondered why it seems the only thing a star athlete can think of to say when the TV cameras pick him up on the sideline is, "Hi, Mom!"?

Is it just lack of imagination? Is there no girlfriend, no former coach, no buddy or brother or sister anywhere who deserves a greeting, too?

We like to think it's evidence of a special bonding between mothers and sons, and Jill, of course, can testify to this five times over.

When Bobby was nine, we arranged for him to fly by himself from Orlando to Chicago to spend time with Jill's parents. Naturally, we would escort him to the plane, and the airline would take respon- sibility for him until Grandma and Grandpa picked him up. His first question was, "Who's taking me to the airport?"

"Who do you want?" Jill asked. "Mom or Dad?"

Bob's answer was sure and certain, to our delight. "You, Mom, be- cause if anything goes wrong, I don't think Dad could handle it. You know everything there is to know, and all Dad knows about is basket- ball and baseball."

And when Grandpa got third-base box seats at the Cubs game where the TV cameras showed the fans to the whole nation on a cable net- work, Jill saw her nickname on Bobby's homemade sign: "Hi, Mo!"

FEBRUARY 4

READ: 1 Corinthians 15:8–11
KEY VERSE: 1 Corinthians 15:10

As a board member of the Baseball Chapel, I was responsible for lining up chapel speakers on Sunday mornings for the Philadelphia Phillies. A young man from Ohio named Cordell Brown had been rec- ommended to me, so in 1980, I invited him to address the Phillies and Pirates before their game at Veterans Stadium. I asked him to come early for a tour of the ballpark.

I was stunned when he arrived. He was a serious victim of cerebral palsy. I had seen more mildly afflicted people in wheelchairs, but he insisted on getting around on his own. He lurched as he walked and had hardly any control of small motor muscles. Eating was a major chore, and he spoke with great difficulty.

As we toured the park, people must have wondered what in the world I was doing with the man. When a couple of dozen Pirates and Phillies gathered for the chapel service, the difference between Cordell and the gifted physical specimens was enormous.

His message was powerful. "If you hit .350 and make $1 million a year, one of these days they'll still close the lid on that box, and then you and I will be the same. I don't need what you have in life, but you sure need what I have. And that's a personal relationship with Jesus Christ."

That was one chapel service I'll never forget.

FEBRUARY 5

READ: Isaiah 25:1–8
KEY VERSE: Isaiah 25:8

Jill recently received a letter from a dear friend who had moved back to Great Britain a few years ago. Helen and Jill had grown close and had corresponded frequently until Helen married and we moved to Florida.

They hadn't communicated across the ocean for a few months, but still Pat was unprepared for the tears that came when Jill finished reading the letter. "What's wrong, Jill?"

"I miss Helen a lot."

Few men are comfortable in the presence of a crying woman, and like most husbands would do, Pat tried to change the subject. Without condemnation, Jill said, "I don't want you to take my attention away from Helen. I miss her, and I just want you to cry with me for a minute."

Jill didn't want Pat literally to cry, though there are times when that, too, is perfectly appropriate and therapeutic. What Jill wanted at that moment was to know that Pat cared and was willing to hold her while she hurt.

That willingness tells a wife that her husband is sensitive, and that it's all right to express honest emotion in front of him. Pat prefers a wife who has the capacity for such love and loyalty toward her friends that she can be moved to tears at their memories.

FEBRUARY 6

READ: Joshua 1:1–9
KEY VERSE: Joshua 1:9

We know in our heads that worry is sin, yet communicating that truth to our souls and hearts is another matter. Who doesn't worry at one time or another?

Here are four practical words to use in handling the inevitable the next time it crops up to trouble you:

1. *Presence.* Claim God's presence. He promises that we are not alone. God is always with us. (See our key verse for today, plus Isa. 41:10 and Matt. 28:20.)

2. *Promises.* Get into God's Word and study the promises. Scholars tell us there are nearly seventy-five hundred of them! A thorough study of the promises of God could take years. They are ours to claim. (See Pss. 4:8; 37:4–5; Prov. 3:5–6; and Isa. 26:3–4.)

3. *Prayer.* We're talking about the real thing. Be specific. Name your worry. Like a tired hiker dumps his backpack on the ground, dump your worry on God. (See Ps. 55:22; Phil. 4:6–7; and 1 Pet. 5:7.)

4. *Patience.* This is the toughest one. No one likes to worry for long. It grates on you, wears you down, and leaves you frazzled. Yet we know we're not supposed to worry; we are to have patience and trust the Lord. (See Ps. 27:14; Isa. 40:31; and Rom. 8:25.)

FEBRUARY 7

READ: Philippians 1:1–6
KEY VERSE: Philippians 1:6

Sarah and Andrea are our little Oriental dolls, but they aren't above a little mischief now and then. The other day Jill noticed a whole fresh banana in the wastebasket in their room. To a health-food nut (Jill prefers "nutrition expert"), wasting a banana or other good-for-you food is a cardinal sin.

Neither of the girls would own up to the crime. When Jill demanded to know the culprit, they pointed at each other. There was no way to tell who was telling the truth, so it quickly became evident to Jill that she had lost the round.

At times like that, Jill admits, she is tempted to throw in the towel. She's tempted to ignore wrongs, clear the table herself, straighten a room, pick up after the kids, put away their sports equipment, and generally let good parenting slip through the cracks.

That's also when she thinks back on one of her favorite books: *Growing Together: Mother and Child* by Lenore Ruth. The author writes, "Ask not that God will make your child what you consider perfect. Rather ask that God will enable your child to fulfill the potential the Maker built in.

"Pray that God will forge an unshakable bond between you and your child—one which becomes a friendship that warms and cheers you both."

FEBRUARY 8

READ: Galatians 5:16–26
KEY VERSE: Galatians 5:22

When Andrea was five, she got in the van after school one day and said, "Look at my report card, Mom!"

Jill was thrilled to find all Satisfactories or Satisfactory-pluses, and she said so.

Andrea beamed. "Do you think I have to have the red plate?"

We have a red plate with the words *Today You Are Special* on it, which we use for various occasions. It might be a child's first day in kindergarten, first lost tooth, first goal kicked, first successful cartwheel, first basket made, first ball caught, or even a day of having been extrahelpful or kind.

We find our kids want and need praise and recognition, and giving positive feedback results in more good behavior than offering criticism does. We see bad behavior habits changing more quickly when we turn on the spotlight instead of nagging.

When Andrea lost her first tooth, she was so proud and happy she just couldn't quit smiling, which of course made the gap show even more. It made everyone else smile, too. We always make a big deal out of things like that, but you'd have thought that losing her tooth was the greatest thing that had ever happened to her.

Pat finally came up with the reason. "Who would she have had to show off to at the orphanage?"

FEBRUARY 9

READ: Psalm 103:11–14
KEY VERSE: Psalm 103:13

Pat finds himself following in the footsteps of his late doting father. James Williams, a schoolteacher and coach, was proud of his son, so eager to watch, to coach, to cheer, that Pat was often embarrassed.

Now that he's a father, Pat understands. He cares; he's there. But most important, he wants to be a godly model to his own boys. One of his favorite poems (author unknown) is this:

A careful dad I want to be;
  A little fellow follows me.
I do not dare to go astray,
  For fear he'll go the self-same way.
I cannot once escape his eyes;
  Whate'er he sees me do, he tries.
Like me he says he's going to be,
  This little lad who follows me.
He thinks that I am good and fine,
  Believes in every word of mine.
The bad in me he must not see,
  This little lad who follows me.
I must remember as I go
  Through summer's sun and winter's snow
I'm building for the years to be,
  This little lad who follows me.

FEBRUARY 10

READ: Psalm 8:3–5
KEY VERSE: Psalm 8:5

Isn't it wonderful that God isn't stuck on one pattern? He doesn't have a heavenly mold into which we must fit. The world produces conformity; God produces individuality. Our God is a God of infinite variety who uses people of all kinds, shapes, and colors, and He has a unique purpose for each of us.

Warren W. Wiersbe has said, "A child's life is filled with wonder, and this sense of wonder enables him or her to see things in life that escape the rest of us. My grandchildren can squat and stare at a flower or insect with an imaginative interest that I hope will never be lost.

"Alas, tests show that a child's creativity—which includes imagination and wonder—diminishes by 90 percent between ages five and seven! When an adult gets to be forty, he has about 2 percent of the creativity he had when he was five."

Physicist J. Robert Oppenheimer said, "There are children playing in the street who could solve some of my top problems in physics, because they have modes of sensory perception that I lost long ago."

What are we as parents and teachers doing to our children during their most formative years to rob them of the imagination, wonder, and creativity with which they were created? Rein in their behavior, but let their God-given imaginations run free.

FEBRUARY 11

READ: John 13:34–35
KEY VERSE: John 13:35

Around our house, we call hugs "tight love." There's no other reason to hug someone than to show love. Our Korean daughters were huggers par excellence from the day they arrived.

When Jill's mother and grandmother, Grandma and Nana, came to visit the girls for the first time a few weeks after they arrived from Korea, Andrea and Sarah could hardly wait. As soon as the visitors came through the door, the girls attacked them with hugs, wanting to be held and carried everywhere.

We had an out-of-town visitor they had never met, but when he arrived around midnight, one of them woke up. Then the other. They knew someone new was in the house, so they begged to be brought down to see who it was.

He smiled at them and said hi, and they both reached out to be held. They ran their fingers through his hair, kissed his cheek, and smiled from ear to ear. They hardly knew any English, but they were communicating in a physical language all their own that they were happy to be in a home where they were loved and treated as special little people. They figured that any friend of theirs was a lover of them, and they were right.

This was around the time that Andrea was learning to pray aloud. Friday was her day to pray for the meal. She always finished her prayer, ". . . and dear Jesus, amen."

FEBRUARY 12

READ: 1 Thessalonians 4:1–12
KEY VERSE: 1 Thessalonians 4:11

Ever notice how economical Abraham Lincoln was with words? "You cannot help men permanently by doing for them what they could and should do for themselves" is an example of his laconic style.

His Gettysburg Address is probably the prime example of his less-is-more style. Biographers quote his wife as saying that he was an extremely quiet man in private, and when he felt the most deeply about something, he expressed himself the least.

As a rule, men are less expressive than women. That isn't all bad. Some wives, according to the apostle Paul, could take lessons from their husbands.

But when a lack of response starts to wear on a woman, danger is on the horizon. The strong, silent type may at first appeal to a woman, but in a lifetime of marriage, he can drive her crazy. She wants input, reactions, and conversation, not occasional tight-lipped monosyllabic utterances.

For years, Jill suffered when Pat seemed to communicate with her only in a surface way. She once accused him of talking to her as if she were "a Philadelphia sportswriter." She wanted time, substance, depth, feeling, and response. Bottom line: she wanted him.

Your wife wants to be a top priority in your life. She doesn't want you to put her ahead of your relationship with the Lord, but she should be priority number two, ahead of children, friends, and job. You can be a better husband than Honest Abe!

FEBRUARY 13

READ: Ecclesiastes 3:1–9
KEY VERSE: Ecclesiastes 3:8

After the death of her eighty-nine-year-old father, actress Kim Novak said, "I had a love-starved childhood that haunts me to this day. My parents never said, 'I love you' or 'You are wonderful.' I can't forget that I never heard those words from either Mom or Dad. Now that they're gone, I'll never get the chance again.

"All I have is the memory of the pride they once showed for me, and although it's not like hearing 'I love you,' it will have to do. All the awards, adulation, and money can't make up for the love from your parents. It's something from which I've always felt cheated."

What a sad commentary, and what a lesson for us! We parents in this generation have had so many articles, books, movies, television programs, lectures, and seminars on this subject that we are completely without excuse for failing to express love to our children.

If a modern Christian parent leaves a child a legacy like that, there is no one to blame except the one in the mirror. But it's never too late to do the right thing. Maybe you never had an example of how to be a parent from your own mother and father. Still, you know what needs to be done. Even if you're past middle age and your kids are grown, do the right thing. Say the right words. Let 'em know.

FEBRUARY 14

READ: Song of Solomon 1:1–4
KEY VERSE: Song of Solomon 1:2

Need a few hints on keeping the romance alive in your marriage this Valentine's Day? Dr. Stanley Platman, former professor of clinical psychiatry at the University of Maryland, has eight:

1. Make "couplehood" a priority over "parenthood." You still want your spouse around when your kids have been gone thirty years.

2. Be physically affectionate. Hold hands, hug, and cuddle. Frequent physical contact, even in public, keeps your love alive.

3. Be unswervingly loyal to each other. When one is attacked or slandered, the other should come to the defense immediately and unequivocally.

4. Keep up your health and appearance. Stay trim and youthful with careful diet, exercise, and frequent physical checkups.

5. Be partners, not competitors. Take pride in your spouse's accomplishments.

6. Give each other space. Don't live in each other's pockets. Too much togetherness can be stifling and monotonous.

7. Make time for each other. Don't settle for leftover time. Spend weekends together sharing simple pleasures.

8. Be adaptable. Life is full of changing circumstances. You may move or have to deal with illness or death in the family. You must be willing to change and be flexible, no matter what.

FEBRUARY 15

READ: Ephesians 6:1–9
KEY VERSE: Ephesians 6:4

"Where are the parents who so value eternity that they would count it a high honor to have their child become a missionary, pastor, or some other calling of career ministry?" asks Dr. Joseph Stowell, new president of the Moody Bible Institute in his book, *Fan the Flame.* "It seems that many parents today want 'more than that' for their children. Perhaps some of us do not want to tell our friends whose children are attending prestigious universities that our child is going to a Bible college or seminary.

"Some parents want to live out their own worldly dreams through their children's lives. We must remember that children are not meant to be extensions of our wish list. God wants them to be an extension of His almighty arm. Granted, a child moving into a secular profession can have great impact for Christ if his values are right. The rub comes where parents discourage their child from seeking an investment in career ministry.

"Gratefully, prayerfully, and carefully placing our children in the treasure chest of the kingdom of Christ by loving and living kingdom values is our highest responsibility and most profound privilege.

"What better way is there to express our love for Him than through our children?"

FEBRUARY 16

READ: Matthew 5:38–42
KEY VERSE: Matthew 5:41

During biblical times in the Roman Empire, a centurion on a mission for the king would typically carry heavy equipment, armor, and supplies. Roman law stated that he could stop any Jew living in the empire and require him to drop whatever he was doing and bear the burden for *one* mile.

The Jew needed nothing else to remind him of his status as a slave, as a humiliated, put-upon creature who was at the beck and call of Rome. Imagine the poor man who gets pressed into such duty. He might be on a walking trip into the city for a day of shopping at the markets. He has a cart, maybe a donkey, a wife, and two or more children. It's hot and dusty, and they have a big day ahead.

A passing centurion need only point at him and hand him his gear, only giving him time to tell his wife where to meet him a mile up the road. She is left with the family, the animal, and the possessions. The Jew would seethe the whole way, wishing for a way to avenge his plight, to put the Roman in his place.

As usual, however, Jesus had a revolutionary word for the Jew. Jesus, the conquering King, came to set things right, but how? By smashing the slave drivers into submission? No. Jesus told the Jews to carry the Romans' equipment *two* miles down the road. Cheerfully go the second mile in every situation you face today. It will revolutionize your life.

FEBRUARY 17

READ: 1 Peter 1:22–25
KEY VERSE: 1 Peter 1:22

Soon after we adopted Sarah, we realized we had a feisty little one on our hands. She required a lot of discipline, always administered in love and only for willful disobedience. She learned and grew from it, but we remember how hilarious it was when she was still learning English.

After a spanking, while both Mom and Dad were dispensing hugs and kisses and expressions of love, Sarah would sob, "I forgive you!"

Jill can never forget a traumatic moment in her childhood when her mother sent her to her room for some offense. She was supposed to think about what she'd done, and *think* she did. The more she thought, the more she feared that she would never be forgiven. The thought scared her to death: *Mother will never love me again.*

Finally, she went to her mother in tears. She apologized for her wrong and appealed, "Please forgive me. You don't have to love me, but please forgive me."

"I forgive you, Jill," her mother said. "And how can I not love you? You are part of me."

Jill remembers that as if it were yesterday, and now that she has eight children of her own, she understands it totally. "How can I not love you?"

FEBRUARY 18

READ: 1 Corinthians 9:1–14
KEY VERSE: 1 Corinthians 9:14

Pat was speaking at King College in Bristol, Tennessee, when the discussion at the banquet table evolved to the subject of televangelists. This was during the height of the controversy over scandals within the ministries.

One woman said she had learned a valuable lesson from her two-year-old daughter. The little girl couldn't help being aware of how important it was to Mommy to watch her favorite Christian TV program, "The 700 Club," every day.

When the theme music came on one day, the little girl squealed, "Mommy, Mommy, God's on!"

The woman carefully explained that Pat Robertson was not God, but that he talked about God. "Well, it's Pat God!" her daughter said.

That was a lesson for everyone at the table. Of course, Pat Robertson doesn't claim to be God, but then neither do most Christian leaders or laymen. However, because we are the only Christ most people will ever see, the only Bible they'll ever read, we have a huge responsibility as Christians. Do our actions and words honorably represent the King of kings and the Lord of lords? Do some people who look at us and want to see Jesus see only Jill and Pat, imperfect and failing? We desire that they would see Jesus.

FEBRUARY 19

READ: Malachi 2:14–15
KEY VERSE: Malachi 2:15

How important is creative romance in a marriage? To a husband, not very. Unless he values his future as a husband. To a wife, it means everything.

Although this is a generalization, most husbands are not romantics by nature. Most wives are. At least, they're sentimentalists. Jill is no different. Pat fits his stereotype, too.

One of the major bones of contention in the marriage crisis in 1982 was that Pat invested all his creativity in his job and had nothing left for the marriage relationship or the family. The man who was dubbed the second Bill Veeck, whose life revolved around schemes to get people to come to basketball games, didn't have the initiative to surprise his wife, to plan something just for her.

How important is it to Jill, even now that the marriage is healthy and everything seems to be going swimmingly? Jill says, "My life is full with caring for eight active children, writing books, cutting records, speaking, singing, enjoying watching Pat build the new team. But if one important ingredient is missing, all the rest loses its excitement. If there is no creative romance from my husband, I'm bored with my life. With romance, everything else is enhanced."

FEBRUARY 20

READ: Psalm 17:1–9
KEY VERSE: Psalm 17:8

Former major-league baseball player Bobby Malkmus is an old friend of ours who lives in Union, New Jersey. He was one of the managers of the Spartanburg Phillies when Pat was general manager and president there, and he was instrumental in Pat's conversion to Christ.

Bobby is good with his hands, an expert in designing and needle-pointing his own creations. Over the years, Pat has commissioned him to do four custom jobs for the Williamses. The first was one that epitomizes Pat and Jill's present relationship: "I'd rather be snuggling."

Then after our marriage had been rejuvenated by the B-E-S-T principles from Dr. Ed Wheat, Bobby needlepointed "Blessing, Edifying, Sharing, and Touching." It's a constant reminder to us both to continue in our resolve to be the best we can be for each other.

Third, one of Jill's favorite songs was made popular by Roger Whittaker, and it sums up her feeling about her relationship with Pat. Bobby needlepointed the title: "You Are the Wind Beneath My Wings."

Fourth, for our children, he needlepointed a message that hangs in the hallway over the front door and reads, "In assurance of our lifetime commitment to you. Love, Mom and Dad."

FEBRUARY 21

READ: Matthew 5:27–30
KEY VERSE: Matthew 5:29

The very mention of baseball tryouts raises the spirits around our house. Baseball is Pat's favorite sport, and Jim and Bob love it, too.

Pat was asked to help supervise the tryouts for twelve-year-olds as coaches selected their teams.

As Pat ran the boys through their paces, it became obvious that one boy couldn't catch. He couldn't hit. He couldn't run. The coaches were concerned about his safety with baseballs flying in all directions.

Finally, someone from the league phoned his home and talked to his mother. "The boy really has no baseball ability."

She pleaded with the coaches to put him on a team. They relented. After a few practices and several near misses where the boy could have been hurt, a league representative called his mother again and insisted that he be dropped from the team.

"I understand," she said. "And I appreciate your concern. It's just that I'm divorced, and I was hoping that you could teach him to play baseball. Every American boy should have that chance, and it's something his father never gave him."

Of course, it's pretty late to be teaching a kid at age twelve the fundamentals of the game. The sad story just pointed up to us again the ravages of divorce and the havoc it wreaks on a family, especially on a child.

FEBRUARY 22

READ: Proverbs 16:9
KEY VERSE: Proverbs 16:9

We enjoyed the wedding of Pat's cousin, Jenny Batchelor, and our good friend from Washington, D.C., Mike Cromartie. After the ceremony, Jenny related the fact that for a long time, they knew each other and dated, but there were no stars in her eyes or fireworks between her and Mike.

As the relationship progressed, so did her feelings, and eventually, they were in love, engaged, and married. Jenny's mother summarized: "You commit yourself to what you know to be God's will and remain true to that. Then, as you work together, if there are to be fireworks, there will be fireworks."

Pastor David Jeremiah puts it this way: "You can't command the emotions, but you can command the will and the emotions will follow the will."

Pat saw similarities between their story and his and Jill's. Pat dated Jill at first because, frankly, she had pursued him. He thought he was pretty smooth, asking the young schoolteacher for her phone number, but that had been her purpose all along.

Then when he showed a little interest, she sparkled with enthusiasm, but he ran the other way. The more time spent together, however, the more God worked in Pat's heart. Finally, the day came when he knew, as if from the Lord, that he was to marry Jill.

She was the one; she was to be the woman with whom he would share the rest of his life. The knowledge of it was fireworks in itself, breaking his shell and breaking him down.

FEBRUARY 23

READ: Proverbs 17:6
KEY VERSE: Proverbs 17:6

The following selection has been attributed to everyone from Kevin Leman to Chuck Swindoll, so the original author is probaby unknown. It is widely known as A Child's 10 Commandments to Parents:

1. My hands are small; please don't expect perfection whenever I make my bed, draw a picture, or throw a ball.

2. My eyes have not seen the world as yours have; please let me explore safely. Don't restrict me unnecessarily.

3. Housework will always be there. I'm only little for a short time. Willingly take time to explain things to me.

4. My feelings are tender. Please be sensitive to my needs. Don't nag me all day. Treat me as you would like to be treated.

5. I am a gift from God. Please treasure me as God intended, hold me accountable, give me guidelines, and discipline me.

6. I need your encouragement to grow. Remember, you can criticize the things I do without criticizing me.

7. Permit me to fail so I can learn from my mistakes.

8. Please don't do things over for me. That makes me feel that I don't measure up. And please don't compare me with anyone.

9. Don't be afraid to leave for a weekend together. I need a vacation from you sometimes, just like you do from me.

10. Please take me to church regularly. I enjoy learning about God.

FEBRUARY 24

READ: John 10:11–16
KEY VERSE: John 10:14

Jill always feels she learns more when she's teaching than when she's listening, so the small Bible study she teaches in Orlando has been a source of good learning.

When the day's lesson centered on Psalm 23, she read today's passage as a supplement. She was particularly struck by the key verse, because she could identify with it. "I tend to relate a lot of things to mother-and-child relationships, because that's me. This passage made me remember when I was in the hospital after having had each of our babies. When it was feeding time and the nurses were bringing the babies to the mothers, I could tell which baby was mine from down the hall. One cry was all it took. Just like Jesus knowing His sheep, I knew my little lambs."

It didn't take long before each baby learned the mother's voice, too. That kind of intimacy is available only through people who are bonded by blood and love. And that is a picture of the relationship we can all have with our heavenly Father.

It's overwhelming to think that He has that kind of connection with His children if they simply desire it and claim it. He knows His children intimately. There's no reason why we can't know Him the same way if we seek His face in prayer and read His Word.

FEBRUARY 25

READ: Matthew 9:35–38
KEY VERSE: Matthew 9:36

In his book, *Restoring Your Spiritual Passion*, Gordon MacDonald tells a story of Sir William Osler, whom he calls "one of the most highly esteemed physicians in modern medical history." Apparently, Osler was not only a genius as a medical practitioner; he also epitomized compassion.

One day in a London hospital he noticed a sad little girl sitting alone with her doll while the rest of the children played together. A nurse told Dr. Osler that the girl had been ostracized because the other children considered her unimportant. Her mother was dead, and her father had paid just one visit.

The compassionate doctor immediately walked to the child's bed. "May I sit down, please?" he asked in a voice loud enough to carry to the other children. "I can't stay long on this visit, but I have wanted to see you so badly."

The girl's eyes were wide with joy. For several minutes the physician talked with her in quiet, almost-secretive tones. He inquired about her doll's health and pretended to carefully listen to the doll's heart with his stethoscope. As he left the ward, he spoke loudly again, "Don't forget our secret!"

He turned to see the once-ignored youngster now the center of attention. He had affirmed her specialness in her own eyes and in the eyes of others. That's the power of compassion.

FEBRUARY 26

READ: Psalm 127:4–5
KEY VERSE: Psalm 127:5

One Sunday morning when we had only (!?) six kids, Jill had to stay home with Bob and Michael, who were battling the croup. That meant Pat had responsibility for Jim, Karyn, Sarah, and Andrea during church.

After the service, a woman told Pat, "I noticed how well your children behaved, especially how they responded to *that look*. My father had *that look*, and we responded the same way, but you don't see it much anymore."

It's true that too few parents can control their children or keep them in line in public with one meaningful glance. It's not that our kids are angels. They get into their share of squabbles and have to be untangled. But they are being taught how to behave (sometimes we wonder if the job will ever be done).

Because of our schedules, moves, and responsibilities, we have had to take our kids everywhere from church to restaurants to banquets (sometimes at the head table) and to some boring adult meetings. At first we felt it a burden to us and the children, but now we look back and see how it helped teach them to interact well with adults.

We were just dumb enough to expect our kids to obey and respond, and somehow, it worked. Sometimes we get what we believe we'll get. Try it.

FEBRUARY 27

READ: Proverbs 14:29–35
KEY VERSE: Proverbs 14:29

Every once in a great while, we hear of a married couple who have never raised their voices to each other. There were times in our past when we would have suspected the honesty of that claim. In our rejuvenated marriage, we see that it's possible.

But what happens when you do blow your top at your spouse? Don't let it fester. Get to work, as soon as you are cool enough, to patch up the relationship in a loving, godly way.

Psychologist Dr. Marc Lipton recommends what he calls a four-*A* approach to soothing a loved one's hurt feelings after you have lashed out in anger:

Apologize. Do it quickly before things get out of hand. A prompt, sincere apology will take the sting out of what you already said.

Assure. When you lash out at someone you love, the individual may fear having lost your respect, your support, and perhaps even your love. Give assurances of love quickly.

About-face. Be very calm. Speak in a gentle voice. Be reasonable and in control. Recoup good graces, and defuse the situation with a brief statement of what made you mad.

Accept. Accept your loved one's explanation without interrupting or arguing and without demanding an immediate resolution. Be satisfied you haven't alienated your spouse.

FEBRUARY 28

READ: Acts 4:1–12
KEY VERSE: Acts 4:12

On this occasion of Pat's spiritual birthday—he was reborn on this date in 1968—share your conversion story with your spouse. You should have known this aspect of your spouse's history long before the engagement period, but perhaps it's been a while since you've rehearsed it.

Salvation stories are uplifting and challenging and frequently moving, no matter how familiar they are. Pat was a twenty-seven-year-old executive in minor-league baseball when the impact of many Christians was driven home in a simple conversation with a college girl who was a member of a Campus Crusade traveling singing group.

Pat was convicted by the truth of the Four Spiritual Laws—that God loved him and had a wonderful plan for his life, that sin had separated him from God and God's plan, that Christ had paid the penalty for his sin and provided a way to bridge the gap between him and God, and that by believing he could be born into God's family.

As a child, Jill went forward at an evangelistic crusade under the clear, dynamic preaching of a young chalk artist named George Sweeting. She responded to the moving of the Holy Spirit in her heart and put her faith in Christ.

FEBRUARY 29

READ: Proverbs 22:17–21
KEY VERSE: Proverbs 22:17

Parents have to keep open minds. Sometimes, because of the way we were raised or because of cultural norms, we tend initially to react negatively to ideas from our kids. When Jim told us he had been invited to a lock-in party at the Orlando Y, we were not thrilled.

How would that have sounded to you? The church youth group rents the Y. The kids are locked into the place so they can't be out on the streets, yet the idea seemed to us, at first, fraught with disaster. The kids bring their sleeping bags, but no one is expected to sleep. They play volleyball and badminton all night, and anyone who falls asleep is the victim of some harmless practical jokes.

But Jim really wanted to go, so we agreed to think about it. We decided we wanted to channel our children into wholesome, Christian activities. It *was* the church youth group, after all, and there would be some times of spiritual exercise. The kids would be locked in, not out, so they would be safe from hazards and temptation.

Jim would lose a night's sleep, but what else is new? At six, they would have breakfast and then be driven home. He might be cranky, but he'd catch up on his sleep. He went with our blessing.

MARCH 1

READ: Psalm 23
KEY VERSE: Psalm 23:1

Linda Kaat called the other day. She's the wife of former big-league star pitcher Jim Kaat, and they are friends of ours from outside Philadelphia. Linda raises sheep, and when we lived in the Philadelphia area, we visited their farm. It was fascinating to see the shearing and dyeing and to hear about the marketing of wool. It looked like fun, but a lot of work, too.

As Linda and Jill were catching up on old times, Pat realized who was on the phone. Linda had just announced that the Kaat farm was expecting twenty-five lambs when Pat signaled to Jill to find out if she was still raising sheep.

"I guess that answers Pat's question," Jill said, laughing.

"What's that?"

"He wanted to know if you were still raising sheep."

"Oh, yes! Once a shepherd, always a shepherd."

How like the Lord Jesus was that comment! It's what we would imagine Him saying, should anyone feel the need to ask. He's our eternal Shepherd, a comforting metaphor that pushes us back to the Psalms and readings like today's.

There will be days in the year when we will want to be led, to be fed, to be rested, to be cared for, and to have our souls restored. There will be days when we will have no courage in the valley of the shadow of death, but we will know our Shepherd is with us.

MARCH 2

READ: Proverbs 18
KEY VERSE: Proverbs 18:24

If your spouse is your best friend and your best friend is your spouse, you're doubly blessed. It's been said that a person who has one true, long-lasting friendship in life is an exception.

Jill once gave Pat a plaque for his desk at work. It read: "Happiness is being married to your best friend."

What is a friend?

A true friend is . . .

. . . one who makes your grief less painful, your adversity more bearable.

. . . one who joyfully sings with you when you are on the mountaintop and silently walks beside you through the valley. Anonymous fans sent us congratulatory messages when the 76ers won the 1983 championship. Very few of our closest friends did.

. . . an earthly treasure God lends you to help prepare your eyes, heart, mind, and soul for the glories He has prepared for you. Jill has one friend in New Jersey who has the unusual ability to relate everything naturally, inoffensively, and wisely to the Lord.

MARCH 3

READ: Hebrews 13:1–6, 16
KEY VERSE: Hebrews 13:16

Is it fair to equate loving with sharing and sharing with loving? Theophile Gautier, a nineteenth-century French poet and novelist, thought so. He wrote, "To renounce your individuality completely, to see with another's eyes, to hear with another's ears, to be two and yet but one, to so melt and mingle that you no longer are you but another, to constantly absorb and constantly radiate, to double your personality in bestowing it—that is love."

And what do some people who are so envied today say about this matter of sharing? Grammy-winning recording artist Kenny Rogers: "Trophies are only important if you have somebody to share them with . . . otherwise, what does it all mean?"

"Miami Vice" undercover cop Don Johnson: "The thing I miss is being able to share all this wonderful stuff with somebody. It's a thrill, but when you can't share it with somebody, it's very empty."

"Dynasty" star Linda Evans: "Are fame and fortune going to keep me company when I'm older? Can you talk to fame and fortune at night when you come home from work, when you're lonely and desperately need someone to talk to? I have everything most women would die for, but what do I really have if I have no one to share it with?"

MARCH 4

READ: Philippians 4:1–9
KEY VERSE: Philippians 4:1

This is the only date in the year that is a command: *March forth!*

It reminds Pat of a rousing sermon he heard at the First Presbyterian Church of Orlando during one of his first Sundays in Florida. The preacher was the sonorous Howard Eddington, and this is the story as Pat recalls it:

On a Tuesday in March of 1858, five thousand men packed the YMCA Hall in Philadelphia and listened to young preacher Dudley Tyng speak on the text: "You that are men, serve the Lord."

His stirring sermon made a penetrating impression on many, though they had no idea it was his last. A few days later, a farming accident forced the amputation of his right arm. He was not to survive the shock to his system.

As he realized he was dying, he called his father and drew him close. His last words: "Stand up for Jesus, Father. Stand up for Jesus. And tell my brethren of the ministry, wherever you meet them, to stand up for Jesus!"

The following Sunday the Y was even more crowded. Tyng's friend and fellow evangelist, George Duffield, read out in the service the words of the poem he had written in honor of his friend, based on his last sermon and dying words.

Years later, George Webb put to music the poem "Stand Up, Stand Up For Jesus."

MARCH 5

READ: Proverbs 25:11–12
KEY VERSE: Proverbs 25:11

Because of the unusual way we spell Karyn's name, her second-grade classmates had a lot of trouble with it. Our boys got a kick out of the notes Karyn received from classmates because, try as they might, they couldn't find the correct spelling.

Journalists will tell you that a cardinal rule in reportage is the correct spelling of someone's name. It's so personal and so important to the individual that few things are more offensive than getting it wrong.

This situation gave Bobby, then nine, a chance to display his gift of kindness. He had been visiting his grandparents in Riverside, Illinois, and when he returned, he had a note for each of us, telling us how much he missed us and loved us.

The one to Karyn was especially sweet. On the front he had written: "To Karny, Karn, Kan, Kany, or Karyn. To you, Sweetie Pie."

Inside, he wrote: "To Karen, Caren. Nothing fancy, nothing funny. Just a simple I love you. I'll get your name right, Karyn. I love you. Love, Bob."

Often we find ourselves wondering if we are as gracious and loving as our kids are capable of being.

MARCH 6

READ: Malachi 2:14–17
KEY VERSE: Malachi 2:14

A few years ago we were blessed with the privilege of introducing the pro-life ministry of Dr. Francis Schaeffer to the Philadelphia area. What a joy it was to meet the great Christian writer and apologist! Pat was most impressed by Dr. Schaeffer's eagerness to pray anytime, anywhere. He even prayed for the city once as we drove along the expressway.

Francis and Edith Schaeffer had five rules to defend and strengthen Christian families. Want to make your family unique and blessed of God? First, take time for daily prayer. Commit everything to God and trust Him to meet even the smallest need.

Second, accept the Bible as final authority. The only standards for living are those that can be supported by Scripture. Dr. Schaeffer so loved his Bible that he admitted to *Moody Monthly* during his last interview before his death that he often reached over and patted it when he awoke in the morning.

Third, encourage family creativity. Model creativity. Transform the mundane into something beautiful and glorifying.

Fourth, recognize the importance of children as being of infinite value, full and responsible partners in the family who can share their deepest doubts and questions without fear of rejection.

Fifth, recognize the beauty of marriage as one life lived to the fullest in a relationship of love and commitment.

MARCH 7

READ: Matthew 20:1–15
KEY VERSE: Matthew 20:14

Karyn had been practicing with a gymnastics team for several weeks, and finally, it was time for their first meet. With so many other activities pulling the family here and there, Jill was the only one who was able to attend.

Karyn was the youngest and smallest competitor in the field, and Jill worried that she would be nervous and scared. As it turned out, Jill was more nervous than Karyn, who admitted to only a "little bit" of fear.

She performed flawlessly on the balance beam and in the floor exercise. Jill was grateful that three other events were going on at the same time so that all the attention wouldn't be focused on a first-time performer. But because Karyn was so tiny, she drew attention anyway. Everyone applauded when she finished, and she won two blue ribbons for her age group.

Naturally, Jill was thrilled when Karyn stepped to the top of the victory stand, but she also immediately felt for the little girls who had been too nervous to do well.

The meet directors had thought of everything, though. The whole event was for beginners and for instruction, not so much for competition. Everybody, even the ones who finished fifteenth in their age brackets, received colorful ribbons. Surely, such a rewarding experience had to be uplifting for each of them.

MARCH 8

READ: Genesis 1:26–31
KEY VERSE: Genesis 1:28

Does it make sense that we, the people God intends to rule and subdue the earth, should be constantly beset by feelings of insecurity? Dr. Clyde Narramore, the Christian psychologist, said in his magazine: "It's no compliment to God, our Creator, when we, His creatures, are disturbed, distraught, downtrodden, and distressed. Yet many of us are crippled by insecurity.

"Negative attitudes about ourselves usually take root because of crushing experiences and/or repeated negative input received during the early years of our lives. Many people have shared, 'My parents told me over and over that I would never amount to a hill of beans.'

"Why would any parent downgrade a child? Because they have problems themselves. They are unaware of how they are crushing their child's potential. It causes the child to grow up thinking that he is no good, that he can never measure up to his parents' expectations, that he is unwanted, worthless, and unloved.

"All this negativity generally translates into a person's life as insecurity. No wonder so many lack self-confidence."

We and our children were fashioned in God's likeness. Isn't that a better message to hear and to send today to the ones we love? Let's encourage our children to accept themselves as unique creations of God.

MARCH 9

READ: Psalm 130
KEY VERSE: Psalm 130:6

The family was at a vacation spot where everyone could swim and Jill didn't have to cook. She had just poured herself some boiling water for a cup of herbal tea and was putting the pot away so no one would get hurt when she heard the scream.

Eighteen-month-old Michael had reached for the cup of scalding water, and it had splashed over his chest and arm and foot. Where the elastic of his pajama top gathered around his wrist, the heat was trapped and burned deep. Jill will never forget the agony of ripping that top off him and hearing him wail as his skin peeled away on its own. Pat got directions to a nearby hospital, then the whole family piled into the van. By the grace of God, Michael was the only one in the emergency room, and he was treated right away.

Jill still feels guilty about it, though Pat has tried to persuade her not to blame herself. Often she strokes the only remaining scar, around Michael's wrist, and reliving the scene makes her cry. When she suffers a minor burn in the kitchen, she realizes how Michael must have hurt. She says, and means with all her heart, that if she could have taken all the pain upon herself, she would have. That is what Christ did for each one of us when He died for us at Calvary.

MARCH 10

READ: Luke 12:4–8
KEY VERSE: Luke 12:7

We were keeping a secret from the kids, something we love to do when we have arranged something truly special for them. For an hour in the car, they tried to guess. They thought of everything from Disney World to Epcot Center to the zoo, but they were wrong.

Finally, we arrived at the Kissimmee Airport, and the secret could be hidden no more. Tethered near the runway was the Sea World Blimp. We had all wanted a ride in it, and the kids became as excited as we were.

As we piled out of the car, Pat told the kids how fortunate we were, "because the air ship is leaving for California Sea World tomorrow and won't be back in Florida for almost a year."

We all crowded around him as he approached the window and told the woman that our names should be on the list. "Yes, they certainly are, Mr. Williams, but I'm afraid we're not flying today. I'm sorry, but the pilots tell us the winds are too severe for such a light craft. We're simply not taking anyone up today. Sorry for your inconvenience."

We were deeply disappointed, and the kids said, "Planes fly when it's windy." But Pat made the point that we must trust the experts with our safety, just as we trust our lives and souls to God.

MARCH 11

READ: Song of Solomon 4:10–15
KEY VERSE: Song of Solomon 4:10

Dr. Benjamin Belden, director of the Marriage and Family Counseling Center in Chicago, offers five suggestions for bridging the gap that often grows between husband and wife:

1. Schedule a marriage meeting at least once a week to discuss important issues. Set the meeting for a time when the children are asleep or occupied and you've both had a chance to unwind from a hard day.

2. Encourage communication. Listen when your spouse speaks and try to understand the point of view. Learn about his favorite sport so you can understand what excites him about a game. Accompany her to her favorite activity once in a while.

3. Use verbal door-openers that won't put your partner on the defensive. Instead of saying, "You never talk to me about your work," approach the subject from another angle. Say, "I feel lonely when you don't share your work with me."

4. Offer support. Constant nagging by either partner will only widen gaps between you. Praise strong points and overlook weak ones. Studies show that couples who idealize and praise each other develop strong, supportive marriages.

5. Be creative in the bedroom. Variety (with which both partners are comfortable) can enhance sexual closeness. Use your imagination (and the Song of Solomon) to keep romance alive.

MARCH 12

READ: John 1:35–42
KEY VERSE: John 1:41

Jill has an aggressive yet inoffensive way of encouraging neighborhood women to get involved in the things of God. She simply talks with these women as if they would naturally want to be interested in God and God-centered activities.

She invites them to church, not asking if they want to attend or have their own church. She simply assumes that they might like to come to ours. She uses the same approach for a Bible study or a Christian women's luncheon. She asks, expectantly, and if they are opposed, they must say so. She doesn't provide excuses or apologize for asking. Too many people begin by saying, "I don't know if this interests you or not . . ."; "Maybe you have your own church . . ."; or "Have you ever thought about coming to a Bible study?"

Jill just informs them of the function, tells them they're invited, and offers to bring them. One neighbor in New Jersey thanked Jill "for bugging me about going to church and Bible study." But she was grateful for Jill's gentle persistence.

Another woman confessed to Jill that she was an alcoholic. Jill had never dealt with that before. She hugged her and said, "We love you anyway." The woman burst into tears. She admitted, "I was encouraged to tell someone, but I didn't know what to expect. You're the first person I've told." She has gone on for treatment and is now living victoriously for Christ.

MARCH 13

READ: Genesis 2:18–25
KEY VERSE: Genesis 2:24

Want to fail-proof your marriage? Dr. Ross Campbell, author of *How to Really Love Your Child*, says that the initiative belongs to the father to take "full, total, overall responsibility for his family."

He adds that by "conveying his love to his wife and children, [the man] will experience unbelievable rewards: a loving, appreciative, helping wife who will be her loveliest for him, and children who are safe, content, and able to grow to be their best.

"I personally have never seen a marriage fail if these priorities are met. Every failing marriage I have seen has somehow missed these priorities."

Dr. Howard Hendricks of Dallas Theological Seminary has said, "Any man with a little bit of money, a Christian education, and some popularity can, with great style, make a mess out of his marriage."

Pat takes responsibility for the major problems that caused the marital crisis in 1982. And his initiative in determining to prayerfully set things back on keel rescued and revived the love that had been there.

Frustrated by your marriage and the state of your relationship with your wife? The ball is in your court.

MARCH 14

READ: Philippians 4:4–8
KEY VERSE: Philippians 4:6

People can really get hung up on prayer. Jill's been a Christian since childhood, Pat for almost twenty years. In our day, we're sure we've heard every kind of prayer from the pompous to the simple.

We believe God simply wants us to talk to Him, like friend to Friend, like child to Father. Would a kid say to his father, "Most gracious Dad, I would that thou wouldst favor me with the blessing of bestowing upon me the keys to the chariot this night so that I might honor thee by dating a righteous maiden"?

Can't we just talk to God? Anyone with children knows that kids are—if nothing else—straightforward in prayer. If they want something, they ask for it. And apparently they believe us when we tell them they can't put anything over on God. They know He sees and hears everything, so they don't even try to fool Him.

Jill's dad tells this story of Bobby when he was three years old. He was visiting Grandma and Grandpa, and it was time for bedtime prayers. Bob and Grandpa knelt by the bed, and Bob began asking God to bless everyone in the family he could think of. Grandpa prompted him, "Thank You for this day."

Bob repeated that and nodded, "And help me not to say shut up and not to stick my tongue out." Shouldn't adults ask God to help them not to do specific things, too?

MARCH 15

READ: Psalm 37:1–8
KEY VERSE: Psalm 37:8

So often, the things we worry most about are things that never happen. Jill worried about how two-year-old Michael would respond in 1987 when she took Karyn to Scotland for several days.

Pat thought it was a great idea as long as she got all the kids farmed out and taken care of. The kindergartners would stay with a friend. Jim and Bob would be watched after school until Pat got home, then he would take over.

That left the little guy. The plan was that Jill's mother and grandmother would come for a visit and take him back home to Chicago with them. That's what had Jill in a tizzy. She's spent a lot of time with Michael, of course. He's always been like a house afire, and they have grown close.

For a week, Jill and Grandma and Nana talked up Michael's big trip. It would be so exciting—so much fun, so much to do. He'd fly on the airplane and see Grandpa. What a great time!

Michael, however, seemed slightly reluctant. He didn't want to talk about the trip as much as Jill.

Jill packed his bag with all his favorite things. She worried and prayed all the way to the airport, hoping she would have the fortitude to make him go if he refused or burst into tears and pleaded for her. He did neither. He walked onto the plane and never looked back. Jill cried all the way home.

MARCH 16

READ: Luke 6:39–49
KEY VERSE: Luke 6:46

How many times in your life have you heard someone say that actions speak louder than words? Sometimes clichés are so old, we forget the kernel of truth they contain. Perhaps by looking at the key verse for today and these other ways of saying the same thing, you'll be able to find fresh meaning in them.

Ralph Waldo Emerson: "What you do speaks so loud that I can't hear what you say."

Oliver Goldsmith: "You can preach a better sermon with your life than with your lips."

Andrew Carnegie: "As I grow older, I pay less attention to what men say than to what they do."

When Grandma Moses was asked at 93 what she was proudest of, she replied, "I've helped some people."

When Benjamin Franklin wanted to interest the people of Philadelphia in street lighting, he didn't try to persuade them by talking about it. Instead, he hung a beautiful lantern near his own door.

People on the dark street saw Franklin's light from a long way off. To each, it seemed to say, "Come along, my friend! Here is a safe place to walk. See that cobblestone sticking up? Don't stumble over it!" It wasn't long before Franklin's neighbors followed his example and began placing lights in front of their homes. Soon the entire city was using street lighting.

Actions speak louder than words. Don't talk about it. Do it.

MARCH 17

READ: 2 Corinthians 8:7–9
KEY VERSE: 2 Corinthians 8:7

Pat speaks nearly every day on behalf of the ball club or in Christian ministry. Of the ton of inspirational material he has gathered over the years, one of his favorite sports-related stories concerns Bill Caraway, who played on the Georgetown football team when the legendary Lou Little was coaching.

With one game left in his career, Caraway reminded the coach that he had not played one minute in an actual game. Coach Little reminded him that it was the league championship game, the most important game of the season, and that it meant a lot to a bunch of people, but he promised to do what he could. Unfortunately, the next day the game was tight all the way into the fourth quarter. Georgetown trailed by 3 points almost the entire way.

With just a few minutes to go, after having tried everything else he could think of, Little sent in Caraway. As the clock ran out, Caraway ran for more than sixty yards and caught a dramatic touchdown pass to win the game. Afterward, the coach sought him out and asked what had made him such a motivated player when he had been so mediocre in practice all those years.

Caraway told him, "My dad wanted me to get an education and play college football, but he was blind and wouldn't have seen me play anyway. But last week he died, so this is the first game he was able to see. I had to succeed. I just had to."

MARCH 18

READ: 1 Timothy 5:1,2
KEY VERSE: 1 Timothy 5:2

Our friend, internationally acclaimed speaker and apologist Josh McDowell of Campus Crusade for Christ, sent us a copy of his *Teens Speak Out: What I Wish My Parents Knew About My Sexuality* even before it had become a best seller.

What an eye-opener it was for us, as our children begin to reach the edge of adolescence! Josh writes that "the Great American Vending Machine promises quickie intimacy that avoids the encumbrance of commitment. Teenagers, bombarded by messages of happiness in relationships through sex, may not want to bother looking for real intimacy. Worse yet, they may not believe it is possible."

Josh was not surprised to hear teens say that much of their understanding of their own sexuality came from observing their parents' relationship. "When children see in their home a marriage based on love and respect, they know that lifelong relationships are possible: They have seen one work. By watching displays of affection that back up affectionate words, children learn how relationships can be built on more than self-gratification."

We thought it was tough growing up in our generation! Kids today have a perpetual onslaught to their senses and incredible peer pressure. We must give them all the help we can.

MARCH 19

READ: Hebrews 9:16–28
KEY VERSE: Hebrews 9:27

Christian sociologist Anthony Campolo reports that fifty people over the age of ninety-five were recently asked, "If you could live your life over again, what would you do differently?"

Among the answers were these:

"I would reflect more, have a deeper life. One with more substance."

"I would risk more. Quit limiting myself because of low goals and lack of confidence in what God wants to do through my life."

"I would do more things that would live on after I'm gone."

The only two things that last forever are God's Word and people who belong to God. The sad fact is, we don't get a second chance at this life. Reincarnation devotees notwithstanding, the Bible, including our key verse for today, is clear that a person will die only once.

Williams James said, "The greatest use of a life is to spend it for something that will outlast it."

More important, of course, is what God's Word says: "Come now, you who say, 'Today or tomorrow we will go to such and such a city, spend a year there, buy and sell, and make a profit'; whereas you do not know what will happen tomorrow. For what is your life? It is even a vapor that appears for a little time and then vanishes away" (James 4:13–14).

MARCH 20

READ: Psalm 8:1–2
KEY VERSE: Psalm 8:2

Jill remembers that as a child she was fascinated with education. Even before she knew the meaning of the word, her mind was storing teaching techniques. Like most children, Jill loved learning by object lessons. When a schoolteacher or a Sunday school teacher used some sort of an object to drive home a point, she stored it that much more solidly in her young mind.

Of course, the most important lesson a child can learn is about Jesus and how He died for our sins and rose from the dead that we might live forever. Some evangelists tell the story and pass around a huge spike, so children can feel the weight of the ugly sharp object that pierced Jesus' hands on the cross.

Or they might use a railroad tie to show children how heavy the horizontal piece on the cross might have been. Anything children can see, touch, smell, or feel will add to the sensory impact on the memory that is made by hearing alone.

Your kids may want to design their own object lessons. When Bob was nine, totally unprompted he showed Jill his own object lesson. A dull and dirty pencil represented us "before we received Jesus into our hearts." Then he stuck the pencil into the electric sharpener and pulled it out, sharp and clean. "And this is what we look like after He becomes our Savior."

MARCH 21

READ: Luke 15:20–24
KEY VERSES: All

Even though we attend the huge First Baptist Church of Orlando, we are members of a small Sunday school class of about thirty. You wouldn't know the teacher's name. In fact, Jerry Fallon started by subbing for someone else.

We could tell from the first class, however, that he was a gifted communicator and that he had done his homework. He taught the story of the prodigal son, comparing it to the Crucifixion. We studied forgiveness—its motivation, which is inherent in God but not in us—and grace—love given freely.

Of course, it's not possible to compare Jesus to the prodigal and God to the father who welcomes him back, for Jesus knew no sin until He became sin on the cross. But *we* can identify with the prodigal.

As you read the familiar story once again, think of the embrace as a symbol of acceptance. Think of the kiss as a symbol of forgiveness and love. The ring is a symbol of authority and trust. The sandals are the sign of a free man, not a slave. The robe is a sign of respect. The fatted calf was butchered and served only when a VIP came to visit.

The prodigal was treated like royalty, loved, forgiven, accepted, and lifted up. Those are the very benefits afforded freely to us as sons and daughters of the King.

MARCH 22

READ: 2 Peter 1:1–4
KEY VERSE: 2 Peter 1:4

When Jill gets tired of the hassle of car-pool driving all over central Florida (it seems), she reminds herself of the benefit of serving others, even when they are often her own kids and too often don't seem appreciative.

Even better, though, is the opportunity to listen to Christian radio programming. Jill enjoys Dr. James Dobson's "Focus on the Family," Dr. John F. MacArthur, Jr.'s "Grace To You," Pastor Chuck Swindoll's "Insight For Living" and, most challenging, Joni Eareckson Tada's "Joni and Friends." Joni is the young woman who was paralyzed in a diving accident two decades ago and has become a shining example of the grace of God as a speaker and writer.

Driving home from the Winter Park YMCA, Jill was fortunate enough to catch Joni's five-minute program when she was speaking on being a partaker of Christ (see key verse). Jill found it thrilling to think of the incredible fact that we finite human beings are partners with His divine nature.

We can *partake* of the Creator of the universe! When people look at us, they need not see us. They can see Jesus. Being good or developing our character is transferred from our responsibility to that of the heavenly Father as long as we are constantly partaking of His Son, Jesus.

MARCH 23

READ: Psalm 139:13–16
KEY VERSE: Psalm 139:16

It was appropriate that Jill was in the last two months of her third pregnancy when we were called upon to chair the world première of *Whatever Happened to the Human Race?* The seminar and film package featured the late Dr. Francis Schaeffer and C. Everett Koop, M.D., now surgeon general of the United States.

Like most self-respecting Christians, we had always considered ourselves basically prolife. Sure, why not? Sounds good. But before accepting an assignment like raising support for and interest in the program in the Philadelphia area, we decided to carefully study the issues.

We became convinced that abortion is wrong. It's sin. It's murder. People say, "What about those babies conceived via rape or incest?" Although such conceptions are statistically minuscule, what about them? Was it the baby's fault? Should the innocent party be put to death? What if the mother's life is in danger? And Dr. Koop says that in nearly four decades as a pediatric surgeon, he has never encountered a situation where the willful killing of an unborn baby was required to save the mother's life.

We know the issues are heart-rending and anything but easy, and our hearts break when virtual children become pregnant. But if abortion is the ending of a human life, and we firmly believe that it is, no reason can justify it.

MARCH 24

READ: Deuteronomy 6:10–19
KEY VERSE: Deuteronomy 6:12

Have you ever noticed our propensity to assign new words to old problems and then tolerate them? Americans gave murder a new name and aborted more than 1 million unborn babies last year alone.

God calls it drunkenness. We call it alcoholism, a disease.

God calls it sodomy. We call it sexual preference.

God calls it perversion. We call it adult entertainment.

God calls it immorality. We call it the new morality.

With the dissolving of absolutes, crime has skyrocketed. A serious crime is committed every 3.5 seconds, a robbery every 83 seconds, and a murder every 27 minutes. We have a half-million heroin addicts, and 43 million Americans say they've at least experimented with marijuana. The United States has over 10 million alcoholics. Suicide is the second most frequent cause of death of teenagers. At least 2 million Americans a year contract gonorrhea.

America once legislated against things God said were wrong. Gradually, we began to tolerate, accept, and even condone what was once unthinkable. The perversion and degradation that once made us blush are now flaunted before the eyes of a nation conceived in the fear of God—not because someone forced it on us, but seemingly because we didn't care.

The Christian no longer has an option. It's essential to become an activist. It's long past time to get into the battle.

MARCH 25

READ: Leviticus 26:1–13
KEY VERSE: Leviticus 26:12

Sometimes you do someone a favor without knowing it, and sometimes the favor is returned without your expecting it. That may never make it to a book of famous quotations, but it represents something that happened to Jill and Karyn on their trip to Scotland in 1987.

They had a layover in Bermuda for an hour, and Karyn began entertaining a four-year-old named Nicholas, who was hiding from his parents under the ticket counter. Once on the plane, Karyn disappeared for several hours, returning shortly before arrival at Heathrow Airport in London.

In the terminal they again met up with Nicholas's parents, who thanked Jill for letting Karyn play with him. The long trip might have been a nightmare for the young child, except that Karyn had read to him, talked to him, and colored with him. His parents asked Jill and Karyn to join them for a snack.

Jill, of course, was glad Karyn had been of assistance. And Nicholas's family was able to return the blessing by guiding Jill and Karyn down a long corridor and onto a bus, which would take them to another terminal to board their flight to Aberdeen. Those directions were never given to them by the airlines, so Jill and Karyn might have missed their plane.

Some might call that chance, coincidence, or luck. We know better. God walked with Jill and Karyn that day in the same way He guided the Israelites out of Egypt and into the Promised Land.

MARCH 26

READ: Proverbs 15:1–2
KEY VERSE: Proverbs 15:1

We make a big thing in our home of blessing one another with words. And not just between the two of us. We bless the kids, and we encourage them to bless one another and their friends. That doesn't mean they go around like pious little chaplains saying, "Bless you, my son, and bless you, sister." They try simply to say nice things to and about one another, and thereby bless others.

While living in New Jersey, we had occasion to see the best and worst examples of blessing. The worst, unfortunately, was exhibited by a couple of baby-sitting sisters (with our houseful, one baby sitter—unless it's Mom—is never enough).

These girls were so mean to each other that occasionally we came home to reports that they had actually come to blows. Finally, we had to speak with their parents and restrict them to sitting one at a time.

It was handy to use the sisters together, but as Bobby said in his eight-year-old wisdom, "They don't bless each other very much."

Fortunately, in Bobby Jones (the now-retired forward of the Philadelphia 76ers), our kids also had the model of what a Christian athlete should be. Bobby's very demeanor blessed others constantly.

MARCH 27

READ: John 11:1–27
KEY VERSE: John 11:25

Many skeptics say the miracles of the Bible stand in the way of their believing in God. The crux of our faith is in the resurrection of Jesus, but to some, this seems the most far-fetched of all. Josh McDowell once set out to write a book to disprove the historical reliability of the Christian faith. In the process of researching *Evidence That Demands a Verdict*, the popular Campus Crusade for Christ representative was led to the opposite conclusion. He says:

1. There's more historical evidence for the validity of the New Testament than for any ten classical pieces of literature combined; 24,633 manuscripts for the New Testament have been identified. The second best-documented piece of literature, Homer's *Iliad*, has only 633.

2. The resurrection of Jesus Christ is one of the most-established facts in history, according to the laws of legal evidence.

3. The Old Testament has 333 prophecies, which are all fulfilled in the person of Jesus Christ.

4. The probability of just 8 Old Testament prophecies about the Messiah coming true is 1 in 1,000,000,000,000,000,000. The probability of 48 of those prophecies coming true is 1 in 100 with 157 zeros trailing behind.

MARCH 28

READ: 2 Corinthians 12:7–10
KEY VERSE: 2 Corinthians 12:9

Doug Coe, a friend of Chuck Colson's with a ministry in Washington, D.C., covered an exciting concept in his newsletter, *Thoughts for Friends*, which Pat received several years ago. He wrote about the opposites of God.

He said that if it's true that as a man thinks in his heart, so is he, a Christian should want to think God's thoughts. A Christian should want to follow God's ways because man's ways are almost always opposite those of God.

In God's way of thinking, if you want to be exalted, humble yourself. If you want to receive, give away. If you want to be rich, become poor. If you want to possess everything, possess nothing. If you want to become a leader, become a servant. If you want to reach others, reach yourself. If you want to save your life, lose it. His strength is perfected in your weakness.

The question then remains, says Coe: How can a man or a woman live as God intends? Only through Christ, by having the mind of Christ. Imagine being given the capability to have the mind of the Lord!

We must keep our eyes focused on Jesus Christ, not on trying to become better and better by the program of man. We need to operate on His program by giving ourselves away to Him.

MARCH 29

READ: Galatians 3:26–4:7
KEY VERSE: Galatians 4:7

Sometimes we try to imagine what happened one day in Korea when a single mother got to the point where she knew she could not raise her own children. She took them to a police station or welfare agency or some other official center where she left them, turned her back, and walked away. What a heavy burden must have gripped her!

There is a distinction made between children who are abandoned—left on a doorstep—and those that are relinquished. In the latter case, the mother is seen when the children are delivered to the authorities.

Jill often weeps when she thinks of the girls' mother having to make that decision, but she believes it was an act of love. That mother knew it was the only chance her children would have of surviving in this world, because of her circumstances.

During the final gymnastics show of the season, we watched Andrea and Sarah in their leotards, their hair braided, doing their routines with such joy and pride. We knew that thousands of miles across the ocean is a woman who thinks of those very two children and wonders how they are doing.

Is it possible that someday she will see the girls on television or get to come to the States herself and somehow run into them? She would never know they were hers. Her grief at having to give them up must be deeper even than our joy in having them.

MARCH 30

READ: 1 Corinthians 13:12–13
KEY VERSE: 1 Corinthians 13:12

It was Labor Day in 1979 that Art DeMoss was called home to be with God. He was a wealthy and generous Christian, but his most outstanding characteristic was his gift of bold evangelism, one-on-one.

Many Christians point back to a chance meeting with him or a sales call on him that resulted in their kneeling to make Christ their Lord and Savior. Rare was the conversation with Art DeMoss that didn't clearly determine the spiritual condition of the visitor.

The day after he died, we visited his home in Bryn Mawr, Pennsylvania to pay our respects to his wife, Nancy, and their seven children. In his home we had always experienced friendly laughter and upbeat talk so we didn't know what to expect.

We should have known. There was an air of triumph about the place. There were also tears, of course, but one of his daughters perfectly summed up the feeling of the family: "We're pretty rejoicing."

What a wonderful way to feel about the passing of a loved one, to grieve, yes, but not to begrudge him the glory of looking upon his Savior face to face. We want to be missed when we die, but what a legacy if someone would rejoice over our new residence!

MARCH 31

READ: Matthew 10:27–31
KEY VERSE: Matthew 10:31

Our family has more than fifty birds in cages and outside in aviaries. Jill reads every bird book she can get her talons on, because though she is the mother of eight children (the oldest in junior high), she considers herself the grandmother of all the birds.

Half our children were the results of Jill's pregnancies and our trips to the hospital. The others were the results of the pregnancies of others and our trips to the airport. Obviously, with eight children, Jill loves being a mother.

She claims to get almost as excited over discovering newly laid eggs as she did welcoming new babies to the family. One day in her bird book reading, she discovered this paragraph in *Handbook of Zebra Finches* by Dr. Matthew M. Vriends:

"When the offspring are about a week old, you can hear the 'food call.' In the darkness of the nesting bowl it could be rather difficult for the parents to see exactly where they should put the food, but nature has provided a beautiful solution: on either side of the black beak are small luminous spots, and two more can also be found on the very tip of the tongue."

Imagine our excitement when we saw those spots for ourselves and knew that it wasn't nature but our heavenly Father who had put them there. All that for a tiny finch, measuring not an inch long and weighing less than an ounce. Surely, we can trust Him!

APRIL 1

READ: Proverbs 15:7
KEY VERSE: Proverbs 15:7

Some years ago Pat was convicted at a camp by a speaker who quoted Scripture after Scripture during his message. Pat was astounded. He learned that the speaker had committed himself to memorizing a verse of Scripture a day for the rest of his life.

Pat felt led to make the same commitment and soon began collecting from friends and acquaintances references to their favorite verses. As he heard their stories of why certain verses meant so much to them, he transferred each of them to a three-by-five card.

When he jogged every morning, he took a card with him and read it over and over, repeating it in his mind and aloud. After a shower and breakfast, he fastened the card to the sun visor in his car and refreshed his memory of it on his way to work.

Every several days, he would haul out his stack of memorized verses and review them. He has found this an enriching, convicting exercise that has added vitality to his spiritual life.

Jill was so impressed that she felt led to memorize a verse *every hour* around the clock for the rest of her life. It's inconvenient to have to set an alarm every hour through the night, and she has had to concentrate on short verses, but she's sticking with it. If this paragraph seems a little hard to swallow, check the date and have a happy April Fool's Day!

APRIL 2

READ: Psalm 119:1–11
KEY VERSE: Psalm 119:11

What happens to our love for the Word of God as we grow older? Do we love it more, or do we find it more of a chore to get to?

There is something sweet and innocent and trusting in a child's love for his Bible and for Bible reading. Our Bobby is going through that period just now, and we hope it becomes a pattern, a habit that will never wane in his life.

With our eight children and the two others who are in our car-pool, the van can get noisy in the afternoons. Still, there's an open space between the two front seats and the back portion of the van that makes private conversation possible. Bobby took advantage of that recently and made his way up to the passenger's seat for a talk with Jill.

He pulled his Bible from his backpack. "I've been reading my Bible, and it's really getting to be . . ." He hesitated. "Well, fun. I like to underline some of the really important verses and the verses that I like the best, but lately it seems like I'm underlining everything!"

Jill noticed that his Bible was open to the book of James. He had heard Pat speak about that recently while suggesting a Bible study method for a group of adults. The underlining and highlighting he got from Pat, too.

We always want to be examples of Christians who love the Word and hide it in our hearts.

APRIL 3

READ: Leviticus 19:1–18
KEY VERSE: Leviticus 19:18

It behooves us busy spouses to remember that when the Scriptures refer to how we are to treat neighbors, that applies to people under our own roofs. Writer Lynn Allison says it's the little things that can sink a sound relationship, such as the following:

1. Blaming and complaining. Don't blame your spouse for your unhappiness. Make peace with yourself first.

2. Looking on the negative side. Most of us tend to pay more attention to mistakes than to what our spouses do right.

3. Making unfair comparisons. The grass only *looks* greener on the other side. Build your spouse's self-acceptance by praising personal characteristics instead of comparing to those of another person.

4. Taking advice from sex experts. You may encourage something your partner finds a turnoff. Discuss the subject with your spouse.

5. Taking your relationship for granted. Put your spouse ahead of everyone else. You'll be glad in your twilight years.

6. Expressing needless jealousy. Faith and trust are the best building blocks for the future.

7. Giving up when things go wrong. Look at couples who have survived peaks and valleys. Hang in there when things get tough.

8. Embarrassing your spouse. By criticizing, even teasingly, you hurt a good relationship. Look for the best, and you'll get it.

9. Dwelling on the past. Bringing up old angers or reminding of past loves can seriously threaten a relationship.

APRIL 4

READ: Psalm 139:7–12
KEY VERSE: Psalm 139:10

Counting gray hairs the other day, Jill realized there were quite a few more than the last time she checked. She attributes this directly to life as a Little League mother.

Somehow when a child is on a team, whether it's named for a big-league club or a local car dealership, it becomes *we, us, our team* to the parents.

Last year was Bob's first, and though he is tiny, he has shone as a young ballplayer. One night, the game was all but over. "We" were down 8–4 with two out in the top of the last inning. It was time for concession speeches. And guess who was up against a fresh, big, hard-throwing right-hander?

Bob.

Pat prayed for a walk. Bobby was no match for the giant. He walked. "Our" Dodgers produced a rally that resulted in a miraculous 5 runs to win the game. The parents went wild.

Pat, certain that Bobby would have learned a valuable lesson, ran from the bleachers and into the dugout to find him. "Bob, what does this teach you?" It's always the right time for a lesson, right? And just like on TV, he thought Bob would come up with the right answer.

In reality, heady with success, Bob said, "I don't know."

Pat smiled and imitated Winston Churchill. "Never give up."

APRIL 5

READ: 1 Samuel 16:6–13
KEY VERSE: 1 Samuel 16:7

One of Jill's dreams has always been to complete her bird collection with a husband (a peacock) and wife (a peahen) team. Ulysses and Julia are her dream come true. They stroll around, acting as if they own the place.

Ulysses frequently fans his gorgeous tail feathers and struts his stuff. He might do this for just us occasionally, but he really gets inspired when his mate, Julia, is watching. Better yet, when Julia is in the yard but *not* looking!

He gets excited, steps in front of her, fans, and turns at just the right angle so she can appreciate the full beauty of his bright blue hues. She yawningly turns away, only to be chased by Ulysses, who seems to be pleading, "Look at me! Admire me! I need you to notice me!"

Poor Ulysses shouldn't have to work so hard for attention, and neither should spouses. Words chosen and spoken carefully can cut down on a lot of strutting. Everybody needs encouragement, even that husband who seems to get lots of admiration and respect at the office. Too often wives yawn and wonder if enough isn't enough. One of our boys told us recently that what really makes him feel good after a ball game is when players on both teams come up and tell him, "You're really a good player."

APRIL 6

READ: Hebrews 4:14–16
KEY VERSE: Hebrews 4:16

On their trip to Scotland in 1987, Karyn and Jill enjoyed Edinburgh, a beautiful old city. High atop a natural rocky fortress stands Edinburgh Castle, a centuries-old tourist attraction.

The Royal Mile leads from the castle to Holyrood Palace, and on that street stands the original house of John Knox. In fact, the Royal Mile takes a jog past his house because historians refused to allow it to be moved or torn down, so important was the religious reformer to the history of Scotland.

A convert from the Catholic priesthood to Protestantism, Knox opposed the Catholic government and rule by women. His biography tells of his flight to Geneva, Switzerland, when Mary Tudor, a Catholic, became queen of England. When Elizabeth I became queen of England, he returned and mounted shrill opposition to Mary, Queen of Scots.

He was chiefly responsible for the return to Protestant rule in that country, yet there was something said about John Knox that is an impressive compliment, regardless of where you stand on his doctrine or politics.

Mary, Queen of Scots, was reported to have said, "I fear nothing but the prayers of John Knox." What higher compliment could be paid to any Christian?

APRIL 7

READ: 1 Timothy 6:3–16
KEY VERSE: 1 Timothy 6:12

Last year Jill caught a television show that confirmed again our opposition to abortion and infanticide. William Christopher (he played the priest on "M*A*S*H") was interviewed on a Christian talk show.

He and his wife have two sons, the second of whom did not respond to them the way the first did. When he was still an infant, tests proved he was autistic.

In this day and age, many people would institutionalize such a child. They might wish he had never been born or might starve him to death just after birth if the diagnosis could have been rendered that quickly. He's not perfect, they reason, so do away with him.

Ned, the Christophers' son, was adopted. What a deal! Damaged goods! Why not trade him back in on a later, better model?

Nothing doing. William Christopher shared how he and his wife felt their lives had been enriched by Ned. They kept him at home during his schooling until he was an adolescent, and only when he became violent and too powerful for them to handle were they forced to get help with him.

Why not before? Did they wish his mother had aborted him? Never. He brought true love into their lives.

Jerry Falwell recently wrote, "Over 1.7 million families put their names on adoption lists last year. A million more want to adopt, but are discouraged by the long waiting lists. How can we fill their empty arms? Every year 1.5 million babies are aborted in this country alone. It doesn't take an Einstein to figure out that if these abortions were turned into adoptions, a myriad of potential problems and heartbreak for childless couples could be solved."

APRIL 8

READ: Proverbs 12:18
KEY VERSE: Proverbs 12:18

John M. Drescher maintains that probably nothing encourages children to love life, to seek accomplishment, and to gain confidence more than sincere praise—not flattery but honest compliments when they have done well.

He tells the story of Sir Walter Scott, who as a boy was considered dull in school. He often was made to stand in the dunce corner with the high pointed hat of shame on his head.

He was approximately twelve when he happened to be in a home where some famous literary guests were being entertained. Robert Burns, the Scottish poet, was admiring a picture under which was written the couplet of a stanza.

Burns inquired about the author of the couplet. No one seemed to know. Finally, a small boy crept up to his side, named the author, and quoted the rest of the poem. Burns was surprised and delighted. Laying his hand on the boy's head, he exclaimed, "Ah, ye will be a great man in Scotland someday."

From that day, Walter Scott was a changed lad. One sentence of encouragement set him on the road to greatness. "In praising and loving a child," said Goethe, "we love and praise not that which is, but that which we hope for."

Longfellow said, "A torn jacket is soon mended, but hard words bruise the heart of a child."

APRIL 9

READ: Matthew 25:31–46
KEY VERSE: Matthew 25:40

If you were to write a classified ad for the job of a servant, it might read something like this: "Wanted: Unsung hero for challenging position. Long hours, low pay, few promotions. Only those totally committed should apply."

Jesus gave His disciples a job description in our Scripture text for today, but it's a far cry from positions most people are looking for— jobs promising excellent benefits, paid sick leave, plenty of vacation, advancement, and a retirement program.

Martin Luther wrote, "God has very finely distributed His gifts, so that the learned serve the unlearned, and the unlearned humble themselves before the learned, in what is needed for them. If all people were equal, the world could not go on; nobody would serve another, and there would be no peace.

"The peacock complained because he had not the nightingale's voice. God, with apparent inequality, has instituted the greatest equality; one man, who has greater gifts than another, is proud and haughty, and seeks to rule and domineer over others, and condemns them. God finely illustrates human society in the members of the body, and shows that one member must assist the other; and that none can be without the other."

"So the last will be first, and the first last" (Matt. 20:16).

APRIL 10

READ: Proverbs 6:6–11
KEY VERSE: Proverbs 6:9

Dr. John Wood Robinson says that the hardest part of any job is probably the beginning of it. Many times it's difficult just to get started. We stand around and wait because we aren't sure of ourselves and we don't know how it's going to turn out.

The important thing is to begin. And beginning and doing our best with the little opportunities that come along will get us a lot farther than just sitting and wishing for a big chance that may never come. An average person putting into action even a very small idea will produce more than the genius whose plans are never carried out.

We should use what we already know, map out a plan, and pitch right in. We can't be sure how any activity will end, but it's surprising how well most things work out once they are tackled with faith and hard work. One idea, when pursued, seems to lead to another, and before we know it, the job itself has been done.

Samuel Johnson once said, "Nothing will ever be attempted if all possible obstacles must first be overcome." Don't wait for a more convenient time! Begin the job now!

Could many of our church boards and committees benefit from this advice? How many worthwhile projects slip through the cracks through simple lack of execution?

APRIL 11

READ: 2 Corinthians 6:1–10
KEY VERSE: 2 Corinthians 6:3

Pat's first love, after Jill and the kids, is baseball. It's his game. He played professionally, was general manager and then president of a minor-league club, and considers himself a knowledgeable aficionado, if not an expert.

In 1966, when Pat ran the Spartanburg Phillies, the manager, Bob Wellman, got thrown out of games three nights in a row. He explained to Pat, "The umps are so poor, I could get thrown out every night if I wanted to!"

Pat often reminds Jill of that. In fact, it has become a buzz phrase. When Jill gets overly frustrated with the kids, Pat says, "Jill, you can get thrown out every night if you want to."

His point is that Jill could spend her every waking moment frustrated at something the kids have done. But why waste all that precious time? It's better to learn to ignore the little things, the childish things, and concentrate on willful disobedience, rebellion, sassy tongues, and dishonesty.

That approach goes a long way in building self-acceptance in children. They want and look for rules, whether they're conscious of it or not. When we nag about every little, normal childlike problem, they feel worthless. When we concentrate only on the big problem areas, we build them up.

APRIL 12

READ: Deuteronomy 8:1–18
KEY VERSE: Deuteronomy 8:3

When we start taking our lifestyle in stride, we try to remember what it was like when we were growing up. Neither of us was poor. We were comfortable, but we certainly didn't have it as cushy as our kids do today. How are parents supposed to help children keep it all in perspective when the kids have everything they need and want—and more?

As a kid, Pat would never have dreamt of playing baseball on a manicured diamond with scoreboards and lights for night play. He was in junior high before he even played organized sports. He would pester his mother until she drove him all over town looking for a ball diamond and a pick-up, sandlot game. To wear a uniform? To have a paid umpire? Or two? The other night in Bobby's game, there were three umpires. That's more than in the minor leagues!

All we can do, short of harking back to the olden days (which parents have been doing for ages) is to encourage the kids to be grateful to God for their blessings, "for it is He who gives you . . . wealth" (v. 18).

We also require them to earn money for things they want. We make them contribute to the family welfare with plenty of chores. And we pray a lot.

APRIL 13

READ: Matthew 16:13–20
KEY VERSE: Matthew 16:16

He was born out of wedlock to a peasant woman nearly two thousand years ago. He never went to college, never wrote a book, never held an office, and never had a family or owned a home. Though He had no credentials but Himself, throngs followed Him all over His homeland.

While He was young, public opinion turned against Him, His followers ran away, He was convicted and sentenced on a false charge, and He died between two thieves. Three days later, He arose from the dead—living proof that He was who He claimed to be, the Son of God.

Nineteen centuries have come and gone, and today the risen Lord Jesus Christ is the central figure of the human race. This one Man's life has furnished the theme for more songs, books, poems, and paintings than any other person or event in history. Thousands of colleges, hospitals, orphanages, and other institutions have been founded in honor of this One who gave His life for all.

All the armies that ever marched, all the navies that ever sailed, all the governments that ever sat, and all the kings who ever reigned have not changed the course of history as much as this one solitary life.

What a privilege to belong to Him!

APRIL 14

READ: Proverbs 4:10–13, 20–22
KEY VERSE: Proverbs 4:12

The family's peacock and peahen, Ulysses and Julia—named after the Grants, of course—apparently married and consummated their relationship. Jill found six eggs produced by Mrs. P. Three hatched and died in a storm. Jill decided to put the other three into an incubator and send the newlyweds packing.

Although it seemed cruel to take Mrs. P.'s eggs away, the Mr. had become so noisy that it would have been cruel and unusual punishment (for the neighbors) to keep him with the eggs. So, taking charge of the potential newborns seemed the lesser of the two evils.

One never hatched, but two were born in the incubator. The kids were fascinated as Jill hand fed the hatchees. One day, however, as she watched, they stood, turned around, flopped over, and died.

Such things are hard to understand and harder to explain, but we always try to take these opportunities to teach the kids about the major issues of life and death and the sovereignty of God. Gloria Gaither has been an inspiration to us as a mother who uses everyday events to bring her children into right relationship with their heavenly Father. While Gloria believes in systematic devotions and study of God's Word, she finds the daily illustrations just as valuable.

APRIL 15

READ: Matthew 7:1–11
KEY VERSE: Matthew 7:9

One of Pat's favorite sportswriters is the great columnist of the *Los Angeles Times*, Jim Murray. Jim told *Sports Illustrated* the story of his youngest son, Ricky. Jim got him a job as a reporter at the *Times*, and everything seemed fine. Many were the days Ricky would call his dad and laugh about the subject Jim had written about in that day's column.

"I don't know what happened," Murray said in the interview. "Dedication [to my column] is hard on the marriage, hard on the family life. Maybe it was the column. Maybe it was the Malibu Beach scene [where Ricky and his family lived]. Maybe it was all of it."

From *Sports Illustrated:*

"In the early evening of June 6, 1982, Jim and [his wife] came home to find a business card sticking out of the door. It was from the county coroner. 'CALL RE: CASE NO. 82-7193.' Case No. 82-7193 was better known as Ricky, age twenty-nine, dead from an overdose."

"I think about it all the time," Murray said, fingering that card, wrinkled from the years it has been in his wallet. "I don't even know if I should say this, but it was always easy for me, the column. It's not like I spent long, long hours on it. I had plenty of time to be with my family. . . . but I don't know. You lose a son and you think, *Was I a lousy father?*"

APRIL 16

READ: 1 Peter 5:1–11
KEY VERSE: 1 Peter 5:5

This issue of humility is perhaps one of the most misunderstood and underapplied truths of Scripture. Some think that only people who have nothing to boast of should be humble. If you make it, become a leader, and have something to be proud of, perhaps you can make an attempt at "humble pride." But Jesus, who alone was worthy of pride, was meek and humble.

The story is told that in 1949, accordionist and band leader Lawrence Welk hired Myron Floren to play in his band. He considered Floren the finest accordionist in the world.

When Welk told his business manager, Mr. Karzas, he was furious. "Welk, you have to be kidding," Karzas exploded. "One accordion is bad enough, but two! Besides, would Benny Goodman hire another clarinetist? Let him go."

Karzas was in the audience the first night Floren played for Welk. He wended his way toward the front during the intermission and beckoned Welk to bend down so he could hear him. He gazed at the band leader thoughtfully and said, very softly and distinctly, "This new accordion player plays better than you do."

"Mr. Karzas," Welk confided in the same soft tone, "that's the only kind of musician I hire."

That's an example of humility, the kind the Bible speaks of, and the kind we are called to emulate.

APRIL 17

READ: Philippians 4:10–12
KEY VERSE: Philippians 4:11

It was a very brisk Sunday morning in Banff, Scotland, when Jill and Karyn were invited to church. Jill was excited about the opportunity to worship in another culture, and she knew the experience would be good for Karyn, too.

As members of a big, lively Baptist church, Pat and Jill are used to a fast-paced and, of course, an easily understood message. In Scotland, the minister's accent made him very difficult for Americans to follow.

The hymnbooks had only the lyrics, not the music, so Jill and Karyn struggled along. A very reserved people, few of the Scots extended greetings. Had she been in a different mood, it could have all worked together to bother Jill. But she was in a foreign country, high on the excitement of being with an old friend, of discovering and experiencing new things. Her friend suggested, "Now, wasn't it boring?"

Jill thought a moment, surprised at her own reaction. For some reason, against all logic, she *hadn't* found it boring at all. She examined her thoughts. She had gone there to worship with other believers. There was no getting around it. In spite of the obstacles, the differences, the coldness of the weather, and even some of the people, she was filled with the joy of God, because she had worshiped Him.

APRIL 18

READ: James 1:1–12
KEY VERSE: James 1:4

In his book, *Further Up the Organization*, Robert Townsend lists ten qualities of a first-class boss. See how many of them apply to being a good husband, wife, parent, church member, or church leader. Townsend says the best boss is

1. Available. If I have a problem I can't solve, he is there. He is forceful in making me do my best.

2. Inclusive. Quick to let me in on information or people who might be useful or stimulating to me.

3. Humorous. Has a full measure of the comic spirit in his make-up. Laughs even when the joke is on him.

4. Fair. He's concerned about me and how I'm doing and makes it obvious to me.

5. Decisive. Determined to get at those little unimportant decisions that can tie up organizations for days.

6. Humble. Admits and learns from his own mistakes openly.

7. Objective. Distinguishes the apparently important from the truly important and goes where he is needed.

8. Tough. Won't let top management or important outsiders waste his time.

9. Effective. Teaches me to bring him my mistakes and what I've learned and done about them.

10. Patient. Bites the bullet until I solve my problems.

APRIL 19

READ: Proverbs 16:1–9
KEY VERSE: Proverbs 16:3

A few years ago, Pat became a Civil War buff. Much as Jill resisted it at first, his enthusiasm piqued her interest, and she began secretly leafing through the piles of books he found on the subject. She leaned more toward the personalities of the famous characters than the battles, and when Pat learned of her interest, he began picking out books she might enjoy.

Since she shares a birthday (not the same year) with Thomas Jonathan (Stonewall) Jackson, he is one of her favorite characters. A special book to her is *The Gallant Mrs. Stonewall* by Harnett T. Kane.

Mr. Jackson, she learned, was a committed Christian who spent an hour a day reading his Bible and praying. Often his wife, Anna, would try to persuade him to skip his devotion or at least shorten it when she knew he was exhausted. "Isn't it time to stop?" she would urge gently.

"Practically time, but *not* time," he told her. "Anna, please understand. I've tried to set regulations for my life, and one of them is Govern Yourself. One lapse invites another; if you slough off once, you set a precedent for the next time."

Later Anna found written in his notebook, "You may be whatever you resolve to be." Truly, he was a man who lived what he believed.

APRIL 20

READ: Psalm 82
KEY VERSE: Psalm 82:6

When Pat was a kid, he was embarrassed by his dad. Jim Williams honked and waved and yelled to his son at baseball games. Once he brought popsicles for the whole team. Pat suffered with the nickname Popsicle for a long time.

Now he understands when Jim and Bob cringe if he makes too much noise at one of their games. He knows what it's like to be a doting father. And he thinks differently about his late father.

What a contrast between a doting parent and the mother Jill saw recently. Outside a convenience store, a little boy, about ten, smashed his hand in the car door. By the time he had extricated himself and taken his mother's wallet into the store for her, he was crying with pain.

Jill left the store behind them, and as she got into the van, she heard the mother hollering, "Do you wanna go to the beach or not?" The boy was still crying, moaning about his hand. "Answer me!" He mumbled something.

"You do? Then shut up!"

Jill was tempted to tangle with the hard-looking woman. She wished the woman had simply taken the time to examine the painful fingers and, more important, to hug a hurting little boy.

APRIL 21

READ: Psalm 39
KEY VERSE: Psalm 39:1

One of the most significant changes in our marital relationship since the crisis of 1982 has been in the way we argue—or don't argue. Arguments are much less frequent now, though we still, of course, disagree occasionally.

Pat has learned to curb his tongue as early as possible when tension arises. His tongue is his gift, and in his prime he could butcher and fillet anyone, his wife included. For a woman who needs positive strokes and reassurance, that is the dead opposite approach of what is required.

Pat didn't even have to be loud to upset Jill in the past. If he was reprimanding her for something, even in quiet tones, she would say, "Don't yell at me."

He'd say, "Jill, I'm not yelling."

"You're yelling with your face."

Pat is careful to point out that his new method is not characterized by simply caving in and conceding every time just to keep the peace. Rather, he listens, he reasons, and he avoids sarcasm or outbursts at all costs. "The problem with those," he says, "is that the wrong word at the wrong time in the wrong tone can become much more of an issue than the original point of disagreement."

We keep short accounts and talk everything out. The battles are over. We love what Pastor David Jeremiah told us: "In forgiveness, it's always your turn."

APRIL 22

READ: Psalm 62
KEY VERSE: Psalm 62:10

Financial analyst Jo Ann Skousen, co-author of *High Finance on a Low Budget*, says millions of women place themselves in jeopardy because they're not actively involved in the week-to-week management of the family's expenses. She claims there's potential disaster should the husband die or become disabled, and she offers these tips for women with men who won't discuss finances:

1. Be willing to take an active part. Some wives are happy to get an allowance for food or personal use, but you should get involved. Ask if you can help by taking care of some of the family's bills. This shows that you're committed to the strengthening of the marriage by being more mindful of how the money is spent.

2. Show him you can be trusted. Some men are sensitive about how much money they make and might not want anyone else to know. Show him you can be trusted by not even telling your mother.

3. Know the best time to start getting involved. March and April are excellent months, because tax forms are being filed. Ask your husband to go over each section with you.

Of course, we assume that any husband willing to share a daily devotional time with his wife will also be eager to keep his wife in the know so she won't flounder if something should happen to him.

APRIL 23

READ: Matthew 22:1–9
KEY VERSE: Matthew 22:9

Bringing unbelievers into the home for a dinner party is an effective evangelism tool if it's choreographed correctly. We invite Christian friends to tell what Christ means to them, and we do not mislead our non-Christian friends about the purpose of the dinner.

We know of people who have held such gatherings in restaurants or hotels, and sometimes there is music or a fashion show or some other preliminary to people sharing. The late Christian philanthropist, Art DeMoss, loved these kinds of events. Once, however, when he grew impatient with all the preliminaries, he said in his inoffensive way, "Let's get on with the testimonies!"

Our good friend, Norm Sonju, tells of a small dinner party he attended with the DeMosses. After the meal, each guest told about becoming a Christian. Several referred to their stories as testimonies.

When it became a certain young man's turn, he said simply, "I don't have a testimony."

Somehow, without embarrassing the young man, Art DeMoss excused himself and took the young fellow aside. They returned a few minutes later, and the young man was beaming. As they rejoined the group at the table, DeMoss said, "Now you have a testimony. Let's hear it!"

APRIL 24

READ: Ecclesiastes 2:4–14
KEY VERSE: Ecclesiastes 2:11

Dick Enberg of NBC is one of the most gifted sportscasters in the business. Pat went to see his old friend when he was in Orlando for an appearance.

Dick told Pat that he had been in a different hotel room on business 250 nights the year before. He had just turned down an offer from the California Angels to broadcast sixty of their home games. "I just can't do that to my family anymore," he said. "Those nights are too precious to us. I sure miss the game, but I'd miss my family even more."

Julius Erving, the former 76er star, is also a devoted family man. During his illustrious career, he received many awards and honors, but on his last tour of NBA cities, he was feted in every one.

Whenever possible, Julius and his wife, Turquoise—he lovingly calls her Turq—took their children with them on the road. Jill reads lips and often noticed Dr. J. say to a stadium guard or an official as he was about to receive an award, "Where's Turq?"

He always insisted that his family be ushered to the floor to share the moment with him. To Erving, there was always something more important than the game, the fame, the glory, and the money, though he appreciated that. Family always came first.

APRIL 25

READ: 1 Chronicles 26:1–19
KEY VERSE: 1 Chronicles 26:18

We dare say this is the strangest key verse in this book, and we don't really recommend your memorizing it. Pastor James Borror mentioned in the Dallas Theological Seminary magazine that he used to recommend our key verse as a joke, telling people it was most familiar and important and would solve all their problems by answering deep theological questions.

Then one day it occurred to him that if all Scripture was profitable (see 2 Tim. 3:16), this strange verse must be worth more than a joke. He studied and found more about its basic meaning: while David was giving assignments for the temple, he stationed two guards at the Jerusalem suburb of Parbar and four more at the causeway that adorned the temple gate.

Borror says the passage illustrates at least three principles: (1) every believer has a job as part of a holy family (see 1 Pet. 2:9); (2) every job is important, even when it doesn't seem to be—after all, the little guard station at Parbar is mentioned in the Word of God; and (3) every believer must be qualified. Today's passage indicates that five qualities were needed for those jobs: fruitfulness, courage, persistence, capability, and dependability.

May we continually be aware that we each have important roles to play, that every job is important, that we should seek to be qualified, and that the single greatest ability is dependability.

APRIL 26

READ: Matthew 6:24–34
KEY VERSE: Matthew 6:24

Christian television host Pat Robertson writes that any well-run company must have a corporate identity. This is partly accomplished, he says, through a unifying mission statement, something that says, "This is what we're here to do."

Without a stated purpose, many businesses flounder. Either they try to do more than they can handle, or they do little of anything at all. John Couch, former executive with Apple computers said, "More organizations die from indigestion than from starvation." In other words, they try to do too many things rather than focus on one thing. The same holds true for individuals. To be successful, people need to have clearly defined goals. Yet most of the people in America and the rest of the world have no goals.

They work at their jobs, go home, watch TV, and go to bed. Then they get up the next day and start over. On Saturday or Sunday, they may go out and play ball.

Robertson submits that no one should live aimlessly. Everyone can achieve amazing things with God's help. Of course, it's possible to achieve goals that are not of God. Nothing is more tragic than someone who has worked all his life in the pursuit of a particular goal, then he gets it and it turns bitter in his mouth.

According to Robertson, the first and continual question each of us has to ask is, What does God want of me? Get your thoughts on God. Tell Him you want to do His will. Then expect Him to show you what you should do.

APRIL 27

READ: 1 Corinthians 10:11–13
KEY VERSE: 1 Corinthians 10:13

Jill often plays the violin, sings, and speaks to church and women's groups. In spite of the positive reactions, she's always a little surprised at the invitations, and she often feels inadequate.

In fact, when she pulls into the parking lot, she finds herself wondering what she's doing there. Her prayer is simply, "Lord, You brought me here. You know how I feel. Please give me clarity of voice and thought, guide my fingers on the violin, and above all, let them see not me, but You."

She enjoys sharing with the audience the many names of our God. One of Jill's favorites is *El Shaddai*, which is also the name of a very popular Christian song she recorded on her second album. She likes it especially because it comes from a root word meaning "the breast," which identifies God as "the Nourisher."

Another beautiful name for God is *Adonai*. Adonai is the Master, the Lord. He commands; we obey. Embodied in the word *Adonai* is the character of God that says, "I never give My servant more than she can handle. I never ask her to do what I haven't first equipped her for."

By this time in her program, Jill is relaxed and communicating, but it's only because she's applying the truths she's sharing.

APRIL 28

READ: 1 Corinthians 3:5–15
KEY VERSE: 1 Corinthians 3:10

Dr. James Dobson has long held the opinion that it's important to guide children into specialty areas so they can enjoy at least one distinctive in their teen years. Perhaps it's athletics. For him, it was tennis; for Pat, baseball and football were his specialties.

For other kids, it might be piano or ballet or karate or gymnastics. The point is, the child will survive peer pressure much more successfully if a talent, a gift, or a bent is recognized and encouraged.

As usual when good advice is heard, others are getting on the bandwagon. Even the National Basketball Association is working with teens. The NBA's program, "Don't Foul Out," emphasizes "Say no to drugs." Many schools and youth organizations have adopted the phrase in an all-out campaign.

However, studies have shown that just telling teens to say no to drugs has little effect unless you have helped them achieve success in their elementary years. Sound familiar? It brings very close to home the importance of giving children every possible opportunity to learn sports, art, music, and other confidence builders.

Could it be that simple? What a waste if we discover that the common denominator among burned-out teens and young adults is a gnawing, yearning sense of worthlessness, chiefly because their parents didn't take the time to help them develop and perfect their God-given talents.

APRIL 29

READ: Romans 12:9–21
KEY VERSE: Romans 12:9

At a retreat for couples in Daytona Beach we asked the participants to think of new ways to keep their love alive, their marriage interesting, and their spouses happy. Jill asked the chairman of the event to send us their responses.

We got some good ideas from the fifty couples. Here are a few:

1. Send a formal invitation to your husband to meet you at a restaurant. Have hotel reservations already made.

2. Develop an annual hobby together, like going to concerts or joining the same health club.

3. Give your spouse the musical instrument he or she has always wanted to play, and arrange for lessons as well.

4. Pack a love note in your husband's lunch.

5. Pack a love note in your husband's pajamas before a business trip.

6. Surprise your wife by folding and putting away all the laundry.

7. Decorate your car interior for Valentine's Day, even if it's not Valentine's Day.

8. Throw a surprise birthday party for your spouse.

9. Give coupons for special freebies, such as "Good for one back rub."

APRIL 30

READ: Colossians 3:23
KEY VERSE: Colossians 3:23

Recently, we had a typical Monday morning. It may remind you of your own home.

Everyone was just a little late getting up, but that kind of pressure motivates Pat. He started a factory line, and he and Jill got the cereal out, fed all the kids, read the devotional, whipped together sandwiches for a bunch of lunches, and got the kids ready for the car-pool just in time.

Pat was psyched. He felt good. "I felt as if we had done our job again, a job we would have to do every school day for the next several years. I was satisfied."

The feeling didn't last long, however. All was not right in Paradise. Jill was in the pits for the same reason Pat was happy. "We are failing," she decided, stunning him. "We throw the food at them, no one listens to the devotional, and everything whizzes by so fast that there's no sense we're even a family. We're doing a rotten job."

Pat tried to reason with her, to soothe her, but soon the crux of the matter was revealed. She said, "No one even remembered to kiss me good-by."

Determined to learn from Jill, even when she occasionally overreacts or maximizes a problem, Pat agreed that the family must get up earlier and make the morning routine a pleasant one.

MAY 1

READ: Ephesians 5:1–7
KEY VERSE: Ephesians 5:2

The same church group that came up with the creative suggestions for spouses we shared April 29 also listed things to do with children. Here are some of them:

1. Date each daughter one at a time.

2. Plant acorns and other seeds with the kids and together watch them grow, identifying each one with the child who planted it.

3. Reward good school performances with a bonus hour of either Mom's or Dad's time to do whatever the child wants.

4. Show kids how it was done years ago and go as a family to chop your own Christmas tree.

5. Have backward night for dinner, especially with younger children. Start with dessert, then main course, and then salad and appetizers.

6. Have everyone come to the dinner table dressed as a famous person and take turns guessing who's who.

7. Have an indoor snowball fight with socks or foam balls.

8. Rotate children as first for the day. The child's name is posted on the refrigerator or bulletin board and is allowed to be first in every activity, sit in the front seat, whatever.

9. Let small children make up their own bedtime stories, pretending that they're reading.

MAY 2

READ: Hebrews 12:1–11
KEY VERSES: Hebrews 12:5–6

When Michael was two, he "helped" Jill in the garden by moving wood divider boards she uses to separate the vegetables. As they came inside, he complained that his hand hurt, and Jill discovered two slivers in his palm.

As she used a needle to coax them out, Michael whimpered and tried to wiggle out of her grasp.

It made Jill think of her heavenly Father and how He tries to draw the impurities out of her life. "How many times have I whimpered and tried to wiggle out of His loving hold? It made something come alive that I once heard Warren Wiersbe say: 'Your loving heavenly Father may allow you to be hurt, but He will never harm you.'"

Pat tells of the time in Chicago when he was in the observatory tower of the John Hancock Building, peering down to the streets. The driver of a car was trying to parallel park into a space with very little room to spare.

At first Pat was amused as the car went forward and back, forward and back, lightly bumping the cars parked ahead and behind it. Then he noticed that just around the corner were several empty parking spaces in a row.

He suddenly knew how God must feel when He knows the best way for us, yet we aren't watching or listening.

MAY 3

READ: Acts 2:17–21
KEY VERSE: Acts 2:17

It seems only yesterday that Pat was twenty-nine and the youngest general manager in the history of professional sports. On this date in 1988 he'll be forty-eight, one of the veterans on the sports executive scene. With fifty staring him in the face, he still looks and acts like a kid in a candy store; he loves his work, his family, and his life that much.

With a wife nine years his junior, and a love of God and of life that keeps him going, Pat likes to believe that age is simply a matter of the mind; if you don't mind, it doesn't matter.

Among his many resolutions for the rest of his life as a father is to expand what he tries to teach his children. For years he has been teaching them the finer points of his favorite sport: baseball. Riding along in the car, he'll make up situations and ask the boys how they would respond and what they would do with the ball.

One day Jill asked, "Why don't you set up other situations from life, like an offer of drugs, a family argument, an injustice, and coach them on how to respond in those situations, too?"

Now the coaching covers a huge range of topics, and the girls can get involved, too.

MAY 4

READ: Romans 12:1–8
KEY VERSE: Romans 12:3

Are you content with who you are? Counselors are discovering that few people are. Our key verse indicates that we should see ourselves the way God sees us, no more (which would be pride) and no less (which would be false humility).

How does God see us? We are special to Him. Genesis 1:26–27 says He created us in His own image. He purchased us with a great price, and if any one of us had been the last person on earth, Jesus would have died for that individual.

We are loved by God (see John 3:16; 15:9; and Rom. 8:38–39).

We are accepted by God just as we are because of what Jesus Christ did on the cross. Now we're free to accept ourselves and others as they are (see John 4:10).

We are forgiven (see Matt. 26:28; Mark 3:28; and Eph. 4:32).

We belong to God (see John 14:11, 19–20). First John 3:1 states, "Behold what manner of love the Father has bestowed on us, that we should be called children of God! Therefore the world does not know us, because it did not know Him."

To live contentedly don't compare yourself to others (see Gal. 6:4). Do good to one another, do what is right because it is right, and share your faith (someone has said that the Christian's goal in life should be to go to heaven and take as many with him as he can). Above all, be thankful (see Eph. 5:20).

MAY 5

READ: Philippians 1:9–11
KEY VERSE: Philippians 1:10

We're glad it's so clear in Scripture that Jesus loves little children. That registers with us.

Recently, during the first really gorgeous day in several weeks, Jill eagerly gathered up several rose bushes and vegetable plants she had bought—just waiting for a day like that—and hurried out to the garden.

It wasn't long before Michael, the youngest at age two, came toddling out to help Mommy "shubble." To Jill, there is little as precious as watching a child try to plant a flower. She showed him how to make a hole in the ground with his finger. When his hand came up, the dirt came with it.

He picked up the plant by its flower and mashed it into the waiting hole. Then he pushed the dirt around it, on it, over it, and practically crushed the whole thing with his chubby, patting fingers.

It was a mess that would likely not grow, but when he turned for Mom's smile of approval—and got it—he shyly scratched his cheek with a muddy finger and beamed from ear to ear. It was as if he thought he'd begun an arboretum, and it was a picture Jill will never forget.

"We shubble more Mommy, hm?"

MAY 6

READ: Colossians 4:2–6
KEY VERSE: Colossians 4:5

Jill's experience in beauty pageants (she finished first runner-up to Miss Illinois in 1972) taught her the positive effects competition could have on a child, if kept in perspective.

So, when Karyn was seven, Jill encouraged her to try out for a singing part in the Disney World extravaganza called the Epcot Christmas Holiday Splendor show. Karyn has always loved to sing for people, and win or lose, Jill thought it would be a good experience for her to at least try out.

More than three hundred other families had the same idea for their children, but only two boys and two girls would be chosen to sing with

Carol Lawrence in the show, which would run two or three times a night for fifteen nights. The children would alternate performances.

What a thrill when we got the call! Karyn had been selected. That was only the start of the grueling daily schedule of rehearsals at home, in the car during the thirty-minute drive each way, and at Epcot.

Jill made a real effort to redeem the time. And the rest of the family pitched in to make the whole thing possible. We'll never forget the shows, and we know Karyn won't either.

MAY 7

READ: Revelation 2:8–11
KEY VERSE: Revelation 2:10

It's a joy to be a part of someone else's life when there's a celebration—a wedding or a birthday party or a graduation. But what do we do, what do we say, when others are suffering?

The church of Smyrna was going through suffering and trial. Jesus Christ, Lord of the churches, speaks to them in the Revelation and offers three words of encouragement:

1. Remember the character of our Lord (v. 8). He is the eternal and sovereign God who has all things, even tribulation, under His control. He faced death and won the victory through resurrection. His victory is our victory. Through Him we are overcomers (see John 16:33).

2. You are not forgotten (v. 9). Smyrna's list of problems was huge. They faced blasphemy, slanderous accusations, and vicious rumors because of their faith. But the key words in this verse are *I know.* When the circumstances seem overwhelming, our Lord who controls all things knows all about our troubles.

3. Look ahead (vv. 10–11). The crown of life, the mark of our victory, is ahead for those who are faithful in difficult days. Overcomers are not undergoers. They will not undergo the second death of Revelation 20:14 and 21:8.

No matter what, we can live and encourage others to live as overcomers through Christ.

MAY 8

READ: 2 Timothy 2:3–13
KEY VERSE: 2 Timothy 2:11

Rev. Don Ogden of Winona Lake, Indiana, defines a *steward* as "a manager of someone else's business." He says that God is in big business, and it's more important than any other business in the world. He is taking miserable sinners and making them over into saints. He is working twenty-four hours a day at refining the rough products so that they more accurately reflect His image in their daily lives.

God decides if we have been good or bad stewards. Poor stewards quit when it's too cold or too hot, too rainy or too snowy, too tiring or too boring. Like soldiers, good stewards endure difficulties because they know that winning the war is more important than being comfortable.

Poor stewards mix up their priorities. Good stewards know what is important and don't let the fun things keep them from their productive tasks.

Poor stewards are like runners who break the rules and take short cuts. Being a faithful steward is not as easy as being an unfaithful one, and sometimes it's a lot less enjoyable; but faithfulness brings the satisfaction of winning the war, seeing the barn filled with a harvest, and receiving the trophy at the end of the race. Who wants to be a conquered, hungry loser, anyway?

MAY 9

READ: 1 Corinthians 7:1–3
KEY VERSE: 1 Corinthians 7:3

At his fiftieth wedding anniversary celebration, Henry Ford was asked how he'd kept his marriage going so strong for so many years. He replied, "By sticking to one model."

Long-term marriages are rare these days. Counselor Dean Clifford wants to know the source of the prevailing notion that a good marriage just happens, that if it's "made in heaven," a husband and a wife won't have to work at it.

Nothing good develops without hard work. So, what is the work of marriage?

First, the will to preserve, the determination to hang in there, no matter what.

Second, respect for each other. Without mutual respect, any marriage is on a shaky foundation.

Third, space and privacy. Too much togetherness is smothering to the individual and stifling to a marriage.

Fourth, frequent expressions of love. Why should the years diminish the need for romance?

Fifth, insistence on slowing the pace. Without long, shared conversations and time for just being together, couples suddenly discover the gap between them seems too wide to be bridged.

Sixth, attention to the sacred. Any marriage is strengthened as it stretches beyond the human and into the divine.

MAY 10

READ: Proverbs 31:25–29
KEY VERSE: Proverbs 31:28

One of the advantages of living in Orlando is having several major-league baseball teams come here for spring training games. The Minnesota Twins are headquartered here, and recently, the New York Mets came over from St. Petersburg for an exhibition game.

Pat looked up his old friend Clint Hurdle, an outspoken Christian who was trying to catch on with the Mets. He had been with the Mets in 1985 when the Cardinals won the World Series and then went to the Cardinals in 1986 when the Mets won the Series. Talk about being in the wrong place at the wrong time!

"I hope you make this club," Pat told him near the batting cage. "Come fall, you could be wearing a Series ring."

Hurdle smiled. "That would be nice, of course, but the only ring that really means anything to me is the one I wear on my left hand—my wedding ring."

Another friend, an aging pitcher and a Christian, also happened to pay tribute to his wife when he and Pat chatted in the locker room. "You know, Pat, I'm really learning to listen to my wife. Over the last year I had three big, significant business deals fall apart. I lost a lot of money."

Pat shook his head. "She knew better?"

"Did she! Five minutes into our conversations with the principals she knew she didn't trust them. If only I'd listened to her."

MAY 11

READ: Acts 8:26–40
KEY VERSE: Acts 8:37

Pastor and best-selling author Charles Swindoll suggests what he calls the Philip Approach to evangelism in *Growing Deep in the Christian Life*. He finds serious problems with the Redskin Approach (where the emphasis is on scalps), the Harvard Approach (where the emphasis is on directionless religious discussion), and the Mute Approach (which says, "I'll just be a silent witness for God").

The Philip Approach, from today's Scripture, contains seven principles that allowed God to best use His servant:

1. He was available. The Lord spoke to him, and he "arose and went" (v. 27).

2. He was led by the Spirit. Verse 29 says the Spirit of the Lord prompted him to get acquainted with a traveler.

3. He was obedient. Philip cooperated; he did what he was told.

4. He used a proper opening. The man was reading Isaiah, and Philip started by asking him if he understood what he was reading. It was a logical, but leading, question. The statesman-stranger invited Philip to assist him.

5. He had tact. Even though he had his foot in the door, he remained gracious, courteous, and a good listener, yet he was sensitive to the time he might speak of salvation.

6. He was specific. He spoke only of the Savior (v. 35).

7. He followed up. What a perfect model for evangelism.

MAY 12

READ: 1 Corinthians 6:12–20
KEY VERSE: 1 Corinthians 6:20

In his *Superenergy Diet*, Dr. Robert C. Atkins says the American population is "diseased. Most American people are eating a totally unhealthy diet and have been eating so poorly all their lives that we accept poor health as the norm, unaware of how well we can really function."

Our family became very health food conscious several years ago when we realized that bodies literally become what we put into them. In other words, if we put live food, such as fresh fruit and vegetables, nuts, grains, and seeds into our bodies, we will lengthen our lives. It's tough for the kids, who report that their peers actually laugh at them for eating whole wheat bread. But the kids understand our commitment.

If we put dead food, that is, processed food, so-called junk food, and food filled with preservatives, into our bodies, we diminish the quality of our lives and hasten our deaths. A good question to consider is, What did I eat today that would have grown had I planted it in the ground?

Without proper nutrition, our bodies lack the necessary building materials to properly replace worn tissues and sustain life. In fact, if our families are existing on junk foods and an inadequate diet, we are literally killing ourselves and our children.

Dr. David Rueben warns, "The greatest threat to survival is not nuclear war. It's what you eat at dinner tonight."

MAY 13

READ: Proverbs 5:15–23
KEY VERSE: Proverbs 5:18

We're grateful for the opportunities afforded us to speak at retreats for couples in churches all over the country. We ministered at one weekend retreat that included a couple celebrating their fiftieth wedding anniversary. They were clearly very happy together.

The gentleman shared openly with Pat and Jill that he had always felt he had married a woman who was far more beautiful than he deserved. In the afternoon sessions, the men were in one room and the women in another, and his wife shared her nickname for him: Prince.

She told Jill and the other women that every day she would send him off by asking how he was and admiring whatever he chose to wear. She'd say, "Let's see how good my Prince looks today." That may sound corny, but he ate it up, and it's worked for half a century.

One afternoon the couples had free time, and most took long walks on the shoreline. Pat had told our story and emphasized the importance of nonsexual touching and holding hands in public. The men looked embarrassed at first, but while we strolled the beach, every time we passed one of the retreat couples, the husband would wave with his free hand and point to his other hand, which was holding his wife's.

MAY 14

READ: Proverbs 29:23
KEY VERSE: Proverbs 29:23

Naturally, Jill worried about the effect of a taste of show business on little Karyn. She wanted the experience in the Epcot Christmas show to be a positive one. She wanted to see Karyn learn some valuable lessons for life, whether or not she continued in a singing or performing career.

Would she become enamored with the glamour? Would she see herself as a performer who was more important than the stagehands and sound people? It was one thing for Jill to remind her of basic truths, but it would be quite another if Karyn didn't see those truths modeled.

Fortunately, Carol Lawrence was not a typical star personality. She treated everyone with respect and dignity, and she was incredibly patient when there were delays or problems.

Jill carefully watched Karyn for signs that she thought she was something special. Of course, Jill wanted her to be aware of her talent and be grateful that she had been selected from such a large field, but she didn't want her to start being uppity.

It was gratifying for Jill to discover that Karyn was still the sensitive, loving child she always had been. When her teacher had surgery after Christmas, Karyn told Jill that she planned a daily bike ride so she could "be alone to think about Mrs. Pluth and to pray for her."

MAY 15

READ: Mark 7:6–13
KEY VERSE: Mark 7:10

We're fortunate to have in-laws on both sides who are loving and helpful. Not all couples do. Have you ever joked, "My spouse sure has better in-laws than I do." Think about it.

If you suffer from in-law troubles, here are four suggestions from Dr. Frederic Flach, adjunct professor of psychiatry at Cornell University Medical College, to keep them from wrecking your marriage:

1. Be committed to each other. Most problems are caused when one spouse maintains primary loyalty to his or her own family. By putting your marriage above all other family ties, you build a union no relative can damage.

2. Be diplomatic. Your spouse can say things about his or her family that you can't.

3. Win your in-laws over. Make them your friends. Send personal notes to them on special occasions, and offer to do little favors for them. If they ask you to do something for them, agree promptly with a smile. If you can't do it, find someone who can. In this way you build a reputation as friendly, eager to help, fun loving, and dependable.

4. Have a "foreign policy." If all else fails, instead of going to war, keep relations open by being personally polite while limiting your visits to defuse the problems.

MAY 16

READ: Exodus 1:15–22
KEY VERSE: Exodus 1:17

On her trip to the British Isles in 1987, Jill was shocked to learn the status of abortion and infanticide in Europe. A friend of hers in the United Kingdom was in the sixth month of her first pregnancy, and she was naturally worried about it.

The friend had been working with handicapped and retarded children, so she worried about the health of her own baby. She told Jill, "Of course, if it's severely retarded, there isn't any decision to make. But if it's mongoloid or just mildly handicapped, I'm not sure what we'll do."

Jill didn't know what her friend was saying. "What do you mean, there's no decision to make?"

Her friend was clearly uncomfortable even talking about it. She averted her gaze. "Well, severely retarded or handicapped babies are simply not fed. It's standard procedure. If it's a mild case, the parents decide whether to withhold nourishment or not."

Jill tried to gently share with her that all of life is of God and is thus sacred. Inside, she was screaming in anger and frustration at a system that would treat human life that way, and at parents who passively let it happen. She prayed that the child would be given its life, no matter what the state of its health at birth.

MAY 17

READ: Song of Solomon 2:10–13
KEY VERSE: Song of Solomon 2:10

Dave Hocking, pastor of Calvary Church in Santa Ana, California, and his wife Carole wrote *Romantic Lovers*. They maintain that romantic love is needed in every marriage. From their book:

"Marriage is based on commitment, not romance. If no romance ever exists in a marriage, it is still a marriage in the sight of God if the man and woman have spoken vows to each other before two or three witnesses. In other words, marriages should be held together even if no romance exists. But, as we read the Song of Solomon we get a clear understanding that God's intention for marriage is that it be characterized by romance.

"The Song of Solomon portrays the man as the lover. He is the romantic one: tender in his approach, lavish in his praise, sensitive to his spouse's needs. Abishag refers to Solomon as her love; it is her favorite word. She, like women today, has a need for the romance of her husband, and she expresses throughout the book how much it means to her.

"Solomon is an example to all husbands today. We need to be romantic toward our wives. Constant encouragement and praise must flow from our lips as we relate to our wives and describe their attractiveness to our hearts. It is not a mere feminine quality to be romantic. Macho men can learn to be romantic too."

MAY 18

READ: 2 Thessalonians 3:1–5
KEY VERSE: 2 Thessalonians 3:1

We'll never forget how saddened we were when we received a letter from our Christian school principal announcing his resignation at the end of the school year. "I have accomplished God's work for me here," he told us. We are happy for him, of course, but anyone committed to sending children to Christian schools knows how hard it is to find a good leader. We've had our kids in Christian schools for more than eight years and have dealt with several principals. The one we lost was a good one.

In a day when people are scared to death to touch a child for fear of sexual abuse charges, he was a hugger. He had nothing to hide and knew no one could ever accuse him of anything inappropriate in private, because he would never dream of such a thing. It was not unusual to see him with his arm around junior-high or high-school boys, in a manly, caring way. He was genuinely interested in all the kids, and they adored him.

Pray for Christian schoolteachers and administrators. Most often they are overworked and underpaid, and for all the complaints and gripes they receive, they get very little corresponding cooperation from parents.

By the time you read this, we assume we will have another principal in place. Our pledge is to help him all we can.

MAY 19

READ: 1 Corinthians 7:5–9
KEY VERSE: 1 Corinthians 7:5

Jill spoke recently for a dinner at Denver Theological Seminary and enjoyed getting to know Dr. Haddon W. Robinson, president of the seminary. Dr. Robinson wrote recently in the seminary magazine that "marital infidelity can be overcome if husbands and wives recognize that marriage is a contract in which husband and wife owe it to each other to be sexually responsive.

"When you marry, you enter into a contract with your husband or wife. Calling marriage a contract may not be very romantic, but that is how the Scriptures look at it [see today's key verse]. In a Christian marriage, therefore, sexual relations should not be regarded as a 'favor' given to the marriage partner, but instead a debt that is owed.

"To have such an attitude demands that you love your husband or wife in an adult, Christian kind of way. A child's idea of love is getting, but an adult's concept of love is giving. So many marriages today are 'child marriages,' where adults behave like babies. They value marriage only because of what it does for them, but they do not see it as a means of investing in the one loved. . . . Take this word from God seriously. As a husband or a wife, you alone of all the people on earth can, with God's blessing, satisfy the deep need of the person whom you married. A man can hire a maid to clean his house or a cook to prepare his food, but only his wife can meet this need for sexual expression with the approval of heaven."

MAY 20

READ: 1 Samuel 9:6
KEY VERSE: 1 Samuel 9:6

In 1962, Pat's first year in professional baseball, he caught for the Miami farm club of the Philadelphia Phillies. One night Pat drilled a fastball between short and third, forcing the shortstop to go deep into the hole, just to get a glove on it. He knocked it down but was unable to make the play, and Pat was safe at first. As he stood on the bag, the scoreboard flashed that most hated letter: *E*. The official scorer, a young sportswriter for the *Daytona News Journal*, had ruled the play an error, not a hit.

Though Pat likes to joke that the scouts said he "may not be big, but he's slow," and that he was already "in the twilight of a mediocre career," in truth he was hitting near .300. When you're trying to do whatever is necessary to make the big leagues, you need every hit you can get. With his teammates' encouragement that he had indeed been the victim of a poor scoring decision, the next day he sought out the sportswriter and talked him into changing the decision. He wound up the year hitting .292, and that hit may have made the difference to put him over .290.

Many injustices will stay uncorrected until we get to heaven, but in the meantime, where we can, we want to make things right. That young man didn't have to change his decision, but he did the right thing.

MAY 21

READ: James 5:13–18
KEY VERSE: James 5:16

Here are some practical suggestions on how we can draw strength from God. Dr. Robert A. Cook, chancellor and former president of The King's College, Briarcliff Manor, New York, writes in *The King's Hour*, the college's monthly bulletin:

Write down what you're worried about. Figure out the worst thing that could happen, then talk to God about it and the pressure will go.

Make your request to God. If you don't ask, God won't interfere.

Sometimes we just want to get away—anywhere. Sometimes God wants to work through us in our present circumstances. Your need may be not to get out of the pressure situation you're in, but to see God work in it.

There is something to be said for *definite* praying. Put little things in your prayers. Pray your way through the day, beginning when you wake up.

One man of God would start each day, "Good morning, Lord. What are You up to today? Whatever it is, please count me in on it."

You can talk over anything with Jesus, and He'll give you the right point of view. God works in the parameters of your mind to guide you. He'll give you His answers to prayer. Trust Him for ideas and guidance.

MAY 22

READ: Proverbs 25:15
KEY VERSE: Proverbs 25:15

Riding home from school in the van, Bob and Karyn were with Jill. Suddenly, Bob made an unusual comment, "Nobody likes me." Bob— of all people. He's unusually cute and very small. He will talk with anyone of any age. He's thoughtful and encouraging.

He had starred in a musical, *David and the Giants,* which was performed for several audiences to rave reviews. And he's the son of the man the papers are saying has almost single-handedly brought pro basketball to Orlando. To top it all off, Bob got a lot of attention from the picture of our family on the front page of the previous Mother's Day issue of the Sunday *Orlando Sentinel.*

We know Bob to be truly humble, even if he enjoys the attention. We've had no reports of his lording it over anyone or being obnoxious. Yet Bob says one of his friends told him he drew all over the picture and chopped it to pieces with a hatchet (a typical childish exaggeration).

"Bob," Jill explained, "it's not your fault. It's not because of anything you've done wrong. Your job now is always to win the game."

"What game?"

"The put-down game. When someone tries to put you down, the last person who talks loses."

As missionary Jim Elliot said, "There's no need for one to apologize for his actions, or defend them, if he's in God's will."

MAY 23

READ: Proverbs 30:24–28
KEY VERSE: Proverbs 30:24

Greatness is often in miniature, says Bob Foster, one of Pat's favorite writers. The weak, the little, and the insignificant can teach us lessons completely unknown to the mighty. Littleness does not mean nothingness. Solomon wisely illustrates this truth in today's passage and uses four puny creatures as test cases.

The ants have a built-in sense of doing the right thing at the right time. From the ant family, learn the lesson of prudence.

The rock badgers are hyraxes, animals that resemble rabbit-sized guinea pigs. They have an uncanny savvy about where to live. Feebleness forces them to well-guarded fortifications. Wise is the man who knows his weaknesses. From the rock badger, learn the lesson of perception.

The locusts went forth to divide the spoil, and not one of them was appointed chief. They pulled together in one accord and got the job done. There is a lesson for those of us who are one in Christ: we are all part of the same unified body. From the locusts, learn the lesson of partnership.

The spider is insignificant, yet he ends up in the king's palace. Even when his work is destroyed, he starts all over again. His motto is Never Say Die! Despite every attempt on the life of Joseph, he ended up on the top of the heap. From the spider, and Joseph, learn the lesson of persistence.

MAY 24

READ: Proverbs 10:23
KEY VERSE: Proverbs 10:23

When Pat was a senior in high school, he spent part of his vacation at a summer resort on the eastern seaboard at Rehoboth Beach, Delaware, with his lifelong buddy, Ruly Carpenter. Ruly's father owned the Phillies, and Ruly would grow up to become president of the club one day.

Pat and Ruly were bobbing offshore on rubber rafts when Ruly began to drift out past the buoys. The lifeguards waved him back in, but

Ruly ignored them and propelled himself farther the other way. It was as if he was determined to head for England.

Ruly waved for Pat to join him. Pat looked toward shore where the lifeguards were standing at the tops of their chairs, waving towels, yelling, and whistling at the boys. He made his decision, flopped onto his belly, and paddled to catch up with Ruly.

The lifeguards in boats quickly caught up with the boys. Both paid the price. Home for the weekend, grounded, lectures. Pat's mother was nearly hysterical. "How far will you be led?" was the question he still remembers. As strong a personality as Ruly Carpenter was, Pat had to learn to be his own man and know when to lead, when to follow, and when to speak his mind.

(He and Ruly remain friends to this day.)

MAY 25

READ: Genesis 2:4–17
KEY VERSE: Genesis 2:7

Max Lucado's *No Wonder They Call Him the Savior* is one of the best pieces of writing we've read in a long time. Here's a sample:

"Now, imagine God's creativity. Of all we don't know about the creation, there is one thing we do know—He did it with a smile. He must've had a blast. Painting the stripes on the zebra, hanging the stars in the sky, putting the gold in the sunset. What creativity! Stretching the neck of the giraffe, putting the flutter in the mockingbird's wings, planting the giggle in the hyena.

"What a time He had. Like a whistling carpenter in His workshop, He loved every bit of it. He poured Himself into the work. So intent was His creativity that He took a day off at the end of the week just to rest.

"And then, as a finale to a brilliant performance, He made man. With His typical creative flair, He began with a useless mound of dirt and ended up with an invaluable species called a human. A human who had the unique honor to bear the stamp, 'In His Image.'

"If you thought He was imaginative with the sea and the stars, just wait until you read what He does to get His creation to listen to Him!"

MAY 26

READ: Philippians 3:10–14
KEY VERSE: Philippians 3:14

When he was called by Chicago Cub TV network producer Jack Rosenberg and asked to be one of several fill-ins for the ailing announcer Harry Caray, Pat was thrilled. He had been a broadcaster during college days, but the chance to cover a big-league game was the opportunity of a lifetime. The game was a May 15 contest against the Astros in Houston.

Pat did his homework and carried with him a mound of information so he would sound knowledgeable. When it was over and Pat had been congratulated by WGN personnel and friends around the country, he placed the experience among his three greatest thrills in sports.

The first was the 76ers winning the world championship in 1983. No matter what you do in sports, your goal is to be number one, the top, the undisputed best. Whatever other successes you may have along the way, nothing can compare to the ultimate goal: the world championship. Second on Pat's list was the awarding of the NBA franchise to Orlando after all the work that went into it. The Chicago-Houston game was third, though Pat admits he had to fight a feeling of intimidation just before it started. When announcer Steve Stone complimented him on his opening remarks, Pat relaxed, knew he could do it, and was home free.

MAY 27

READ: Psalm 107:29–31
KEY VERSE: Psalm 107:29

Pat was impressed by the Cub pitcher, Greg Maddux, in the Houston game. He was a twenty-three-year-old who looked about twelve, yet he had the poise of a veteran and pitched brilliantly in the 3–1 victory.

The writers asked him about his poise after the game, wondering if anything fazed him.

"I get intimidated sometimes," he admitted, "but I try not to show it."

That reminded Pat of his own performance and how he wanted to teach the kids the same thing. In trying to accomplish this, he has told them: "There will be times in your life when you will be frustrated, intimidated, or downright scared. If you can cover your fear, your actions might follow the illusion.

"Don't panic. Don't go to pieces. Though your stomach may be doing flip-flops, stay in control. Don't let them see you sweat. Look and act as if you're in charge, and you'll feel as if you are."

It's important to let kids know that this advice is not just for show, to make phonies of them. These techniques build confidence.

We want our kids to learn to be like the duck: calm, cool, collected, and seemingly motionless above the water but paddling like crazy underneath.

MAY 28

READ: 1 Thessalonians 5:12–13
KEY VERSE: 1 Thessalonians 5:13

Though he has never met former big-leaguer and now manager of the Texas Rangers, Bobby Valentine, Pat has always been impressed with the good things he has heard about Valentine.

Unlike many big-league managers, who seem to take pride in living up to the image of being ornery loners, Valentine believes that he's on the job twenty-four hours a day, three hundred and sixty-five days a year. He believes that love is spelled t-i-m-e, and he offers it by talking and listening to players, fans, and the press. During the off-season, he spends his time speaking at banquets, coaching kids, signing autographs, and promoting the Rangers.

He's the kind of coach Pat would like the boys to have. Jimmy's coach was particularly encouraging last year. He took Jim out of a game in the last inning to give another boy a chance to play third, and what the coach said to the new player made Jim's night.

The coach probably didn't even realize Jim overheard it. It wasn't for Jim's benefit; it was for the substitute's. The coach said, "You've got some big shoes to fill."

It's hard to calculate how much of a thrill and a boost that was for Jim. May all coaches learn to be encouragers.

MAY 29

READ: James 1:17–27
KEY VERSE: James 1:17

Our eldest son was born on this date in 1974, and we will never forget holding him for the first time—the weeping, the disbelief, and the awesome responsibility. In the National Basketball Association draft the next day, Pat entered our son's name, James, and vital statistics as a pick of the Atlanta Hawks.

He's a good kid and has taught us much about the value of giving praise to a kid. We've learned that it's important to praise a child's performance, not his personality. When Jimmy was little, after he had been given a kind word praising his character ("You've been a real good boy"), he often responded with bad behavior.

Why? He may have been fearful he could not live up to the goodness expected of him. Children seem to feel they must deny what they sense isn't true. So now we tell him what he has done correctly or well, and he responds with more of the same positive behavior.

We've also learned to praise him for what he is responsible for, not for what he cannot help. Acts of kindness and generosity are worthy of praise, but not his hair or eyes. (He gets enough compliments on those!) It's valid to compliment him on how he *keeps* himself looking sharp, but not for the looks God gave him.

MAY 30

READ: Matthew 7:21–23
KEY VERSE: Matthew 7:21

We have heard it said that there are four types of faith: head faith, dead faith, devil's faith, and heart faith.

Head faith is merely an intellectual assent to what is written about Christ. From this, many people presume themselves to be Christians. The evidence of being born of God will be judged by the Lord Himself on the Judgment Day (see key verse).

Dead faith is an appropriation of ritual, taboo, or doctrine. It's found not only in Christians, but also in people of other religions. A Muslim has no illusions about Muhammad living in him. He knows that Muhammad is dead and his ashes are at Mecca. He fasts, tithes, and prays, and for all of that, he has a dead faith. We dare say that many so-called Christians have a similar faith.

Devil's faith is an emotional response to God's Word, a fear of hell and pleasure at the prospect of heaven. The epistle of James says of the devils that they also believe and tremble (see James 1:19).

Heart faith means appropriating Jesus Christ. It means to personally receive Him as He is presented, Prince and Savior, Lord and Christ. Paul describes this kind of faith in Romans 10:9.

MAY 31

READ: Mark 10:1–9
KEY VERSE: Mark 10:9

If we have a marriage guru, it's Dr. Ed Wheat, author of *Love Life For Every Married Couple*. In a 1983 interview with *Christian Herald* magazine, Dr. Wheat was asked about the misconceptions couples have about marriage. He answered:

"The key misconception that almost every couple has is that if they do what comes naturally, everything will be all right. But if you do what comes naturally, you'll be wrong almost every time. We're all basically selfish; it's our sin nature. . . .

"A lot of young women have the idea that their husbands will know how to love them physically, emotionally, and spiritually. It's a real shock when he doesn't. . . .

"If you want a great relationship, you're both going to have to work at it. No one starts out wanting a poor marriage, but we're all so ignorant. I'd been through medical school and I didn't know how to love my wife the way I should. But there's no place for embarrassment or pride. You've got to learn all you can and do all you can to put your learning into practice. . . .

"A good place to begin is to study marriage in the Bible. Then get hold of some good Christian books and tapes on marriage. If people aren't serious enough about their relationship to do that, I can't help them. If they put into practice the principles in my books, they wouldn't need to see me."

JUNE 1

READ: Matthew 5:13–16
KEY VERSE: Matthew 5:16

It was incredible how friendly people were to Jill and Karyn in the United Kingdom. Everywhere they went, they met people willing to help them with directions and advice. After standing in line to buy post cards, Jill was informed that she didn't have the proper change. The woman behind her simply paid her bill and walked out with a smile.

Jill had to wonder if she would have done the same if the situation had been reversed. Pat says yes, she would have. He remembers what he learned the first time Jill's father took the train from Chicago to Philadelphia to come for a visit. Anyone who knows Mr. Paige knows that he can strike up a conversation and build a friendship with just about anyone. Sure enough, when Jill went to pick him up, he had a new friend to introduce.

He was an Australian traveling across country. Jill asked him where he was staying in Philly so she could drop him off, but he said he hadn't arranged accommodations yet. Immediately, Jill replied, "You're coming home with us."

When Pat got home from work that evening, he wasn't even surprised. The Aussie friend stayed four days and was even recruited as the kids' Bible reader one morning. Pat says Jill can't help it. It's a habit.

JUNE 2

READ: Ecclesiastes 1:1–11
KEY VERSE: Ecclesiastes 1:11

Since 1983, this date has not slipped past unnoticed by the Williamses. That was when the Philadelphia 76ers finally got their victory parade down Broad Street after having delivered on a promise to their fans: they had won the National Basketball Association championship after years of near misses.

Pat spent twelve years as general manager of the 76ers. He served three separate owners and endured some of the most gut-wrenching, heartbreaking losses imaginable.

But the real reason June 2, 1983, is so memorable is that it came close to being a nonevent for Pat, even after all the years of work had paid off. The previous December, two things became very clear. First, the 76ers were the best team in the NBA, and they seemed likely to win the title. That was nothing new and there was no guarantee, but that time it looked more certain. Second, it was obvious that the marriage was on the rocks.

Jill had confronted Pat on what he still refers to as D-day. After ten years of marriage, she finally got his attention, God helped him begin to salvage the relationship, and the whole story resulted in the book *Rekindled.* But Pat had vowed in December, "Without Jill, I don't even want to be part of the victory parade."

The whole family basked in the thrill of it together.

JUNE 3

READ: Matthew 15:1–4
KEY VERSE: Matthew 15:4

From an ad in the *Orlando Sentinel,* early last year:

"Loving Daughters Seek Loving Man for Loving Mom!" Age: 46.

Marital status: Wishes she had one.

Religion: Enjoys her faith in God. Listens to and sings Sandi Patti music. Sings in church choir.

Family: Spends a lot of time with her parents, has four daughters— none of us live with her but one of our cats does because he's in love with her cat.

Family ties: Stronger than a granny knot.

Good points: Sense of humor, attractive, open-minded, adventurous, slim, supportive of daughters.

Bad points: Likes anchovy pizza.

Looks for in a man: Easygoing, sense of humor, nonsmoker, strong will, strong faith, strong ears.

Likes: Visiting with family, friends, and neighbors, and leisurely weekends.

Dislikes: Singles meetings, singles bars, singles parties, single living.

Goal in life: Red-haired grandchildren (however, we are not yet ready to supply her with these).

Most precious possession: Four daughters who love her.

JUNE 4

READ: 2 Timothy 3:10–17
KEY VERSE: 2 Timothy 3:15

Ron Coriell, director of public relations for Cedarville (Ohio) College, warns of the danger of imbuing children with the wrong values. By praising their physical appearance, grades, or athletic achievements, we run the risk of communicating that our values lie in looks, smarts, or skills.

Our key verse indicates that God places a high priority on wisdom. How do discerning Christian parents raise wise children to the glory of God? By using the Source Book of God's wisdom. Coriell suggests seven ways:

1. Read Scripture (see 2 Tim. 3:15). Start with just ten minutes a day, perhaps in John's gospel, and read the life of Jesus.

2. Talk about Scripture (see Deut. 6:7). Relate Scripture even to mundane things that happen during the day, wherever possible.

3. Guide with Scripture (see Ps. 119:105). The Bible is still God's road map to successful living.

4. Comfort with Scripture (see Ps. 119:50). When troubles overtake little ones, apply the healing scriptural salve.

5. Obey the Scripture (see Ps. 119:101). The Bible helps children understand sin and their need for a Savior.

6. Memorize Scripture (see Ps. 119:11). Start with short verses.

7. Sing the Scripture (see Eph. 5:19; Col. 3:16). We have no excuse for not allowing Christian music to permeate our homes.

JUNE 5

READ: Deuteronomy 3:28
KEY VERSE: Deuteronomy 3:28

When Andrea was five, she went with her six- and seven-year-old sisters, Sarah and Karyn, to have her ears pierced. She saw the tears, and knowing she didn't *have* to have it done, she chickened out and begged off.

A few weeks later, she worked up her courage and, with no bugging or encouragement from anyone, went to Jill and told her she wanted her ears pierced, too, just like the big girls.

A little soreness and a few tears later, it was done. The girls all looked smashing in their little pierced earrings.

The next day, Andrea showed us a note she had received from Karyn. Without prompting, Karyn had written to congratulate her on her courage and on getting it done. "I'm so proud of you," she had written.

Not much later, we learned that she had written a similar note to Bob for his performance as David in a musical. It reminded us of a note she wrote to Jill when Jill was down with a severe headache, and of the note Bob had written to Karyn about how he knew her name and would pronounce it and spell it right.

These are the times when it's gratifying to be parents. To see that something we've been talking about and trying to model has gotten through. Blessing is a major part of the B-E-S-T program, and we always want to practice it.

JUNE 6

READ: Isaiah 40:28–31
KEY VERSE: Isaiah 40:31

At times, the life of an oyster appeals to us, says writer Steve Goodier. No work. No toil. When the oyster is hungry, it just opens its shell and food rushes in. What a life! Freedom from want!

But consider the eagle. Survival is difficult, at best. The eagle has been given no home; it must build a nest among wind and rocks, hail and snow. Daily, the elements challenge the eagle. To eat, it must fly, search, and capture. To survive, it must be strong and alert.

By no coincidence, America chose the eagle, not the oyster, as its national emblem. The Bible speaks of mounting up with wings like eagles, not of clamming up in shells like oysters (see key verse).

The eagle may have a tough life, but it's the better for it. Our lives may be even tougher, but given the chance, God can renew our strength and enable us to mount up with wings when we face difficulties.

God can do that—given the chance. But as the passage indicates, it happens for those who wait upon the Lord, not those who clam up like oysters. Little will happen in a life closed to God's energizing power. Much can happen to those who learn to wait.

JUNE 7

READ: Isaiah 50:1–11
KEY VERSE: Isaiah 50:1

The shocking reality of divorce hit us full in the face the other day. A good friend's wife sued for divorce, seeking custody of their two-year-old son. Much wringing of hands, vows, pledges, and prayer preceded the preliminary hearing.

It was a disaster. Our friend was ordered out of the house, not just by his wife, but also by the judge. When he requested two-week-on/two-week-off visitation, he was laughed at. The judge told him he could see his son Tuesday evenings and all day on Saturdays.

Our friend is devastated, and we have to admit, so are we. Where will it all end? Why don't people go for help before it's too late to do anything? These people will be scarred for life. And think of the little boy.

People love to talk of the myth of no-fault or friendly divorces. In reality, it never seems to work out that way. Do you know any divorced couples who are really friendly to each other now? People learn to become civil, but the love is gone, the caring is gone. Cynicism has taken its place.

Kids become emotional tennis balls, batted back and forth between the opponents. Nobody wins. Everybody loses. But no one loses like the innocents. The children.

JUNE 8

READ: Revelation 20:13–15
KEY VERSE: Revelation 20:13

Pat's long-time friend is former football star and outspoken Christian Alan Ameche. The great fullback played at the University of Wisconsin where he won the Heisman Trophy. He then went on to play for the Baltimore Colts, where he acquired the nickname The Horse.

He finally settled in the Philadelphia area where he became a partner in business and also became deeply involved in the Fellowship of Christian Athletes.

Some years ago, in an attempt to surprise and honor him, Ameche's children surreptitiously gained permission from the University of Wisconsin to borrow the films of Alan's glory days there. They invited friends in, enjoyed a feast, set up the projector, and ushered everyone to chairs before the screen.

Imagine their surprise and chagrin as reel after reel showed nothing but a few passes and kicks, no Ameche running plays, unless they were the garden variety of grinding out a few yards. Where were the great plays, the long runs, and the tackle-breaking performances that won him the Heisman? They had been taken, one at a time, over the years to make highlight films.

That story made us think that there are clips from the films of our lives we wish were gone forever. But when we stand before God, it'll all be there, every play.

JUNE 9

READ: Luke 12:7
KEY VERSE: Luke 12:7

Whenever we wonder whether God is really interested in the little details of daily life, we think back to the evening Bobby was born. It was more than two weeks before the projected date that June 9 night in 1977, so we had no idea Bob's arrival was imminent.

Pat was at Temple University scouting a summer-league basketball double-header when Jill knew the time had come. She remembered that she had a phone number for Temple on a tiny scrap of paper she had thrown away a few days before, assuming she would never need it.

On her hands and knees, she riffled through the garbage until she turned up the number. It didn't even say Temple on it, but she remembered the shape of the paper. Who in the world would be answering the phone at Temple this time of night? Surely the administration offices were closed.

She dialed, hoping. Maybe the phone lines were directed to a security guard somewhere who could find Pat or ring the gym. The number rang and rang.

It was between games. Pat had chatted with friends and was walking past one end of the court, when a phone installed in the wall rang. Why not? "Hello?"

"Pat? It's Jill . . ." What are the odds?

JUNE 10

READ: Psalm 62:1–8
KEY VERSE: Psalm 62:8

Whenever we hear stories of children being hurt or killed by accident at home, our hearts go out to the parents. Any thinking person has to share that heartache. We also recommit ourselves to the cautious care of our little ones, to the best of our abilities.

The truth is, the person or persons in charge of toddlers must be constantly vigilant. Jill still suffers from guilt and remorse from the time Michael grabbed a cup of hot water when she turned away for just a moment. We shudder to think how much more serious Michael's accident could have been if the water had hit his head or face or eyes.

Some years ago, John Candelaria, an outstanding Pirate pitcher who is now with the California Angels, had a son who received brain damage and finally died as the result of an accident in a swimming pool. Recently, Marques Johnson, the pro basketball player, admitted his fifteen-month-old son to the hospital in critical condition after he was pulled from a pool. The child later died.

Grim, depressing stories. Parents have to know where little ones are every second of the day. It's tedious, boring work until it fails. We can only trust God and do the best we can.

JUNE 11

READ: Revelation 5:11–14
KEY VERSE: Revelation 5:13

Worship can be a difficult topic for many Christians. How are we supposed to go about it? Some may be used to a church that worships noisily while others are more familiar with a conservative, quiet church.

Our friends at Walk Through the Bible Ministries in Atlanta maintain that worship is easier when we understand four terms: *praise, honor, glory,* and *power.*

We *praise* God by recognizing Him as the Creator, noticing the things He has made—blades of grass, sunsets, rainbows, fragile flowers, and mighty oak trees—and thanking Him for each.

We *honor* God by giving Him the credit that is due Him. Did your child get an *A* on a recent test? Who got bragged on? The child or the One who gave the gift of the sharp mind?

We give God *glory* by magnifying His name. When we tell someone else about Him, there are twice as many people to worship Him.

We recognize God's *power* when we acknowledge that He, and He alone, is able to meet our needs each day.

Pick one of the four words and talk about it and practice it today. Worship involves giving our powerful God the praise, honor, and glory He deserves.

JUNE 12

READ: Isaiah 26:1–6
KEY VERSE: Isaiah 26:6

The other day everything got to Jill. Every gripe she ever thought of came to the surface, probably because she suddenly began feeling like everyone's chauffeur and slave. Endless hours seemed wasted in driving to and from gymnastics, soccer, baseball, youth group, and school car-pool.

She lashed out at the most convenient person—Pat. In a less-than-sweet tone, she let him know that the family never seemed to be together anymore just to relax. Coaches use every daylight hour for practice, and teachers who have the kids eight hours a day monopolize their time with homework at night.

She was afraid the kids would grow up without ever again sitting around the family room for checkers or charades or the occasional good TV program. She told Pat he was the one setting the frenetic pace and the children were not going to know how to relax.

Pat sat and listened seriously. At the end of the tirade, he agreed, and in taking it so well, he made Jill feel as if she might have come on a little strong. "You're right, Jill. I *will* try to learn to relax more and be an example to the kids. Many times God speaks to me through you, and I sense this is one of those times."

It only made Jill wish she'd shared her feelings a little more calmly.

JUNE 13

READ: Luke 16:1–13
KEY VERSE: Luke 16:1

Christian financial expert Larry Burkett says that most individual tension, strife, anger, and frustration are caused directly or indirectly by money. Over 80 percent of the waking day for the average individual is spent thinking about, talking about, and pursuing money.

As we earn money, we enter a training ground for God to develop (and for us to discover) our trustworthiness (see key verse). Here are six other ways God works through our finances:

1. He will use money to strengthen our trust in Him. We must accept our positions as stewards and turn the money over to Him (see Matt. 6:32–33).

2. He will use money in our lives to prove His love for us (see Matt. 7:11).

3. He will use money in our lives to prove His power over this world (see Rom. 10:11–12).

4. He will use money to unite Christians through many shared blessings (see 2 Cor. 8:14–15).

5. He will use money to provide direction for our lives (see Gal. 6:9).

6. He can also use money to satisfy the needs of others (see 2 Cor. 9:12).

God will never use money to worry us, corrupt us, or build our egos, nor will He allow us to hoard it (see 1 Tim. 6:6–8).

JUNE 14

READ: Mark 6:31–32
KEY VERSE: Mark 6:31

For many years, Pat didn't know the meaning of taking a vacation. Oh, he might get away for a few days, but he was always on the phone, eager to get back, making contacts when he was gone, and generally not taking a break at all.

Jill couldn't believe it when she discovered that he never took the opportunity to go sightseeing or even sunbathing when he went to some of the most exotic cities in the United States for business meetings, games, or negotiations.

On the honeymoon in Aruba, Pat wasn't really happy until he found a hotel where he could read the big-league scores from the States on a large message board. After being married several years and having a few kids, getting him to a vacation spot was like stopping Dr. J. once he was in the air with the ball palmed and ready to slam home.

The family would go to the cottage at Eagle's Mere, but after a day or two, Pat just sat with his ear glued to the phone, and nearly every time he found a reason he just had to go back early.

With Pat's resolve to be the B-E-S-T husband and father he can be, he has learned to turn off the phone, forget the job, and spend time with the kids and with Jill. He has learned what it means to really relax, to go on a media fast, and to become better in his work when he does get back because he's rested.

JUNE 15

READ: Proverbs 18:22–24
KEY VERSE: Proverbs 18:22

Dr. Anthony T. Evans, a friend of ours, is one of the most dynamic young black preachers in America. He is very popular as a sports chapel speaker as well. Recently, in his ministry publication, *The Urban Alternative,* he paid tribute to his wife. We've included some excerpts:

"Knowing my temperament, personality, vision, and His call for me, God chose the perfect partner [in Lois]. Who would have thought He would take me more than three thousand miles to a country that I had barely heard of, Guyana, South America, to introduce me to one of the most beautiful and talented ladies in the world, the lady who was to become my wife?

"In this day of family crisis and marital disintegration, it is wonderful to have a woman standing by your side in the ministry who provides the help, support, and encouragement as well as the reproof and accountability that is needed if you are going to minister on behalf of God in an effective and credible manner.

"Lois has also stayed by my side through twelve years of schooling, bearing the hardship with me in establishing a local church, hurting when I hurt, laughing when I laughed. Her willingness to share both the pain and the joy is my delight. And she is an excellent model of motherhood for our children."

JUNE 16

READ: 1 Corinthians 8
KEY VERSE: 1 Corinthians 8:1

For some reason, Jill hadn't slept well. And after having driven around all day in a van that needed a wheel alignment, she developed a nasty headache. Such maladies are infrequent, but when they come, they come on strong.

Fortunately, Grandma was visiting and immediately took over dinner and bedtime chores so Jill could go straight to bed. When Jill stirred at about nine and prepared to get something to eat, she noticed a folded piece of paper on the nightstand.

Squinting against the light, she discovered a note from seven-year-old Karyn. She had drawn a three-story house, some flowers, and a valentine. And she had written: "To Mom—I love you!!!!! When you get sick, my heart is broken. Love, Karyn." Who can put a value on such encouragement?

Pat is capable of his own brand. One morning after a late night of watching the NCAA basketball tournament, he reached over and woke Jill up early. "Jill," he said, "for fourteen and a half years, the grass has always been greener on my side of the fence."

When Charles Colson was sick in the hospital, his twenty-eight-year-old daughter Emily mopped his forehead with a cloth and held his hand. Finally, he insisted that she get back to her office in Boston. She said, "I can always get another job, but I can't get another dad like you."

JUNE 17

READ: Proverbs 15:5–10
KEY VERSE: Proverbs 15:5

Pat was general manager of the Atlanta Hawks in 1974, so we lived in Georgia and were privileged to sit under the preaching of Dr. Charles Stanley of the First Baptist Church.

In his *How to Keep Your Kids on Your Team*, Dr. Stanley writes to fathers, "You are the head of your family, and your children are subject to you spiritually before they are subject to the pastor. As a Christian, you have the responsibility of explaining to your children how to be saved.

"If a godly father asks for permission to baptize a son or a daughter he has led to Christ, I happily answer yes. Nothing in the Bible says that pastors are the only ones who can baptize others.

"Think about it for a moment. Think about that child standing ready for baptism, and he hears his father say, 'I baptize you in the name of the Father, the Son, and the Holy Spirit.' That is an experience the child will never forget. . . .

"Notice I said a godly father, not a perfect father. I simply mean a man whose testimony is above question. He loves the Lord and is trying to build a Christian family and keep his kids on his team. What greater joy could a father have than to baptize his own children?"

JUNE 18

READ: Deuteronomy 3:23–27
KEY VERSE: Deuteronomy 3:26

Today's key verse is not a pleasant one, but there is value in our reflecting on the biblical reasons why some prayer requests are denied. By avoiding those things that cause God to say no, we can experience more yes answers to our prayers. A few of the most significant reasons why God says no are these:

Because of a sinful life (see Ps. 66:18).
Because of spiritual disobedience (see 1 John 3:22).
Because of an unforgiving spirit (see Matt. 5:23–24).
Because of unbelief (see James 1:6–7).
Because of family discord (see 1 Pet. 3:7).
Because the request is outside His will (see 1 John 5:14).
Because of improper motives (see James 4:3).

Recently, Pat went to pick up one of the boys after school. It's unusual to have just one child in the car at a time, but it was also God's timing. "Dad, I have something to tell you, and you're not gonna like it. I looked on someone else's vocabulary test for one of my answers today."

"I'm glad you told me. And what happened?" Pat asked.

"I got it right, but I felt terrible, so I told the teacher and then asked God to forgive me," he said.

"And He did. You know that, don't you? Because of 1 John 1:9."
Our son nodded and quoted the verse.

JUNE 19

READ: Psalm 37:18–24
KEY VERSE: Psalm 37:23

We're big on total trust. To us, either God is in control, or He isn't. The idea that God set things in motion long ago and is now bored or uninvolved doesn't cut it.

Pat had already been in Orlando, trying to whip up interest in an NBA franchise, when Jill started the long trek by van from New Jersey with the kids. The van was jammed, and the top was loaded with bags full of stuff tethered to the luggage rack.

They weren't far out of Jersey when it happened. The wind caught one of the bags, worked it loose from the restraint, billowed it out, and sailed it off the top of the van. Jill caught sight of it floating down and bounding along the highway.

She pulled off and drove back to get it, grateful that there had been no damage. Inexplicably, she felt compelled to make room somehow inside the van for all the bags on top. It wasn't easy. Everybody had to move. People were cramped. She wondered if it was necessary.

Soon the wondering was over. Within an hour she was driving through a raging thundershower. The bags never would have survived it. The rest of the way to Orlando, Jill drove through rain.

Would God Himself cause a bag to fly off a van just to spur a lonely mother to protect herself and her brood? You betcha, for the "steps of a good man are ordered by the LORD."

JUNE 20

READ: Proverbs 3:19–26
KEY VERSES: Proverbs 3:21–23

Jimmy Piersall was an all-star outfielder for the Boston Red Sox in the 1950s and 1960s, and he wound up his major-league career with a sparkling fielding percentage of .997 and a lifetime batting average of .272. His book and the film that resulted from it, *Fear Strikes Out*, told the poignant story of his overcoming mental illness. His father had been overbearing and was the cause of much of his trouble.

He now works in community relations for the Chicago Cubs and speaks as a former ballplayer to various groups. What does he tell the kids he speaks to? He tells them they have to develop enthusiasm for something. "They have to find something they really like doing and then go out there and work hard at it. I tell them I used to hate school myself."

He also tells kids that the first impression they give their teachers is the one that's going to last. "And they'll have to do their homework sooner or later, so they might as well get it done now. You know what causes mental illness in a kid? Not being ready, not being prepared."

He also says that no matter how poor a family is, there's no excuse not to have clean clothes every day. "Kids need to get into doing the little things, the important things that go into creating a good self-image."

JUNE 21

READ: Psalm 127:3–4
KEY VERSE: Psalm 127:3

Judy Markey, a columnist for the *Chicago Sun-Times* and News America Syndicate, tells of a question put to twenty-two third graders: What's the hardest thing about being a dad?

The kids had on-premises daddies, not a divorce in the bunch, and all fathers had white-collar jobs. According to the children, the hardest thing about being a dad is that dad isn't there enough to be a dad. Nearly 85 percent of the kids said, "He's always gone." And being away on business trips wasn't the only reason for dad's absence. Even when he was in town, he was gone before breakfast and didn't get home until eight.

Some dads got home by six, but one child said, "He's usually too wiped out to play." Another said, "I don't really see my dad, except on weekends."

One boy wrote, "I think birthdays are the hardest. Dads always feel bad because they don't really know you well enough from day to day to know what you want for your presents."

Writer Markey summarizes, "But maybe what [that boy] actually wants isn't really *presents* from his dad. It is something even rarer. It's *presence*."

What's needed, even in most Christian homes, is a radical re-arrangement of priorities. Nothing else will work. If kids aren't high on the list, they'll lose out to other things every time, and in the end, the parent-child relationship will lose something very special.

JUNE 22

READ: Psalm 90
KEY VERSE: Psalm 90:12

There's never a wrong time during the year to set goals, measure your old ones, or just talk about where you are and where you want to be. This year, we, with the three oldest children, wrote out our goals.

Pat determined to study five books of the Bible, run over one thousand miles, reflect more, risk more, and do more things that will last after he's gone. He also pledged to spend more time with Jill and with the kids.

Jill committed herself to keep in better touch with friends, be faithful in personal Bible study, be the B-E-S-T wife and mother, successfully breed and raise parakeets, and be more like Jesus.

Jim vowed to get good at the guitar, learn the Bible, get on the honor roll, and learn to use the computer well.

Bob wanted to improve and be a good piano player, be a better person (kind, helpful, loving, and obedient), learn more about the Bible, be in some plays, and keep his room neat.

Karyn set goals of finishing second grade with A's, being better at reading, obeying better, learning more about the Bible, and becoming a better gymnast.

We know many people get hung up on goals, and some set too many or make them too difficult. We like to view them as guidelines for action.

JUNE 23

READ: Acts 13:14–23
KEY VERSE: Acts 13:23

Jill spends so much time in the van that she considers it her home away from home. Sometimes all the running gets to her, but being a "plain old mother" was something she always wanted to be. She just flips on the local Christian radio station and tries to glean something to grow on whenever she gets the chance.

Recently, she heard a sermon from today's passage about Paul preaching in the synagogue, the talk some have called his Antioch address. It became apparent to Jill that the same character traits God exhibited in His treatment of the Jewish nation, He also exhibits toward modern married couples.

In verse 17 His sovereignty is evident as He chooses the people of Israel. Today He chooses a man and a woman to marry and live together in His will.

In verse 18 we see how God in His patience put up with their grumbling in the wilderness. He displays that same patience with us when we grumble about our spouses, our marriages, and our situations.

In verse 23 we see that He sent His Son according to His promise. Our first step must be to accept the promise of His love gift in Jesus Christ. Then we know that if we follow His principles for marriage, as outlined in His Word, He promises to bless our union.

JUNE 24

READ: Proverbs 4:3–5
KEY VERSE: Proverbs 4:5

Pat had the privilege of speaking at Grace Seminary in Winona Lake, Indiana, and then visiting the old homestead of the late evangelist Billy Sunday. Pat was fascinated with the place, which was said to look almost exactly as it had—inside and out—in the days of the evangelist.

Billy Sunday was a professional baseball player, was converted, and then became one of the most dynamic preachers since D. L. Moody. God seems to raise up these men in every generation, from Jonathan Edwards to George Whitefield to D. L. Moody, from Billy Sunday to Billy Graham.

As Pat was shown a photograph of the happy young Sunday family many years before, a sad story accompanied it. His guide said that two of Sunday's children had died of alcohol-related accidents. How tragic in the family of a preacher to whom alcohol was an anathema.

Late in her life, after her husband had died, Sunday's wife made a statement to Billy Graham indicating what might have caused her children's tragedy:

"When you travel, as you surely must, don't make the mistake of taking your wife with you when your children are young. When you are gone, they need her, not anyone else." To the benefit of his family, Billy Graham heeded that advice.

JUNE 25

READ: 2 Peter 1:1–14
KEY VERSES: 2 Peter 1:5–7

Sometimes people accuse those of us who are sports buffs of pushing our kids into athletics just because we like it. Some parents may do that, but we don't count ourselves among their ranks. We'd like to think that if our boys, for instance, had no interest in baseball or soccer, we'd be just as happy to have them play the flute in the marching band.

However, since our kids *are* interested in sports and want to participate well and improve, there are several reasons why we encourage them. We see sports as an important part of their education. For example, in sports they learn the value, the benefits, and the limitations of competition. They'll be competing in some way for the rest of their lives, so they might as well become fully acquainted with it.

The physical fitness derived from competitive sports is gained through a much more pleasurable and less boring exercise than riding a stationary bike or jogging, as valuable as these are.

As important as anything else they learn from sports are the qualities of emotional control, discipline, how to be coachable, the ability to think under pressure, loyalty, and teamwork.

JUNE 26

READ: Romans 8:1–11
KEY VERSE: Romans 8:1

We fall into the same trap any other parents fall into, that of worrying about the job we're doing with our kids. We want to be perfect parents, and we want perfect kids. The more we listen to the experts on the radio and watch them on TV (and yes, read their books), the more guilty we can become.

Guilt feelings can compound the problem. We see and read how they could and should be, and we wonder why they're not. What's wrong with us? The guiltier we feel, the more uptight we can become with our kids, and before we know it, they can't do anything right. Little things upset us more. Their public misbehavior irritates us more. In general, we're all a bit more miserable.

Dr. S. Bruce Narramore, author, speaker, and dean of the Rosemead Graduate School of Psychology at Biola University, reminds us that when Jesus died on the cross to pay for our sins, "He didn't ask us to be something we're not. He took us just the way we were.

"One of the greatest lessons in life is the knowledge that we can accept ourselves with our imperfections—our tempers, our moods, our schedules, our frustrations, even our occasional desires to get away from it all. Guilt is defeating, and a defeated parent can never be his best."

JUNE 27

READ: Ecclesiastes 12:12–14
KEY VERSE: Ecclesiastes 12:12

As voracious readers, we only occasionally run across a truly good book, one that sticks with us a lifetime. One such book is the life story of Glenn Cunningham. The most tragic part of that story came early in his life when Glenn and his older brother were up early in the morning to do their job at the local school in Elkhart, Kansas.

They loaded the stove with firewood, and Glenn's brother doused the wood with liquid from a kerosene can. When he lighted the fire, the explosion killed him, rocked the building, and burned Glenn's legs badly. Due to a mix-up, the can had contained gasoline.

Glenn's doctor recommended amputation, but his parents couldn't bear the thought of it after having already lost one boy. They begged the doctor to wait one more day to decide, and they continued putting him off day after day, the whole time encouraging Glenn that he would one day walk again.

When the doctor finally removed the bandages, he discovered that the toes on Glenn's left foot were nearly burned off and one leg was more than two inches shorter than the other.

Yet through determination and perseverance, Glenn Cunningham became a world record holder in the mile and was named the outstanding athlete to perform in New York's Madison Square Garden during the first century of its existence.

JUNE 28

READ: Ecclesiastes 11:9–10
KEY VERSE: Ecclesiastes 11:9

One of the more inspiring baseball players who has ever lived is Ernie Banks, the former great Chicago Cubs shortstop and first baseman. He hit 512 career homers, although the Cubs never won a pennant while he was with them. Two years in a row in the late 1950s, he won the Most Valuable Player trophy while playing for a second-division team.

Ernie always had a smile for everyone, along with a limerick or a poem. Without fail, his cry was, "It's a beautiful day in the friendly confines of Wrigley Field, so let's play two." He loved the game, people, and life that much.

Pat appreciates the story Ernie tells of his father, who hardly ever saw the sun. He worked from before dawn until after dark so that Ernie would have the opportunity to play ball. He was selfless and sacrificial in his quest to give Ernie whatever he needed to realize their dream: the big leagues.

Finally, the day came when Ernie signed his contract with the Cubs. Would he run out for a drink, celebrate with his friends, call a press conference? No, he had business to attend to first. With part of his small cash bonus, he hurried to a local Western Union office and sent a wire directly to his father. It contained three words:

WE DID IT!

JUNE 29

READ: Amos 3:1–8
KEY VERSE: Amos 3:3

No one argues the fact that God intends permanence for marriage. We contend that compatibility is a prerequisite to permanence, and it doesn't come naturally. In fact, it's pretty much unnatural. But compatibility sparks romance, a quality every marriage needs. So, how do we cultivate compatibility?

By working on communications skills, especially listening.

By planning a daily debriefing time, at bedtime, while fixing dinner, whenever is best for us. We keep it sacred and uninterrupted.

By spending time together, even if we're involved in separate projects. We don't have to converse to be near each other.

By reading the same books. We do a lot of this, and it gives us more than enough to talk about.

By exercising together. We both benefit, mentally and physically.

By taking time for joint devotions. You've already got a head start on that one, especially if you've come this far.

By concentrating on improving our sex life. This deserves our best efforts.

By setting aside time to evaluate our marriage once a year.

JUNE 30

READ: Revelation 7:9–17
KEY VERSE: Revelation 7:17

One of Jill's favorite hymns, which she often performs on the violin, is "Come, Thou Fount of Every Blessing." It's a great song of praise to God, but there is a sad story surrounding it.

Two strangers were sharing a coach, a miserable-looking man and a happy-faced woman. She was reading the words to "Come, Thou Fount . . ." and was so encouraged and taken by them that she showed them to her unknown companion.

The man scowled as he studied the lyrics and then tears slowly rolled down his face. "Madam," he said, "I am the poor, unhappy man who wrote that hymn many years ago, and I would give a thousand worlds—if I had them—to enjoy the feeling I had then."

Robert Robinson had drifted out of fellowship with God until he became a mere shell of the man he had been. He knew the awful bondage of sin.

When Jill plays this song in concert, she quotes the haunting last lines:

> Prone to wander, Lord, I feel it.
> Prone to leave the God I love.
> Here's my heart, O take and seal it.
> Seal it for Thy courts above.

That is our prayer for the end of this month. Is it yours, too?

JULY 1

READ: Proverbs 6:20–23
KEY VERSE: Proverbs 6:23

When Jill read of the National Teacher of the Year in 1987, she was reminded of her own days as a teacher. Donna Oliver, of Burlington, North Carolina, was given a crystal apple by President Ronald Reagan for being chosen from the 2.5 million public-school teachers for the thirty-sixth annual award by the *Encyclopedia Britannica*, the Council of Chief State School Officers, and *Good Housekeeping* magazine.

Mrs. Oliver's tips for other teachers apply equally to parents. She says you've "got to have a genuine love for teaching. You've got to do it because you want to.

"Have a strong knowledge base and keep current.

"Establish procedures and policies at the very beginning.

"Make it exciting. You have a product to sell.

"Have respect for your students. If you do that, you almost command that they respect you."

Jill particularly appreciated the counsel about setting guidelines early. That's something she applied while teaching, and she was often complimented on the orderliness of her classroom. Her principal told her once that he knew he never had to be embarrassed to walk into her room. She says, "I didn't start by being their friend. I established and maintained authority. Fifteen years later, many of those little friends still keep in touch."

JULY 2

READ: 1 John 4:7–21
KEY VERSES: 1 John 4:12–13

At the historic Moody Memorial Church in Chicago, just a few months before we were married, former pastor Dr. Warren W. Wiersbe counseled us in his pastoral office. He said the three essentials for a happy marriage are (1) the will of God, (2) the Spirit of God, and (3) the love of God. We took careful notes, and though we didn't really learn these lessons until after ten years of marriage and a major crisis, the principles remain sound.

Dr. Wiersbe said young people must ask themselves, "Is it God's will for me to marry?" He drove home the point that one should never marry to run from problems. "The key to a happy home is *understanding*, so don't marry a stranger. And remember, men say, 'I think. . . ,' but women say, 'I feel. . . .'"

We listened, and we thought we heard, but we were deaf. We didn't know. We had no perspective. Neither of us was getting married to run from problems, but we were definitely marrying strangers.

And that line about what men say compared to what women say . . . thinking about it, meditating on it, and discussing it might have saved us a lot of grief. Though we heard it ten years before we started practicing it for keeps, we know it's more important to have the graces of the Spirit than the gifts of the Spirit.

JULY 3

READ: Psalm 31:19–24
KEY VERSE: Psalm 31:23

Faithfulness seems to be a disappearing character quality.

Don Sutton, the major-league pitching star and future Hall of Famer, is a friend of Pat's and a regular attendee of the Baseball Chapel program. He says, "I've read there are sixteen basic personality types and my type wants to be dependable, accountable, and responsible. I don't need trumpets and flags when I come in, but I do need a pat on the back on my way out.

"When I'm through, I want people to say about me, 'You could always count on Don Sutton. He cared about the people he played with.' That could not always be said about me, but I'd like to think it's true now. At least, it's what I want."

Even if Don wasn't a friend, we would accept those words as challenges to our own lives. We know that Don and his wife went through struggles similar to those we went through, but due to the ministry of marriage and family counselor, speaker, and author Tim Timmons, they were started back on the right road.

It took determination, hard work, and total dependence on God to pull them back together, but they agree it has been more than worth it. In marriage, in baseball, and in life, Don Sutton wants people to say that he could be counted on. Knowing him, we're sure they will.

JULY 4

READ: 2 Timothy 3:14–17
KEY VERSE: 2 Timothy 3:16

Eighty-nine percent of Americans will not read the Bible today, according to a Gallup Poll, and it has nothing to do with this being a national holiday. Pollster George Gallup, Jr., says our frequency of Bible reading has "remained virtually unchanged over the years. People revere the Bible, but they don't read it. That's what it comes down to."

Several years ago Pat committed himself to studying his Bible every day. And he wasn't talking about breezing through a selected reading chart or a proverb a day. He decided to read a book of the Bible every day for a month, making notes and using a commentary by a recognized conservative evangelical to learn, really learn, the salient points contained in each verse.

He realized, as the late Reuben Archer Torrey said, that mere intellectual study of the Word of God "is not enough; there must be meditation upon it. It must be revolved over and over in the mind, with a constant looking to God by His Spirit to make that Word a living thing in the heart."

Has it been difficult to maintain a schedule that takes at least a half-hour a day and sometimes more? At first, sure. But now it's become a habit, a good obsession. No matter where he is or what he is doing, Pat carves out the time and makes it inviolate. It has enriched his spiritual life beyond measure.

JULY 5

READ: Matthew 28:16–20
KEY VERSE: Matthew 28:19

In April 1987, Press Maravich died of cancer at age seventy-one. He coached basketball at Louisiana State University, and his son, Pistol Pete Maravich, was the best player he ever coached.

Pete was the only college player in history to average more than 40 points a game; a ball-handling, passing, and shooting wizard. With his floppy socks bouncing, Pete would bring the ball up the court and shoot from anywhere. One time, he'd fire one in from just past the midcourt line. The next time, he'd hit a teammate at the baseline with a thirty-five-foot, behind-the-back pass while looking elsewhere. Most who saw him agree he was the most exciting player in basketball history.

Pete played for the Atlanta Hawks when Pat was general manager there in the early seventies, and one of the toughest things Pat ever had to do was tell Pete he was trading him to the New Orleans Jazz for several players and draft picks.

After he became a Christian in 1983, the story goes that Pete would ask kids playing basketball in the school yard if he could talk to them about God. They always refused, of course. Then he would say, "What if I play you one against five and beat you?" A few minutes later, victorious, he would share his faith.

Pete had the joy of leading his own father to Christ a couple of years before Press died.

JULY 6

READ: 1 Timothy 5:1–16
KEY VERSE: 1 Timothy 5:8

Pat reads just about anything he can get his hands on, especially if it will enhance his role as a husband and father. After reading *His Needs, Her Needs* by Willard F. Harley, Jr., Pat has been trying to meet Jill's basic marital needs.

He tries to meet her need for affection with plenty of hugs and kisses. He also tries to show how much he cares with a steady flow of words, cards, flowers, gifts, and common courtesies.

He attempts to meet her need for intimate conversation by talking with her at the *feeling* level. He tries to listen with sensitivity, interest, and concern, conveying a desire to understand her, not to change her.

He tries to meet her need for honesty and openness by explaining his plans and actions, because he regards himself accountable to her and wants her to trust him and feel secure.

He meets Jill's need for financial support by taking the responsibility to provide for the family. Now, with eight children, it becomes more important for him to stay at the level of his profession that will make them secure.

He endeavors to meet her need for family commitment by putting his family first. He doesn't play the fool's game of working long hours to get ahead while his family languishes in neglect.

JULY 7

READ: Proverbs 31:30–31
KEY VERSE: Proverbs 31:30

Jill also learned a few things from Harley's *His Needs, Her Needs.*

She tries to meet Pat's need for sexual fulfillment by studying her own response and communicating to him what brings out the best in her. Each learns to satisfy and enjoy the other.

Jill attempts to meet Pat's needs for recreational companionship by developing mutual interests so that he repeatedly associates her with the pastimes he enjoys most.

She seeks to meet his need for her attractiveness by keeping fit with diet and exercise, and she dresses and makes herself up in a way that makes him proud in public and in private. People think that as a former beauty queen, she has an advantage in this area, but just like anyone else, she must work at it. Jill knows that Pat's love for her doesn't depend on her looks, but she feels he's worth the effort. Striving to always look her best is a gift of love to him.

She endeavors to fulfill his need for domestic support by creating an atmosphere of peace. She manages the home, giving him the opportunity to spend time with the family recreationally.

Jill meets Pat's need for respect by understanding his achievements better than anyone, as an expression of admiration for the man with whom she has chosen to share her life.

JULY 8

READ: Psalm 52:1–4
KEY VERSE: Psalm 52:2

Today's passage is a sad one, but all too true. How often do our tongues trip us up and get us into trouble?

We watched with sadness late one night in 1987 when the general manager of the Los Angeles Dodgers, Al Campanis, was interviewed by Ted Koppel on "Nightline." The purpose of the program was to reminisce about the breaking of the color barrier in big-league baseball forty years ago when Jackie Robinson became the first black player.

Koppel asked Campanis, who had been in baseball since long before Robinson broke into the league, how he would assess the progress made in the last four decades and why there weren't more blacks in management and front-office jobs.

Campanis said, in essence, that it was clear blacks didn't have all that it took for those kinds of jobs. When Koppel clearly gave him a chance to dig himself out, Campanis only made it worse by harking back to other racial myths about the sparsity of black swimmers and quarterbacks.

Within twenty-four hours, Campanis had tried to apologize. Within forty-eight hours, his long, illustrious career with the Dodgers ended in his being fired. All because of a few ill-chosen words, reflecting a bigoted view of man. That little hunk of tissue behind our teeth can spread ruin far and wide.

JULY 9

READ: Proverbs 22:1–16
KEY VERSE: Proverbs 22:6

We appreciate some of the writing of Christian psychologist Clyde M. Narramore, probably because it seems our home is a laboratory for his suggestions to devout Christians who want to ensure that children will follow in the faith when they grow up.

He offers several ideas, but one of his most important is proved in our interaction with Karyn. Dr. Narramore insists that parents must let children know they love them. He says it must be expressed in words as well as actions.

We have a very good friend named Tanya Crevier, who Pat believes is the best ballhandler in the world. She grew up in a family of eleven children, where the parents frequently told all eleven they loved them. Tanya says, "That makes me feel so secure. I don't need to run around looking for love in all the wrong places. You parents, don't ever tire of saying to your kids, 'I love you.'"

Pat likes to tell the kids he loves them all the time. When he queries Karyn, "How do you know I love you?" she says, "Because you always tell me."

A friend of ours tells his kids so often that they sometimes respond, "Yeah, I know."

He says, "You want me to quit telling you?"

"No."

Another hallmark of Dr. Narramore's advice is to develop open two-way communication. Learn to listen, not just lecture. Hear what they say, and what they *don't* say.

Bob is our big talker. He could dominate any conversation. Yet if we're not careful, we can shut him off quickly with the wrong word. We also try to avoid excessive criticism. It tells children they are not acceptable. Correction should be a positive experience.

JULY 10

READ: Psalm 119:162–168
KEY VERSE: Psalm 119:163

One thing Jill is happy about in her marriage is knowing she can trust Pat implicitly. For whatever faults he may have had or still has, lying isn't one of them. Even during the crisis years, when she felt neglected and used and dumped on, she never had any reason not to trust his word. Sure, she got tired of promises to reform, but he never intentionally misled her.

UCLA psychologist Gary Emery says that many men lie to women on a regular basis. "If a man is obviously less than six feet tall, he will say he is two or three inches taller than he really is. If he is an inch or two under six foot, he will almost always claim to be a six-footer."

Dr. Emery says men also lie about being lost. "A man hates to ask anyone for directions if there's a woman sitting next to him in the car—it's like admitting he's incompetent."

Men lie about not minding that their spouse has a romantic past, about why their car won't start, about their sports ability and history, about being afraid, about how they truly feel about what a woman is wearing, and about their health. "If they are feeling ill, they seldom admit it," says Dr. Emery. "Even when asked."

Trust must be the cornerstone for a Christian marriage. A lying husband is a harbinger of deep trouble.

JULY 11

READ: Galatians 5:13–15
KEY VERSE: Galatians 5:13

Sometimes we Christians are so busy that we never see the benefit of volunteer service. Volunteering to do things, such as delivering meals to needy people (not just from church but from the community), stuffing envelopes for a worthy charity, or driving senior citizens to their appointments, not only benefits others but provides an incredible amount of bonuses as well.

"Volunteers find new talents and report greater contentment," says Sara Steele, professor of adult education at the University of Wisconsin. She headed a study of 1,100 volunteers in various programs nationwide.

"Soon after they begin volunteering for things, people start to see themselves as valuable. Eighty-six percent said they gained leadership skills, and eighty-two percent improved their decision-making ability, and about the same percentage found that they increased their organizing and problem-solving ability."

Christians have an even more altruistic motive for community service. We should see it as a chance to serve Christ by serving "the least of these" and also as a chance to witness.

While living in New Jersey, Jill volunteered to lead a kids' choir in a small church. It required many hours to rehearse for two major cantatas and several regular performances, but the church was grateful and it was a fulfilling experience for Jill.

JULY 12

READ: Deuteronomy 6:4—9
KEY VERSE: Deuteronomy 6:7

Okay, we'll admit it. Much as we'd like to come across as Supermom and Superdad, the truth must be told. If we weren't strict with our supervision of the tube, even our perfect children would have the television on all day long.

But when we say we're strict, we didn't know how strict until we found out how many Christian kids seem to watch everything there is to watch. Apparently, we're among the strictest parents going, even among Christian families.

We're firm, we have to say that. No one watches TV without our permission. There's none of this casually plopping down on the couch to see what's on. We watch with a plan, with a purpose. People wonder why teenagers seem to mope around uninspired, but they haven't thought of relating it to television, which we firmly believe robs children of opportunity to think and create and use imagination.

Not to mention the other horrors of television. If you haven't watched with your child for a while, try it. Don't tell yourself that it's just the Road Runner and Wile E. Coyote slapsticking their way across the desert. Cartoons have come a long way from there, baby. Nothing influences children today more than television. Yet we wonder why it's so hard to keep them interested in the things of God.

JULY 13

READ: Matthew 25:14–30
KEY VERSE: Matthew 25:29

When you've been in professional sports as long as Pat has, you never know who you're going to run into from the past. Not long ago, Pat was in the Orlando airport when he was tapped on the shoulder. He turned to see former major-league infielder Denny Doyle who had played second base for the Spartanburg Phillies in 1966 on his way to the big leagues.

Denny runs a baseball camp in Winter Haven, Florida, and he told Pat a story affirming our view (which is actually James Dobson's view) that children must be presented opportunities to develop a specialty and excel at it.

Denny said that several years ago a man named Lefty Martinez brought his eleven-year-old son to the Doyle baseball camp, asking if they could determine whether the boy had big-league potential. Denny told him the kid was talented and obviously had the desire, but it was too early to be able to determine ultimate potential.

"Tell me this then," Mr. Martinez pressed. "Would he have a better chance living in Florida than in New Jersey?"

"Well, sure. Only because he could play virtually the year around and get more experience."

The next year, Lefty Martinez called Denny Doyle from his new home in Florida. A decade later, Dave Martinez is with the Chicago Cubs.

JULY 14

READ: Philippians 3:7–14; Luke 16:13
KEY VERSE: Philippians 3:13

Dr. George Sweeting, chancellor and former president of the Moody Bible Institute of Chicago, was Pat's pastor at Moody Memorial Church when Pat was general manager of the Chicago Bulls in the late sixties and early seventies. Pat always enjoyed hearing Dr. Sweeting speak on single-mindedness because Pat wanted that to be a hallmark of his life.

Dr. Sweeting likes to quote Britain's great prime minister, Benjamin Disraeli, "The secret of success is constancy of purpose." That, Sweeting submits, is what the apostle Paul had in mind when he said, "But this one thing I do" (Phil. 3:13).

Dr. Sweeting believes that single-mindedness is the most indispensable quality of all. A versatile person is all too often the man John Dryden described in one of his poems:

> A man so various, that he seem'd to be
> Not one, but all mankind's epitome:
> Stiff in opinions, always in the wrong;
> Was everything by starts, and nothing long;
> But, in the course of one revolving moon,
> Was chemist, fiddler, statesman, and buffoon.

D. L. Moody used to say, "Give me a man who says, 'This one thing I do,' and not 'These fifty things I dabble in.'" Too much versatility can render us ineffective and spread us too thin.

JULY 15

READ: James 3:1–18
KEY VERSE: James 3:8

Some of our children's coaches think all they're teaching is baseball or soccer. Little do they realize that they're modeling lifestyles, language, temperaments, and a host of other qualities, good or bad, for kids.

Some coaches obviously love the kids. They talk to them and to the parents, keeping them informed. They are encouraging and friendly. Others really seem to know their athletics, but they never say a word to the parents. The children take this in, too. They may not know what to make of it, but it is making an impression.

Jimmy has been fortunate enough to have had several coaches who have been great people to know. One was Jim Shanahan, who coaches in the Merchantville, New Jersey, league. He's a fun-loving man who loves the kids, and they know it. He made up a nickname for each kid on the team (and even some of their brothers and sisters). Bobby became Sox because he always wore a Chicago White Sox hat. Jimmy was Jim-bo.

When we moved to Florida, we heard from Coach Shanahan several times. We've been grateful to have had such a positive influence on Jimmy during his formative years, both in the realm of sports and in life.

JULY 16

READ: Psalm 8:6–9
KEY VERSE: Psalm 8:9

We have to admit that sometimes we are embarrassed by what is passed off as excellence in Christendom. Maybe the music is less than the best, the bulletin is full of misspellings, and the platform "performers" are not up to par. (Not in *our* church, of course!)

Now that could sound uppity or condescending, and we must clarify that we're not talking about humble ministries short on funds or talent. We're talking about ministries that have the resources to compete with the world.

In the sports and entertainment world, shoddy performance is not tolerated for long. Yet in the Christian world, it seems there's a proclivity to shooting ourselves in the foot. With all the shenanigans and failures the cause of Christ has suffered over the past few years, we don't need a lack of excellence on top of those things for people to ridicule even more.

Have we abandoned excellence? Dare we? Excellence is God Himself. His very name is excellent (see key verse). His works, His salvation, and His loving-kindness are excellent. The closer we are to God, the closer we are to excellence.

We heard women who work backstage for Phil Donahue being interviewed about their jobs. "Our job," one said flatly, "is to make Donahue look good."

Our job as Christians is to make Jesus look good.

JULY 17

READ: Psalm 34:1–7
KEY VERSE: Psalm 34:4

Any professional will tell us that worry is an energy consumer. We should channel that energy to finding constructive solutions.

To avoid waking up in the middle of the night in a cold sweat, try these four steps before you hit the pillow:

1. Pray. That sounds easy and didactic, but you'd be surprised how many Christians save it till they're at the end of themselves, out of options, and desperate.

2. Stop mulling over your worry. Come to a decision, even risk being wrong. Much worry is caused by indecision.

3. Having made your decision, stick to it. Don't make the mistake of never expecting to make a mistake.

4. Decide where thought ends and worry begins. Clear thinking is constructive. Worry is destructive. If you fail after praying and deciding and sticking to it, don't worry about it.

When Bob was a baby, his head grew faster than his body, and in the course of one year, he was in and out of every hospital in the Philadelphia area. He underwent every test imaginable. Jill couldn't eat or sleep.

Finally, we decided between us in prayer that Bob was God's very special loan to us. No matter what the outcome, He was in control, and Bob belonged to Him.

The doctors finally concurred that Bobby was just a smaller-than-average kid and found nothing abnormal in any of his tests. He has always been a vibrant, vivacious kid who believes that "the best things come in small packages."

JULY 18

READ: Psalm 34:11–22
KEY VERSE: Psalm 34:12

We think it's fun and stimulating to do your own paraphrasing of Scripture passages. One that has been done many times is 1 Corinthians 13. Jill has done that more than once. Try doing it for each other. You might want to try a different passage, but it's important that you both try the same one and compare the results.

Here's an example, one of Jill's paraphrases of 1 Corinthians 13:4ff.:

Love is incredibly patient.

Love is thrilled to be kind.

Love does not envy.

Love does not act proud.

Love does not show off.

Love doesn't seek the spotlight.

Love keeps calm when life is not.

Love looks for the best in people.

Love will not glory in that which is wrong.

Love completely provides for its loved ones in all things.

Love searches for good and assumes the best.

Love is full of anticipation (see key verse).

Love lasts through thick and thin.

Love never fails or gives up.

JULY 19

READ: Psalm 119:9–24
KEY VERSE: Psalm 119:11

We enjoy hearing on the radio the famous Christian psychiatrists Frank Minirth and Paul Meier of the Minirth-Meier clinic of Dallas, Texas. It was especially gratifying for us to hear them suggest ways for truly changing our lives and making ourselves indestructible. They say the key is making God's Word a power in our daily living.

That strikes a chord with us, because ever since Pat has been committed to a rigorous daily schedule of Bible reading, study, and memorization, we as a couple and as a family have become much more disciplined as well.

We've found it important to read something from the Scripture each day. We suggest that you needn't be legalistic about it. If you miss a day, that's okay; but strive to read some verses each day.

Write down the nuggets. As a verse speaks to your life and your circumstance, write it on a three-by-five card. Take it to work with you or tack it up in the kitchen where you can read it several times a day. Drs. Minirth and Meier do this, in spite of their busy schedules. It's not unusual for people to see them sneaking a peek at the cards they pull from their suit pockets several times a day. They consider it positive brainwashing. What you put into your brain is what's going to come out of your mouth and your life.

JULY 20

READ: Acts 5:1–11
KEY VERSE: Acts 5:9

When Michael was two and a half, Jill took him, along with her grandmother and mother, to Epcot Center. They all walked and walked and rode and rode and bought and bought. Jill's biggest concern was keeping track of Michael in the crowd.

After they had found their way out of the boat ride through the Land Pavilion, they picked up a few souvenirs. They made it all in one piece and began the long hike around the World Showcase Lagoon, stopping at each country's pavilion to see the displays and shops.

About halfway around the lagoon, something fell out of Michael's pocket. As Jill picked it up, her mouth fell open. It was a small watermelon napkin ring from way back at the Land Pavilion.

Like his Mom, Michael is addicted to watermelon, and he had grabbed the trinket and put it in his pocket. Some people might think that Jill should have just forgotten about it because, at $1.25, it seemed such a minor item.

But Jill places great importance on honesty, and she took the opportunity to explain carefully to Michael why they were going all the way back to return the napkin ring. An hour later, it was back in the shop.

JULY 21

READ: Proverbs 1:1–5
KEY VERSE: Proverbs 1:5

From the column of Russ White, a former sportswriter who now writes about religion for the *Orlando Sentinel*:

"One of the most loving father-son pictures I ever saw is of Hall of Fame hockey player Gordie Howe and his sons Mark and Marty. They were teammates for the Houston Aeroes and for the Hartford Whalers. The picture I like so much is of Gordie with his arms around his sons after they had played a game for Team Canada against the Soviet National Team. Pride and joy replaced the stitches and scars on Gordie Howe's weathered face. Imagine a man being both father and teammate to his sons. Imagine.

"I also recall Mark Howe telling me about how great a *dad* this hockey player had been. Somehow, Gordie always had time for his boys, for his family. Baseball Hall of Famer Fred Lindstrom couldn't give his son the same gift. When Lindstrom died a few years ago, I remember his son saying, 'My father never played catch with me. He never had the time.'"

That reminded Pat of a sad quote from Mickey Mantle, the legendary Yankee slugger. He often said it was the time his dad and grandfather spent pitching to him when he was a kid that made him into the hitter he was. "But my four boys never got any time with me when they were growing up. They could have been big leaguers. They should feel cheated."

JULY 22

READ: Hebrews 6:9–20
KEY VERSE: Hebrews 6:18

Pat became a Christian while president of the Spartanburg Phillies minor-league baseball team in 1968. He was naive in the faith, of course, and he thought that the huge success he experienced over the next five years had something to do with his conversion.

He was hired as business manager of the Philadelphia 76ers the next year. A year later he was hired by the Chicago Bulls and became, at twenty-nine, the youngest general manager in the history of pro sports.

For the next three years, things went famously for him. The Bulls were drawing huge crowds, signing good players, and winning games. Pat met Jill and got married. What could have been better? He was speaking, sharing his faith, moving up and out. He wasn't in the Word as much as he should have been or as much as he is now, but he didn't know any better. God was smiling upon him.

In the spring of 1973, the roof fell in. His coach turned on him, the owners pulled the rug out from under him, and the press took shots at him. He couldn't make it add up. Through the counsel of close Christian friends, he realized that the glory years were the unique ones. He discovered that growth comes only through adversity. He's had his share of trials through the years and realizes these difficult times have been arranged by God to make us more like Christ.

JULY 23

READ: Galatians 6:6–10
KEY VERSE: Galatians 6:9

Many minor tasks that must be done in the Lord's work attract little or no attention. Yet the faithful Christian who tends to those details makes a valuable contribution to the work, whether it's emptying wastebaskets, directing traffic, or typing letters.

Legend has it that the architect of a magnificent cathedral promised a large reward to the person who made the most important contribution to the finished sanctuary. As the building went up, people speculated about who would win the prize. The contractor? The woodcutter? The stonecutter? The artisans skilled in gold, iron, brass, and glass? Perhaps the carpenter assigned to the detailed grillwork next to the altar?

Because each workman did his best, the completed work was a masterpiece. But when the moment came to announce the winner of the reward, everyone was surprised. It was given to an old, poorly dressed peasant woman. What had she done?

Every day she had faithfully carried hay to the ox that pulled the marble for the stonecutter.

When God gives us a job to do, we must not be concerned over its greatness or insignificance or whether it carries an impressive title. Rather, God expects that we will be faithful. There is no small task that we do for Him.

JULY 24

READ: Proverbs 24:13–14
KEY VERSE: Proverbs 24:14

It isn't always the child who gives you the most feedback who's catching all your input. We used to worry that because Jim was so quiet and inexpressive as a child, he was not paying attention to us. When we read stories to him, he would appear uninterested. In fact, he might look elsewhere, walk around, or even play while we read.

But when we got to the questions at the end of the stories, he would stop and listen. And he always answered each one correctly. He had been listening all along. It's still happening. Jim is more alert than he sometimes appears. Who knows? Maybe he does it on purpose.

Recently, during the baseball game, Jim was playing third base. Just before the pitch, Pat—and everyone else—heard Jim call out, "Watch for the bunt!" He charged in toward the plate, and sure enough, the hitter bunted.

Jim was in perfect position to field it and throw him out. Pat was amazed. It had not been a bunting situation; there was no runner to move over. As Jim's team headed for the dugout, Pat ran down to ask, "Jim, how did you know he was going to bunt?"

"I watched their coach, Dad. I know their signals, and I saw him flash the sign."

Watch those quiet ones. Often there's more happening inside those heads than we realize.

JULY 25

READ: Matthew 7:24–29
KEY VERSES: Matthew 7:24–25

When Jill was young and her family consisted of her, her sister, and their parents, life was a lot less complicated. They were able to plan and take one really nice family vacation every year, and nothing interfered with it.

The Paiges still reminisce about the fun they had at dude ranches, on train trips and cruises, and at all the American landmarks. Those experiences gave Jill a sense of family that she didn't realize was unusual until she discovered that Pat's family mostly went their separate ways, even in the summer.

Jill's biggest problem now is finding time for the whole family to participate in an activity together. Nothing big, she insists, even just a trip to the playground will do. Unfortunately, something every day of the week, including Sunday, takes away individual members of the family.

Coaches who schedule practices on Sundays are especially irritating. Jill is worried that if her sons do not learn how important family is, when they grow up, they may experience the same crises she and Pat did.

Commitment, she feels, is important, as long as it's to a good cause. Commitment to family should take precedence over any other commitment except the commitment to God.

JULY 26

READ: Proverbs 21:25–26
KEY VERSES: Proverbs 21:25–26

In 1986, the Philadelphia 76ers won the lottery in the player draft and were awarded the first pick from the list of eligible college players. We wound up trading the pick away, but first we interviewed likely candidates, flying them to Philadelphia for physicals and tryouts.

One we brought was the huge North Carolina (Chapel Hill) center, Brad Dougherty. We wanted to know, among other things, what was so special about the program at North Carolina and its coach, Dean Smith. All of us had witnessed the incredible sense of family the coach generated there.

The coach had somehow engendered a love among the players and himself that was unique or at least enviable among college teams. One of our assistant coaches, John Gabriel, asked Dougherty to explain it. His answer was a lesson to Pat, as it should be to any parent.

He said, "From the day we report as freshmen, Coach Smith impresses upon us that we are responsible. We are responsible for ourselves. It's our responsibility to get up in the morning. It's our responsibility to get to class on time. It's our responsibility to graduate. Our responsibility to get jobs.

"Once we've handled our responsibilities, Coach Smith is free to do his, which is to meld us together, teach us the fundamentals, and coach us to victory. We love him for it."

JULY 27

READ: Joel 2:28–29
KEY VERSE: Joel 2:28

We spent a day at the beach talking about things: the team, the house, the kids, Jimmy in particular. We try not to keep calling him Jimmy, but it's hard. He's our first born, so he'll always be our baby. But he was turning thirteen. For the first time, we were going to be parents of a teenager.

We were scared. What were we going to do with this stranger in our house? We decided we would have a talk with him. A big talk. We would confide in him, tell him straight out that this was a new experience for us and for him.

We told him we weren't perfect. Neither was he. "There will be mistakes made on both sides. We're going to have limits. We're going to say no, maybe more than the parents of your friends will. All we can do is our best. You too."

We told him that the one thing we asked above all else was that he continue to talk to us. "Don't go silent on us. Tell us your fears, your concerns, your joys, your failures. Let us have input. We want to be open and transparent with you in advance."

We told him we wanted to go through the experience together and that we needed him to help teach us how to be parents of a teen. After a lengthy walk and talk we asked if he had any questions. Yes, just one, "Mom, what book did you read with all this stuff in it?"

JULY 28

READ: Genesis 9:3–7
KEY VERSE: Genesis 9:7

What is happening to morality? Oh, we've all wrung our hands over the state of the world, but what about the condition of the church?

One of our boys mentioned the other day about how many of the students in his Christian school classroom were from single-parent homes, the parents divorced.

At the Bible study she teaches, Jill has heard Christian parents of professing Christian teens worrying aloud about their daughters' sexual promiscuity and "what's a parent to do about birth control?"

Do we tell them not to do it, and then tell them to protect themselves if they do? We've heard John MacArthur say that giving birth control pills to unmarried women is merely accommodating their immorality.

At least one partner has been sterilized in one-third of all the couples who are at childbearing age in America. Why? Because kids confuse and complicate divorce. If you can keep from having children, you can "easily" end the marriage and leave. Children, most couples feel, are just in the way.

The rules seem to have changed, but the Bible hasn't. It becomes more and more difficult to raise godly children in this generation when there are fewer and fewer examples of godliness for them to imitate, even in the church.

JULY 29

READ: Proverbs 17:17–21
KEY VERSE: Proverbs 17:17

In our new home state of Florida, we see lots of retirees. Some are vigorous and on the go. We get a kick out of some of their bumper stickers. One says, No Job, No Phone, No Hassle, No Boss (and No Money!).

For some, however, that sentiment is more truth than humor. They seem to have punched out on the big clock of life. They hang around as if there is nothing to do. Of course, some are ill or tired and have deserved a lot of do-nothing time, but for those who really can't think of anything constructive to do, we have a suggestion.

Kid sitting.

You got it. There may be a limit to the number and the ages of the children you might want to handle. But what a ministry! Many young marriages would be immeasurably improved if the parents could get away for a weekend or even an overnighter, or if a mother could have a morning to herself. The residents of the Country Cove Retirement Hotel in Woodstock, Illinois, conduct a Christian preschool called Grandma's House. Both moms and the elderly residents benefit from this program.

One critical time in a growing family's life is when a new baby arrives. Some people's parents move in for a while and help out, but not always. Don't ask what you can do; just call and say when you'll be there and what you plan to do. You'll never be more appreciated or feel more useful.

JULY 30

READ: Luke 18:18–27
KEY VERSE: Luke 18:22

We seldom take our kids to shopping malls because of the communicable disease they catch as soon as we enter. It's called the Gimme Syndrome. They want everything they see, and they can't understand why they can't have it.

The last time we made the mistake of strolling through a new mall as a family, one of our kids discovered a scooter made in England. Of course, he just had to have it. We decided against the purchase and left the store.

All through the mall, we heard about it. We have to wonder if these aren't lines that are exchanged between all children and parents in newsletters to every part of the country:

"We could all share it."

"I'll pay you back out of my own money."

And if we say he doesn't have that much, "I'll do extra jobs!"

"It's really neat. We don't have anything like it."

Our whole society is afflicted with this syndrome. The middle class now lives like the upper class lived in the fifties. If you were around then and can recall, remember what you thought of a family that had a big house with more than one bathroom and more than one car? Maybe they had color TV and the latest appliances and toys. They traveled. Enough said?

JULY 31

READ: Ephesians 5:25–27
KEY VERSE: Ephesians 5:25

Christian sociologist Anthony Campolo is convinced that "most men in our society turn into clods shortly after marriage. They treat their wives with indifference. They become preoccupied with sports. And, worst of all, they stop listening to their wives. The deadening effect of an absence of attentive listening makes wives very vulnerable to advances from anyone who shows genuine interest in them.

"We must come to see that the more we succeed in training boys to love power, the more we create men who lack the sweet sensitivity, compassion, and humility that are essential for loving. Boys must be taught that women are to be loved rather than controlled.

"If there is to be hope for the institution of marriage, men must learn that the desire to dominate their wives must be set aside. They must be delivered from the love of power so they can be free to love."

In his book *Who Switched the Price Tags?* Campolo suggests that "there is no secret formula or magical recipe. There is no mysterious process that is the result of extensive research. There is only the age-old truth that those who do loving things will have loving feelings. The only kind of a fight a Christian couple should have is a fight in which each tries to outdo the other in love."

AUGUST 1

READ: Zechariah 8:14–17
KEY VERSE: Zechariah 8:17

The first day of any month is filled with the promise of new beginnings. We want to see ourselves in the best light, put behind us subpar performances, and promise to our family, friends, and coworkers that we will do our best.

In *Further Up the Organization*, Robert Townsend writes of promises: "Keep them. If asked when you can deliver something, ask for time to think. Build in a margin of safety. Name a date. Then deliver it earlier than you promised.

"The world is divided into two classes of people: the few people who make good on their promises (even if they don't promise as much) and the many who don't. Get in column A and stay there. You'll be very valuable wherever you are."

Abraham Lincoln respected and practiced honesty and abhorred dishonesty. He once entertained a guest who saw Lincoln's small son peeking at him from another room. He lured the child to his lap by promising him his watch charm. Later, as he was preparing to leave, Mr. Lincoln reminded him of his promise. "Oh, that charm?" the man said, laughing. "I couldn't part with it. It's been in the family for generations."

Lincoln replied, "Then, sir, I ask that you never visit this home again. I don't want my son to remember me as entertaining liars."

AUGUST 2

READ: John 15:1–11
KEY VERSE: John 15:5

All sorts of exotic plants thrive in Florida's climate. Though Jill has long been an avid gardener, many of the plants are unfamiliar in our two-acre Little Plantation, as the previous owners so aptly named it.

They were genuine horticulturists, and it seems they planted at least one of everything somewhere on the property. Our favorite is the jasmine that has taken over our two sets of iron gates at the entrance to the driveway. We are intoxicated by the sweet fragrance as we jog past in the morning or stroll past in the evening.

Jill wanted to bring some of that beauty and fragrance inside the house, so she cut some branches and put them in water. What a treat it was that first day to catch the scent at the entrance and then smell it again inside! But by the next day, the scent inside had faded. The cut branches had little aroma left.

We couldn't avoid the stark lessons from the jasmine branches. The longer the branches were separated from the vine, the less beautiful and fragrant they were. The only solution would have been to bring the plant itself inside and somehow anchor it in the ground. Separated branches first fade, become less fragrant, then curl up, and eventually die. When we separate ourselves from Christ (our Vine), we also will fade and wither spiritually.

AUGUST 3

READ: Romans 15:1–12
KEY VERSE: Romans 15:2

Pat is crazy about his daughters. He believes in telling them often and profusely that he loves them and that they are beautiful. He is careful not to equate his love with their beauty because he wants them to know that one is not dependent upon the other. Both Pat and Jill are also very careful to speak of the beauty as God-given, and make sure the girls understand that beauty begins inside, then shows outside as a pleasant attitude and a happy smile.

Verbalizing his love and admiration is one way to build their confidence, but Pat is also cautious to avoid flattery and to give genuine praise. He wants the girls to go into adulthood knowing that at least one important male in their lives thinks they are the greatest.

One day as he was leaving to take Bob and Jim to baseball practice, Pat stopped on the way to the van to say good-by to Sarah and Andrea. He hugged them and kissed them and told them they were beautiful. They beamed.

As Pat got into the van, Bobby said, "I know why you told the girls they are beautiful. It's because you feel you're at baseball practice too much with us boys and you want to make them feel good."

It was a fairly insightful comment for a nine-year-old, and Pat had to examine whether he was just assuaging guilt. He was happy to tell Bob that he might be partly right, but Dad meant what he said to the girls, too.

AUGUST 4

READ: Psalm 147
KEY VERSE: Psalm 147:3

One thing we don't mind getting up early for is going to California to be on James Dobson's radio program. During the years when we were reading everything he wrote (we still do!), we never expected to meet him, let alone be interviewed by him.

But when the story of our rescued marriage was released, we were invited. Recently, we went back for another taping of two programs. That's what required the early rising.

We were stunned when Dr. Dobson told us that as a result of the first two shows we had taped, he had received more than nine thousand letters. We knew that the book had engendered a lot of reaction and that many, many spouses had identified with our problems. We had received a ton of letters, but nothing close to nine thousand.

Dr. Dobson told us that the magnitude of the response placed the programs among the top ten he had ever done on "Focus On the Family." The ego stroke of that response was tempered quickly when we thought of the pain and suffering we endured for ten years to make that book and those programs not only possible but necessary.

We wouldn't want to go through that again for anything. And we hope you won't have to go through that either.

AUGUST 5

READ: Hebrews 4:11–12
KEY VERSE: Hebrews 4:12

In James I. Packer's excellent book, *Knowing God*, he tells why knowing about God is crucial. "As it would be cruel to an Amazon tribesman to fly him to London, put him down without explanation in Trafalgar Square, and leave him to fend for himself, so we are cruel to ourselves if we try to live in this world without knowing about the God whose world it is."

Packer makes the point that the world becomes a strange, mad, painful place and life a disappointing and unpleasant business for those who do not know God.

"Disregard the study of God," he says, "and you sentence yourself to stumble and blunder through life blindfolded, as it were, with no sense of direction and no understanding of what surrounds you. This way you can waste your life and lose your soul."

The best way to know God, of course, is to study His Word. That's what makes the Bible so special. It's a library of sixty-six books written over fifteen hundred years by more than forty authors (two of which were kings, two priests, two fishermen, two shepherds, a statesman, a tax collector, a military leader, a scribe, a cup bearer, a former Pharisee, and the list goes on). Despite the wide divergence of its authors, the Bible presents one major theme throughout: the restoration of humankind.

AUGUST 6

READ: 1 Kings 16:29–34; 22:17–26
KEY VERSE: 1 Kings 22:21

Before and after our taped interviews with Dr. James Dobson, we were privileged to be able to chat with him. He mentioned the importance of teaching children that everything they say and do is being recorded in God's book.

He used the illustration of the wicked King Ahab and Queen Jezebel who had no idea that their actions would be recounted for centuries in the most important Book of all time.

It's too easy for children to think that because they can't see God, He can't see them either. We don't believe in portraying Him as some cosmic bogeyman who's spying on them and hoping to catch them doing something wrong.

Rather, we like the biblical concept of a God who is all-knowing, all-powerful, and everywhere present. He is the perfect, eternal combination of mercy and justice. When we make the mistake of emphasizing only the love of God, we give children—and adults—the impression that nothing they do can harm their relationship with God.

True, nothing, not even their sin, can separate them from His love and salvation. But surely, as Dr. Dobson says, our deeds are being recorded. Children should know that just as God knows us and loves us and protects us, so He sees and hears and knows what we do, even in secret.

AUGUST 7

READ: 1 Timothy 5:17–25
KEY VERSE: 1 Timothy 5:22

Twenty years ago, we heard a few sermons about marriage partners keeping themselves pure, particularly from sexual sin. It was understood, a given. There was immorality, of course, but those who engaged in it knew it was wrong and suffered the consequences. Today adultery is so rampant that we have to wonder if even professing Christians have stopped believing it's wrong.

Pastors and other Christian leaders caught in immorality just move on to other ministries. Marriages and families break up, and while love and forgiveness abound, repentance and a true sense of sin are lacking.

There's never a wrong moment to remind ourselves of something very practical: how to control the sex drive. It's a complex issue and one not easily dealt with in a brief devotional, but there is a clear place to begin. We must accept God's moral law as absolute and right for ourselves: "But put on the Lord Jesus Christ, and make no provision for the flesh, to fulfill its lusts" (Rom. 13:14).

The apostle Paul told Timothy to flee youthful lusts (see 2 Tim. 2:22), which indicates that we are not to stand and fight that temptation. Too often, by the time we resolve not to go any further, we've gone too far already. Flee, run, do what you have to do to stay pure. You will save yourself a lifetime of guilt and remorse.

AUGUST 8

READ: Ephesians 1:3–6
KEY VERSE: Ephesians 1:5

Everybody we knew thought we'd gone over the edge when we started thinking about adopting two more children in November of 1985. Two more adoptees! How many kids do you want? Ten?

Many people asked Pat if he was really going to let Jill do it again. The fact was, he was pushing for two more kids as vigorously as Jill was.

People talk about how adding one baby to a previously one-child family doesn't make that big a difference. But when a third is added, it's Katie bar the door. We found that once we had a houseful, what's one or two more? Maybe we won't quit till we have ten, who knows?

Because of our ages and the number of children already in our family, we were elligible only for those children classified as special-need. Everyone seems to want infant girls, so the older or handicapped children or siblings (especially boys) are harder to place.

We wanted a boy and a girl or two boys. We felt that getting two at a time made it easier for each one. However, we didn't know that this time would take at least twice as long as the first time.

Somewhere along the line we heard or read that natural born children can be disinherited by law, but an adopted child can never be disinherited. That gave us a whole new view of our position as adopted children of God.

AUGUST 9

READ: Proverbs 3:27–30
KEY VERSE: Proverbs 3:27

We were telling a preacher's wife of our desire to add two more adoptees to our six children, and she shared a sad story. Following the Vietnam War, she felt compelled to adopt an orphan. Her husband said absolutely not. She is still living with the disappointment of that unfulfilled dream.

If you've thought about it previously, or if by reading about our experience, you've started to consider it, at least check it out. You don't have to make any commitments until you're ready.

We have never regretted our choices. Only a few months elapsed between June of 1983, when the girls' Korean mother relinquished them, and the time they became the answer to our prayers. The magnetic bonding between the girls and us was hard to describe, but when we first held those sweet Oriental dolls, who had been flown halfway around the world, we knew nothing would ever tear us apart.

And as our family expanded, our dream expanded. Three years later, in 1986, we were praying for two more children.

AUGUST 10

READ: Psalm 61
KEY VERSE: Psalm 61:2

The Holt agency told us that Korea was closed to sending special-need adoptees to families as large as ours, so we had them check the situation in the Philippines. For months we heard nothing, even though we had long since turned in the mountain of required paper-work.

For months we prayed and hoped and waited for something, anywhere, to open up. The beginning of 1986 came and went, and with the summer, Pat resigned from the 76ers and moved to Orlando.

By the end of the year, the Philippines possibility had fallen through. Our good friend from Holt, Susan Cox, herself a Korean adoptee, told us that a staff member had just returned with a pessimistic report. With the political and military turmoil and the Aquino government in transition, adoption from the Philippines had virtually been halted.

Rather than cooling our jets, this just frustrated us more. We wanted to adopt. Pat told Susan to cancel our application for a Philippine adoption. "We'll look on our own for something in South or Central America."

"Hold on," she said. "Before you do that, let me exhaust every possibility. You're one of our special adoptive families."

The next day she called with an announcement.

AUGUST 11

READ: Psalm 105:1–12
KEY VERSE: Psalm 105:1

"A miracle has happened," says Susan Cox of the Holt agency. "We just received air express from Korea photos and medical records on two special-need children, identical twin boys. They were born in 1980. Korea now tells us they will allow special children to go to larger families. Shall I send the photos?" You can guess the answer.

A few days later, we're in love again with children we've never met. The pictures of the tiny guys melt us. Their names are Chae Sang Hyung and Chae Sang Wan. We'll call them Thomas Jonathan and Stephen Joseph. Our other kids are ecstatic and supportive.

In our hearts and minds, the twins are already our children. We tell Holt we want them as soon as possible. But they won't come before some nearly heart-stopping news six weeks later.

Pat gets a call from Betsy Guinn at Holt, informing him that they have received a cable from Korea. No more special-need orphans will be awarded to families with more than four children. Betsy tells him, "We said, 'But, what about the Williamses' boys?' A week later a return cable said, 'The Williamses' boys may come but no more after that.'"

Pat tells Jill. We both cry. We know they're coming, but we still don't know when. We're struck by the moving of the hand of God in this and how close we came to missing out on the twins.

AUGUST 12

READ: Psalm 107:1–16
KEY VERSE: Psalm 107:1

On April 16, 1987, Pat got a call from two of the women at Holt. They were having a good-natured fight over who would share the news. Holt had received a cable just seconds before, informing them that the Williamses' children were ready. "Make flight arrangements."

Pat's knees were shaking as he phoned Jill. She whooped and hollered.

Then Jill called our son Bob in Chicago where he was visiting and asked if he could guess what was going to happen in two weeks. "The twins will arrive." He yelled and laughed.

When Jill told the girls, they jumped and danced around the room. When Jim heard, he asked, "Do I finally get to tell my friends?"

We had been waiting and hoping and praying for so long. Our minds were swirling. We had to find the boys a bedroom in a house that would be bulging with a family of ten. We had to set up beds, go through the older boys' clothes to see what would be available for the newcomers, register them in school, and find the Korean dictionary.

It was the kind of activity that did anything but take our minds off the impending arrival. Instead we got more psyched up. Waiting for the news of precisely when that plane would land, we were like a bunch of five-year-olds waiting for Christmas.

AUGUST 13

READ: Proverbs 27:10
KEY VERSE: Proverbs 27:10

Little could go wrong at that late stage of the process, so we wanted to tell everyone. We learned a few lessons, just as we had the first time around. Some of the people we told were precious. Others were not. We can take good-natured ribbing about a big family, but lack of interest hurts the worst.

One woman we told is, admittedly, not known for her conversational skills, and perhaps we should have known better than to tell her. Between every sentence, she tried to change the subject. She wasn't the least bit curious about the boys, their ages, their country, what we were going to name them, when they would arrive, or anything.

Frankly, she represents the kind of friend we don't want to be. Had we been bragging, that would have been one thing. But we weren't. We were simply sharing our good news about how the Lord had blessed us. We were hoping that, as the Bible says, the person who cries with us would also rejoice with us.

When we encounter someone like that, any joy we want to share is— at least temporarily—doused, just like what happens when water is tossed on a fire. All the air in our balloon can be let out with the pinprick of one word. On the other hand, others multiplied our delight by their encouraging reactions.

AUGUST 14

READ: Ecclesiastes 4:10–15
KEY VERSE: Ecclesiastes 4:14

Jill called Carol, one of her dearest friends in New Jersey, to tell her the news and found herself on the receiving end of some. Carol, who has two teenagers and a toddler, was pregnant again. Though forty-two, she was happy about her pregnancy.

She was worried that others might say she was too old, but her husband—a real encourager—said, "Carol, if God thought you were too old for this, it wouldn't have happened."

That would be encouraging to people who are older and still want children of their own. Of course, you should get medical advice, but we

151

believe if you really want an answer, the Lord will give it and provide the peace to accept it.

Carol's pregnancy made Jill think about her own decision to follow her doctor's advice and quit having children. She had had Michael when she was thirty-five. Even though she is always attracted to newborns and tiny infants, she is able to say she has peace about the decision.

Carol offered one of the best comments we received. She said, "What a tribute to Sarah and Andrea, that you would have had such a good experience adopting them that you want to do it again."

AUGUST 15

READ: Proverbs 20:7
KEY VERSE: Proverbs 20:7

One of the requirements of international adoption in the state of Florida is the fingerprinting of the parents. We had it done at the Orlando Police Department where we were aided by Nancy Ramsey.

We told her we were adopting two Koreans, and that would swell our number of children to eight, half of which were adopted. She raised her eyebrows. "Why in the world would you do that?"

Pat told her, "The Lord has put it in our hearts."

"Now," she said, "your job is to make them your friends when they grow up. That'll be a test of your success. I raised four, and the best part is, now they are my best friends."

On the first day of May, the plane arrived. We had picked up the kids at school after a half-day so they could go with us. You'd think we'd be old hands at it by now, but our legs were jelly. The only thing we knew about the boys was that they were twins, they were healthy (though smaller than the normally small Korean), and they were the products of an unwed mother who did not believe in abortion. For that, we were grateful.

The scene was much the same as last time, but the boys were old enough to walk with their escort. As they approached, we looked at them and loved them as our own, even though we'd never met.

AUGUST 16

READ: Psalm 143
KEY VERSE: Psalm 143:8

We're all smiling at them on the way home, trying to communicate in our own ways. They appear happy, at least curious. They remove their shoes before they enter the house. It will take days before they quit doing this. (Jill, however, decides she likes the custom.)

We assume bedtime will be traumatic, and they don't let us down. They have seen pictures of us and our home, and they are excited. But now it's nighttime, and they are exhausted, scared, lonely, and confused.

They're also old enough to speak Korean clearly—and loudly. But when they sob and cry out for their mama from the orphanage, they are hard to understand. We use the Korean dictionary as we try to soothe them, to tell them that we are their forever family and we love them and they are in their forever home.

They wail, mourning, grieving their loss. Though the orphanage was nothing compared to where they are now, it was home. It was comfortable and predictable. Everything here is foreign (that may be the understatement of the year). At least there are two Korean faces for them to look at, faces of girls about their age.

Now, in bed in the dark, that doesn't help. Jill lies between them, trying to understand their cries, sobbing because she can't.

AUGUST 17

READ: Psalm 144:11–15
KEY VERSES: Psalm 144:11–12

The next night it starts again, only a little earlier this time. They got so little sleep after the long plane ride that they are in desperate need of rest. Jill is more determined than ever to understand, to make out the Korean words, look them up, and answer the boys.

"Musowo, musowo," they lament. Finally, she had made it out. She rushes for the dictionary. She wants to teach them their American names soon, too, but for now, if it's more soothing to call them by their Korean names, so be it.

"I am afraid," she declares. "They're saying, 'I am afraid.'"

Back to bed with the boys, she begins speaking earnestly and very quietly in very broken Korean. They recognize her attempt at the words and stifle their sobs to listen. "I am your mama. I love you. I'm going to be your forever mama. I will always be with you. Don't be afraid. I will be here. I love you. Be quiet." They are still afraid, but there has been real communication at last.

During the next day, they are fine. They come into the kitchen and point to the freezer atop the refrigerator. It sounds as if they are saying "ice cream" with Italian accents, making each word two syllables. Ecstatic over their first English words (she thinks), Jill looks up *ice cream* in Korean. *Isu Kurim.*

AUGUST 18

READ: Luke 11:5–10
KEY VERSE: Luke 11:8

This passage can be a troubling one, much like the story of the woman who hounded the judge until he relented, not out of mercy but because of her persistence. It seems we should plead with God and call upon His grace, but these stories seem to indicate that dogged persistence reaches Him, too.

The other night Pat came home from work to find a young vacuum cleaner salesman in the middle of a pitch that had begun at four-twenty in the afternoon. He said a friend had given him our name. (It's a good thing he didn't tell us which "friend.")

A salesman from way back, Pat had never encountered anyone like this fellow. He had an answer for every objection, a comeback to every question. He even weaseled out of several conversation-ending signals, several outright noes, and several hints that we were busy, his time was up, and we were not going to make a one-thousand-dollar decision without sleeping on it.

Of course, the unbelievably fantastic price was available only that evening. Somehow, in spite of it all, we resisted. But Scripture is clear that if a friend persistently pleads with us in the night for bread, we should not turn him away.

And our God will hear *us* if we persistently come before His throne.

AUGUST 19

READ: Deuteronomy 1:34–40
KEY VERSE: Deuteronomy 1:38

Before we knew whether or not the Orlando Magic basketball team would be awarded a franchise in the National Basketball Association, we lived from week to week on pins and needles. We had moved our family of eight from New Jersey, where Pat had been at the top of the profession as general manager of a winning team for twelve years.

We couldn't plan for the future in Florida until we knew something for sure. We hoped, we prayed, and Pat worked toward the goal, but it seemed that every time we expected final word from the league, the decision was postponed.

We tried to encourage each other, but it was always good to get a dose from the outside, too, especially from someone who truly knows and understands. One day, during the worst of the turmoil, Jill received this note from Carole Sonju, wife of the general manager of the Dallas Mavericks:

"Just wanted to drop a note to encourage you to hang in there. What you are going through now is not easy or fun, but God is faithful and as you seek to follow Him, He will enable you to go through anything (even the NBA!). I understand the frustrations and disappointments you face now, and if there is anything I can do, even just to listen, please call. Also, please know I am praying for you."

AUGUST 20

READ: Romans 5:1–5
KEY VERSE: Romans 5:3

We've found that whenever we try to be outspoken about our faith in a secular setting, it's common to be asked to defend God. Have you ever been asked why God allows tragedies? How can a loving God allow airline crashes, terminal illnesses, divorce, and bankruptcy? Are these God's will?

Dr. John A. Huffman, Jr., minister of St. Andrew's Presbyterian Church in Newport Beach, California, says we can only answer those questions when we understand that God has three kinds of will. He quotes Leslie D. Weatherhead's book, *The Will of God*, to explain:

First is His *intentional* will. No, God never intended for there to be sickness, death, and broken relationships. These have come as His creation rebelled and followed Satan.

Second is His *circumstantial* will. God works in the very midst of our sufferings and can help us develop in positive ways both through the sufferings we bring upon ourselves by our own sin and through the innocent suffering that is ours due to the broken nature of the world in which we live.

Third is His *ultimate* will, which will be accomplished through Christ's victory when all human history shall be set straight at His second coming. Dr. Huffman concludes that "the peace of God has a way of undergirding us, even in the most difficult hours, giving us a serenity, a balance, a purpose."

AUGUST 21

READ: 2 Timothy 2:14–26
KEY VERSE: 2 Timothy 2:15

Pat and Jill had a layover in the Houston airport, and each took advantage of the extra time. Pat finished up his daily Bible study, and Jill got in some industrial-strength people watching.

Suddenly, from a long distance, she spotted a face she recognized. She asked Pat, "Isn't that _____?"

Sure enough, it was.

His was a sad story. He had played for one of the NBA teams Pat had managed. Late in his career, he had been traded to a team that was contending for a playoff spot. But down the stretch, when the most crucial games were on the line, he disappeared.

The excuses were lame; nothing was ever really explained. He was unceremoniously cut from the team, though he still had a few good years left of real athletic ability and earning power. Maybe it wasn't fair; maybe he had a legitimate excuse to let the team down. But still, he was branded undependable and unreliable.

Now that his basketball skills have long since eroded, he's desperate to catch on in some other area of the sports world. But that reputation still follows him, haunts him, and mocks him. No one will take a chance on him. All because of one lapse, one big mistake. How we must educate our children to the dangers of laxity!

AUGUST 22

READ: 1 Corinthians 13:11
KEY VERSE: 1 Corinthians 13:11

Our friend, Rev. David L. Bailey, has run a home for delinquent boys in Alloway, New Jersey, for over twenty years. He's got plenty of experience in making a boy into a man and in pondering the difference between a boy and a man.

Here's what he says:

"A boy gripes. You name it, a boy will gripe about it. A man comes to grips with problems and works on solving them.

"A boy cons everyone. A man is never phony.

"A boy cops out on every responsibility. He can't stay with it. A man hangs tough and sees everything through to the end.

"A boy talks tough. A man *is* tough.

"A boy runs from problems, runs from home, runs from people who want to help. A man wants answers, not escapes.

"A boy badmouths people in the worst language he can think of. A man knows when to keep his mouth shut, and how to keep it clean.

"A boy puts down everything and everybody. A man lifts people up and helps them.

"A boy goes along with the crowd. A man does his own thing, God's thing."

Who's the head of your household? A man or a boy? Psychologists call men who never grow up victims of the Peter Pan Syndrome. The real victims are their wives and children. The Bible calls them sinners, worse than infidels. God gives men the power to be men.

AUGUST 23

READ: Mark 16:14–18
KEY VERSE: Mark 16:15

We've always been impressed with Becky Manley Pippert, author of *Out of the Salt Shaker and Into the World* and *Pizza Parlor Evangelism.* Her views on and her modeling of lifestyle evangelism have challenged us and pushed us to see more victory in personal evangelism.

We're the types who like to get involved when a Billy Graham film or a big evangelical meeting comes to town. But even more important is looking for ways to share our faith in easy, conversational ways with the many people who cross our paths.

We can't claim a big list of people we've personally led to Christ, and it wouldn't be appropriate even if we could. But our job is not to win them. Our job is to tell them, plant the seed, and let the Holy Spirit of God do the convicting and winning.

Someone once asked Becky Pippert how a person could be an effective witness if he or she had no non-Christian friends. Becky said, "If you're always surrounded by Christians, you're not being biblical. The Scriptures and Jesus emphasize that fellowship and nurture are to build us for the explicit purpose of going out into the world. Our purposes for being on earth are to become like God and to bring others who don't know Him into relationship with Him."

AUGUST 24

READ: Matthew 7:12–14
KEY VERSE: Matthew 7:12

The famous psychiatrist, Dr. Karl Menninger, was answering questions from the audience after a lecture. Someone asked, "What would you advise a person to do if he felt a nervous breakdown coming on?"

Many people probably expected him to say, "Call a hot line or a friend or a psychiatrist." To their astonishment, he advised, "Lock up your house, go across the railroad tracks, find someone in need, and help that person."

The longer we live, the more we realize that the people who want to help themselves can do so only by helping others. It's the golden rule, the basic law of success. People who begin by asking how they can find success solely within themselves are doomed from the start.

For us, this has meant opening our home to strangers, to people in need. It has also meant adopting four Korean orphans. We're not blind to the fact that our adopted children are better off and live better lives than they might have otherwise, but the real rewards have been ours. We can't imagine our lives without these four precious children, added to the four who were born to us. Making them our own has forced us to look outside ourselves, and we are forever the richer.

AUGUST 25

READ: Psalm 63:1–8
KEY VERSE: Psalm 63:3

A strange thing happened one week in 1987. It was as if we lived a whole year inside seven days.

First, we were informed that Orlando had been awarded an NBA franchise to begin in 1989. The news came after months of working and wondering. Then, we were informed that our house in New Jersey had sold. Finally, our twin Korean boys arrived.

We expected to be ecstatic on each count, let alone all three at once. But at the end of it all, we were melancholy.

"Are you down?" Pat asked Jill one night.

She raised her eyebrows and nodded. "You?"

He shrugged and shook his head, bewildered. "I'm in a valley."

We tried to determine if the anticipation had made everything anti-climactic. Or maybe it was the stress of two little ones in the house who were scared to death and wore us out. But that wasn't it. We decided that we were just learning a lesson. Things, events, or happenings will never satisfy the soul's thirst for God. We are not to depend on circumstances. Even after mountaintop experiences, the valleys are there. We were forced once again to lean on the Shepherd.

Maybe we were learning what Corrie ten Boom meant when she said, "I've learned that I must hold everything loosely, because when I grip it tightly, it hurts when the Father pries my fingers loose and takes it from me!"

AUGUST 26

READ: Matthew 18:1–6
KEY VERSE: Matthew 18:5

At a recent Baby Dedication Sunday at the First Baptist Church in Orlando, our pastor, Jim Henry, gave four admonitions to parents:

1. Live Jesus Christ in front of your child. He will catch more from how you live than from what you teach. In fact, all your words will ring hollow if your actions send another message.

2. Bring your child to church every Sunday that it's humanly possible. You'll be establishing a foundation the devil can't take away.

3. Pray for your child by name every day.

4. Pray that somewhere God has established another Christian couple who are raising up a godly little person to be your child's spouse.

A friend of ours reports that his mother prayed for her children before they were born! She prayed for their salvation and for their future mates; she prayed that they would live godly lives. How significant it was to this man's bride-to-be when she learned that her mother-in-law prayed for her before her fiancé was ever born!

The myriad responsibilities of raising a child for Christ in this day seem overwhelming. But the four principles above, though they aren't as easy as they may appear, are a good place to start. The rewards are more than worth the effort.

AUGUST 27

READ: Proverbs 23:7a
KEY VERSE: Proverbs 23:7a

Notice that the passage today is a half-verse long. That way, you can read it, meditate on it, memorize it, and make it part of your life in a matter of moments. The verse itself will prove its own point.

Our former pastor, Warren Wiersbe, wrote, "You are what you think. You sow a thought and you reap an action. You sow an action and you reap a habit. You sow a habit and you reap a character. You sow a character and you reap a destiny. Destiny begins with thinking."

The truth of it hits home with Jill when she ponders what she thought about in her heart as a child. She literally became what she thought about. It wasn't *that* long ago, but she didn't have all the sophisticated toys that kids have today. She spent more time with dolls and simple toys that required lots of imagination.

For Jill, two themes permeated playtime, whether she was conscious of themes then or not. First, she was a mommy. She always said that what she wanted to be when she grew up was "just a plain old mother."

Second, she was a teacher. She would line up her dolls in rows, sometimes adding her little sister to the class, and teach them. Often she pretended to be a Sunday school teacher. Other times, she was a schoolteacher.

She grew up to be a mother (of eight), a schoolteacher, a Bible study teacher, and a Sunday school teacher.

What are your children playing with? What do they want to be when they grow up? What are they thinking in their hearts?

AUGUST 28

READ: 1 Corinthians 9:24–27
KEY VERSE: 1 Corinthians 9:27

Fifteen years ago, Dallas Cowboy coach Tom Landry spoke to the annual convention of the Evangelical Press Association a few months after his team won its first Super Bowl. He listed four qualities of a champion:

1. *Faith.* The Bible calls faith a confident assurance that something you want to happen will happen. In athletics, faith is believing you can win. It's believing in your coaches, your athletes, and your team. The Bible is full of men of faith. How about Moses? How many of us would have led those Jews through the Red Sea with the Egyptians on their heels? That's faith, and faith helps us develop patience and strength of character.

2. *Training.* It's amazing how people rationalize success. I've discovered that the harder you work, the luckier you get. God uses people who are willing to train and study and let the Holy Spirit put everything together for them (see key verse).

3. A *goal.* Our goal was the Super Bowl, but the necessity for a goal is also there in the Christian life. The goal of the apostle Paul is clear in Philippians 3:13–14.

4. A *will.* People determined to do something for God are people who have wanted to do something for God. They had the will. Christians have a big advantage here. We can submit our wills to the will of God, and that combination is tough to beat.

AUGUST 29

READ: Joshua 24:14–25
KEY VERSE: Joshua 24:15

Dr. Nick Stinnett of the University of Nebraska supervised a study of several intimate families nationwide, families that exhibited a great deal of happiness and parent-child satisfaction. He focused on families with two parents and at least one child living at home. Dr. Stinnett discovered six common characterisics in these families:

1. They show a high degree of *appreciation* for one another and help one another feel good about themselves. Every few months, one

household of five meets, and each person spends one minute praising every other member of the family.

2. These families spend quality *time together* in large quantities. They genuinely enjoy being together, and when faced with outside demands, they limit their obligations and involvements so family time is not lost.

3. They have good *communication* skills and patterns and spend a lot of time talking together.

4. Members of strong families are *committed* to promoting one another's welfare and happiness.

5. These families participate in *church together* and are committed to a spiritual lifestyle.

6. They have an ability to *cope with crises* in a positive manner.

AUGUST 30

READ: Ephesians 4:25–32
KEY VERSE: Ephesians 4:32

Today's verse is one to remember and apply. Pat's philosophy about promoting professional basketball is that on any given day, he may run into someone who doesn't know whether the ball is stuffed or inflated. Many of the questions he gets are naive, but he avoids being condescending, sarcastic, or snippy.

We saw both sides of the teaching of Ephesians 4:32 when we encountered a singer one night and a government worker the next day.

Country singer Crystal Gayle had a concert in Kissimmee, Florida, and after having seen her at the Magic Kingdom birthday bash at Disney World, we made sure to be there. Afterward, Pat suggested we try to meet her and have her autograph our tickets.

She was radiant, a tiny five-two woman with hair down to the tops of her heels. She took the time to chat, and we were impressed with how down-to-earth she was for being such a big star.

The next day we had to call the Immigration and Naturalization Service in Miami in connection with our efforts to adopt the two Korean boys. We needed to know certain steps and the timing of procedures in our new home state, much of which was different from our first adoption.

The woman asked brusquely if we had ever been involved in international adoption before. "Yes," Jill said, "we adopted two Korean girls a few years ago."

"Then you should know what happens," the woman said curtly.

AUGUST 31

READ: Hebrews 2:14–18
KEY VERSE: Hebrews 2:17

It was thrilling and fascinating to finally be able to communicate with our new Korean boys. For a while we felt the way God must have felt when He couldn't communicate with sinful man until He became like us.

We found a Korean woman who agreed to come and talk to our boys, after they had been with us about three weeks. We had been able to teach them only a few words for certain objects, and we struggled with the Korean dictionary to try to understand them.

At first they were shy with the woman, perhaps wondering if she had come to take them away again. Eventually they warmed up, and we got to ask all the questions that had been burning in us since they had arrived.

We learned they had a grandma in Korea, whom they missed. They didn't mention a father. They had been in two orphanages. One of the boys had been accidentally scalded by water, the other one injured slightly when hit by a taxi.

They liked it at our house because the food was good, and although they didn't understand the concept of forever, they caught that they would be with us until they were big, which made them smile. We were able to have the woman tell them in their own language that we loved them and that we would always be their parents.

It was one of the highlights of our lives.

SEPTEMBER 1

READ: James 2:1–13
KEY VERSE: James 2:1

On our trip to China several years ago, we learned as much about ourselves and people in general as we learned about that beautiful, mysterious country. We traveled with our missionary friends, John and Donna Bechtel, before China was officially opened to the West.

In the ancient capital city of Xian, where very few Westerners had ventured before us, many Chinese stared, and some followed us around. Jill's hair was permed, and many wanted to touch it. Our friend Lynne had blonde hair and was also the object of much interest.

As the people stared at us and we looked back into their eyes, we smiled, but they didn't. Donna Bechtel explained that the Chinese consider Westerners ugly; we, who spend millions of dollars every year trying to make ourselves beautiful!

Of course it's only natural that one race should consider itself the norm and outsiders abnormal, even ugly. That's one of the bases for racism in America.

We naturally think that our four Korean children are the most beautiful in the world—along with our four homegrown ones. God created everything and everyone, and each and every race is beautiful in His sight. If our goal is to be more like Him, we won't have room for racial prejudice.

SEPTEMBER 2

READ: Romans 13:8–14
KEY VERSE: Romans 13:13

It's been more than a half-century since Prohibition, and to most of us, that seems like ancient history. Detractors can make us think that was a dark blot on the landscape of our free country. We hear horror stories of gangsters, speakeasies, and the futility of trying to legislate morality.

What really did happen between 1920 and 1933? Was there an adverse effect on society? Consider the following statistics:

1. Crime decreased 54 percent.
2. Ninety-seven of the ninety-eight Keely Alcoholics Clinics closed for lack of patients.
3. Deaths related to alcohol abuse dropped 43 percent.

And what has happened since Prohibition's repeal in 1933?

1. Public drunkenness has increased 350 percent.
2. Violent crime has spiraled.
3. At least 50 percent of all traffic deaths are alcohol related.
4. America has more alcoholics today than ever before in history.
5. Family violence, incest, rape, and a host of other alcohol-induced crimes are rampant.

And now activists are pushing to have marijuana and cocaine decriminalized.

Maybe Prohibition wasn't so bad after all.

SEPTEMBER 3

READ: Psalm 55:16–23
KEY VERSE: Psalm 55:16

Before we adopted our twin Korean boys, when we had "only" four homegrown kids and two Korean daughters, Pat found a typical schedule Jill had drawn up for an afternoon. Remember, this was a normal day, probably something like your own.

Pat noted that it covered just a smidgen over three hours:

3:00—Pick up all kids but Karyn and Bob. Go directly to Y.

3:45—Drop off Sarah and Andrea. Go to Winter Park High School.

4:00—Drop off Jim. Go to Kim and Kate's [car-poolers].

4:20—Go back to school. Pick up Karyn and Bob.

4:30—Go back to Y. Pick up Sarah and Andrea. Drop off Bob and Karyn. Go home. Drop off kids. Go back to Y.

5:30—Pick up Bob at Y. (Stay there.)

6:00—Pick up Karyn at Y soccer field.

6:10—Pick up Jim at Winter Park High School. Pick up dinner on the way home. Do not pass GO, do not collect $200 [just kidding].

When Jill decided as a child that all she wanted to be when she grew up was a plain old mother, she didn't know that some days she would feel just plain old.

SEPTEMBER 4

READ: Acts 8:18–25
KEY VERSE: Acts 8:23

Today's Scripture passage is not a pleasant one. You can hear the cry in Simon's voice when he implores Peter to "pray to the Lord for me, that none of the things which you have spoken may come upon me" (v. 24).

But consider the key verse, where Peter tells that same man (who thought the gift of God could be purchased by money) that he is "poisoned by bitterness."

Bitterness *is* a poison. Jill was bitter for many years because she felt neglected and used by Pat. Only when she got her deepest feelings out into the open was there an avenue for healing.

In his book, *Lee: The Last Years*, Charles Bracelen Flood reports that after the Civil War, Robert E. Lee visited a Kentucky lady. She took him to the remains of a grand old tree in front of her house. She cried bitterly that its limbs and trunk had been destroyed by artillery fire.

She looked to General Lee for a word condemning the North or at least sympathizing with her loss. Instead, Lee said, "Cut it down, my dear madam, and forget it. It is better to forgive the injustices of the past than to allow them to remain and let bitterness take root and poison the rest of your life."

Does bitterness lurk in your heart? Expose it. Then burn it.

SEPTEMBER 5

READ: Psalm 41
KEY VERSE: Psalm 41:2

Pat is a great admirer of Los Angeles Laker coach Pat Riley. The 76ers have carried on an exciting rivalry with the Lakers for many years, and the 76ers beat them for the world championship in 1983. Riley guided the Lakers into the play-offs for seven straight years.

Now in his early forties, Riley and his wife Chris have been married since 1970. They went through difficult times in their marriage after Chris dropped out of college and Pat's basketball playing career came to an end.

Chris helped Pat because, as he has admitted, basketball was his whole life. Finally, he got back into the game as a broadcaster, then as an assistant coach in Los Angeles, and finally as head coach.

We really identify with the Rileys because they have an adopted son. Pat and Chris tried to have a family on their own for six years, and when they were unsuccessful, they adopted James.

Pat Riley says his priorities have changed with this addition to his family. He adds that if a couple can endure the trauma of finding out they can't have children, submit to the tests, and go through what they have to go through to adopt, the adoption itself is the easiest part. Needless to say, we've found this true, too.

SEPTEMBER 6

READ: 1 John 2:1–11
KEY VERSE: 1 John 2:5

The epistle of 1 John is a beautiful little letter that carries tremendous weight in doctrine. In it we find three ways to deal with sin in our lives, and the second and third will outstrip anything any secular humanist psychologist can hope to come up with.

First, we can try to *cover* our sin. But, "if we say that we have fellowship with Him, and walk in darkness, we lie and do not practice the truth. . . . If we say that we have no sin, we deceive ourselves, and the truth is not in us" (1 John 1:6, 8).

Covering won't do it. Who do we think we're fooling? God is the only Person who matters, and we can't hide the truth from Him. The only answer is the next option.

Second, our sin can be *confessed.* One of the great promises in Scripture appears in 1 John 1:9 where we are told that because of two of God's most wonderful attributes, two powerful transactions take place as a result of confession: "If we confess our sins, He is faithful and just to forgive us our sins and to cleanse us from all unrighteousness."

Third, our sin can be *conquered.* What joyous, freeing, exhilarating news to the sinner! The key is in abiding in Jesus Christ (see today's Scripture portion). No sin in a person's life is greater than the faithfulness and justness of God.

SEPTEMBER 7

READ: Philippians 3:1–14
KEY VERSE: Philippians 3:14

In 1987, when the Gary Hart scandal hit the newspapers all over the country, we were stricken by one account. It told of Donna Rice, the woman who had visited him and found herself in the middle of the controversy.

Apparently, shortly after graduating from college as a Phi Beta Kappa and a cheerleader, she pursued an acting and modeling career in New York. Later she revealed to a Fort Lauderdale newspaper reporter that she was a Southern Baptist from a Christian home and that she felt her life in New York was full of sins.

After a Billy Graham crusade in 1985, she said of her time in New York that the lure of the world had pulled her away, that she had been drifting from living for Jesus Christ. "I've been wanting to do this for a long time," she said. "I'm coming back."

This was from a girl who was reputed to have dated Prince Albert of Monaco and Frank Sinatra, Jr. We will probably never know the true story of what went on between her and Senator Hart, so we can't say whether all the allegations have any bearing on her resolve to "come back" to Christ.

The lesson here is to avoid the lure of the world and the danger of being swept away from our first love of Christ. Instead, we must press toward "the upward call of God in Christ Jesus."

SEPTEMBER 8

READ: Proverbs 2
KEY VERSES: Proverbs 2:10–11

Both Donna Rice and Gary Hart maintained that nothing immoral took place during their celebrated meetings. Regardless, Senator Hart's presidential aspirations died for lack of judgment.

We learned the hard way that appearance is just as important as fact. In 1986, after *Rekindled* had become a best seller, we were here and there promoting the book and found ourselves in Minneapolis at a convention of book distributors.

Jill was to sing and Pat to speak, in that order. Each had flown in from a different city, so only brief greetings were exchanged before the event got underway. Jill said she was going to call home to check on the kids, then sit out at the book table and catch up on correspondence after she sang. Pat agreed, joking that she had only heard the speech he was about to give "around eight thousand times."

Jill joked during her performance that she and Pat only saw each other briefly when plane trips happened to coincide. When she left the platform after she sang, people jumped to alarming conclusions.

The rumors started. The next thing we knew, people thought our marriage was on the rocks. Ever since then, we have endeavored to take nothing for granted and to show clearly in public the way our marriage is in private—reborn and whole. In this age when gossip runs rampant, even among church members, we are trying to avoid even a vague appearance of evil (see 1 Thess. 5:22).

SEPTEMBER 9

READ: Proverbs 31:10–16
KEY VERSE: Proverbs 31:16

When we were first married, we had a major disagreement that neither of us was aware of at first. Pat was a busy general manager of a professional sports team, well paid, and happy to have Jill handle the money. Jill was working, too, so there was no shortage of funds.

Jill, however, had grown up in a home in which the husband and father handled the finances. She thought Pat was copping out on his responsibility. Eventually, she said so.

When she complained for the umpteenth time, Pat finally explained how he viewed the situation. His explanation shocked Jill, but she started thinking about just what it meant in the marriage. He said he trusted her so much that he saw her as vice president of their little corporation. "I'll provide the income, and you handle the outgo."

Little by little, it dawned on Jill that Pat had placed her in a position of honor and responsibility. As she talked with other wives whose husbands wouldn't let them buy a candy bar without a major discussion, she realized how fortunate she was to be in such a position.

Many husbands refuse to give their wives a chance to prove that they might be the better of the two in managing the checkbook. It's important for a wife to learn how to do it, at least, in case she should be forced into it through the death or disability of her husband. But how much better if the heart of her husband safely trusted her (v. 11) by being confident in her while freeing his life to be able to spend more time with the family!

SEPTEMBER 10

READ: Proverbs 17:27–28
KEY VERSE: Proverbs 17:28

The joy of our lives as we grow older will be watching our children grow up. We love seeing them pass through their many stages now, and we seem to have them at all ages (though three of our four Koreans were all born in 1980).

But when they get into and through high school and college and start dating and falling in love, what delight we'll derive from observing that process! One of our goals is, at some point, to quit parenting them.

Make no mistake, we'll still be their parents, always and forever. But at some point, probably when they start bringing home our grandchildren, we must stop parenting and start grandparenting.

There's a crucial difference. We've seen the sad situations of grandparents not letting their children parent their own kids. Whenever the grandchildren are at grandma and grandpa's, they have two sets of parents, everyone telling them what to do.

Just as bad is when the parents exercise discipline and the grandparents, right in front of the child, usurp their authority or overrule them.

We will be ready to give *solicited* advice, but we want to let our kids make their own decisions when they're parents. We want to enjoy a mutually respected friendship between adults.

SEPTEMBER 11

READ: Psalm 62:5–8
KEY VERSE: Psalm 62:7

Too many people sit around trying to discover their spiritual gift rather than exercising some easy but effective ones that will benefit others. Even if they decide in the long run that whatever they tried should not be their specialty, certainly no harm has been done.

Waddy Spoelstra, Pat's old friend, has the gift of encouragement. He was a sportswriter for many years with the *Detroit Free Press* and founded Baseball Chapel under major-league baseball commissioner Bowie Kuhn's leadership.

Waddy never misses a big event. When the NBA franchise was awarded to Orlando, we received a note of congratulations from him. When the boys arrived from Korea, a note soon followed from Waddy.

He doesn't miss any special occasion, happy or tragic. It's as if it's a full-time job for him. Pat knows dozens of people who get the same kinds of notes from Waddy. What an example he is to people who feel there's nothing they can do for the kingdom!

All it takes is a little time and energy. You have to get an up-to-date list of names and addresses of your loved ones and spend a little on note paper and stamps, but the results are more than worth the investment.

SEPTEMBER 12

READ: Matthew 20:2–28
KEY VERSE: Matthew 20:26

Gordon MacDonald recounts Robert Sherwood's *Roosevelt and Hopkins*, which tells of the partnership between President Franklin D. Roosevelt and Harry Hopkins. In the book is an account of a conversation between Roosevelt and Wendell Willkie, who had just been defeated by Roosevelt in the 1940 election.

Willkie was about to head for war-torn London, and he had been invited to the White House for a brief visit with the president. Roosevelt told him that he would appreciate it if Willkie would visit with Harry Hopkins, whom Willkie would find in London on another assignment.

Willkie asked Roosevelt, "Why do you keep Hopkins so close to you? You surely must realize that people distrust him and resent his influence."

Roosevelt said, "I can understand that you wonder why I need that half-man [an allusion to Hopkins's extreme physical frailty] around me. But someday you may well be sitting where I am now as President of the United States. And when you are, you'll be looking at the door over there and knowing that practically everybody who walks through it wants something out of you. You'll learn what a lonely job this is, and you'll discover the need for somebody like Harry Hopkins, who asks for nothing except to serve you."

SEPTEMBER 13

READ: Isaiah 54:1–13
KEY VERSE: Isaiah 54:13

Pat read an interesting article in a discarded paper he found on an airplane. The ten behaviors kids want most from their parents were identified in an interview with 100,000 children aged ten to fourteen from twenty-four countries and various social backgrounds.

Children reported that they

1. Didn't want parents to argue in front of them. Voices should rarely be raised, and then only behind closed doors.

2. Wanted to be treated with the same affection as other children in the family.

3. Didn't want to be lied to. It's rare you can put one over on a kid, and of course, a Christian parent would never want to.

4. Wanted mutual tolerance from both parents. Inconsistency in one is bad enough, but when mom and dad don't agree, it's much worse.

5. Wanted friends welcomed in the home.

6. Wanted comradeship with parents. You should be close, leaving enough room for proper respect of each other.

7. Wanted parents to answer questions. Nothing is more frustrating for a youngster than to be ignored.

8. Didn't want to be punished in front of neighborhood kids.

9. Wanted parents to concentrate on their good points, not weaknesses.

10. Wanted parents to be constant in their affections and moods.

Parents would do well to take these comments to heart.

SEPTEMBER 14

READ: Exodus 20:1–17
KEY VERSE: Exodus 20:14

Some people say the Bible is difficult to understand. Maybe. But have you ever noticed that it seems particularly clear, simple, and straightforward at its most crucial points? Like our key verse for today. You can't get any more forthright than God Himself saying, "You shall not commit adultery."

Yet Robert S. Welch, features editor of the *Journal-American* in Bellevue, Washington, reports that the United States has the highest divorce rate in the world. He says that at the current rate, stepfamilies will outnumber biological families in just three years! More than half of all marriage partners commit adultery, and four times as many unmarried Americans live together as in 1970.

Welch makes the point that "in a country supposedly bent on the pursuit of excellence, we settle for 'fair' to 'poor' when it comes to families. If half our major businesses or schools failed, we'd be in a panic. But we accept divorce as some sort of scheduled stopover on the flight to fulfillment.

"Plenty of people in their twilight years have wished they could wind back the hands of time and wrestle on the rug with their three-year-old or take an evening walk with their spouse. Nobody, lying on his deathbed, has ever said, 'I wish I'd spent more time at the office.'"

SEPTEMBER 15

READ: Psalm 100
KEY VERSE: Psalm 100:4

As soon as we learned that Orlando had been awarded an NBA franchise, we prepared to settle in the area. We were already there, of course. In fact, we had bought a house. It wasn't adequate for our large family, but renting was prohibitive. We figured that if we got the team, we could always do some remodeling, tear out a wall here or there and add extra living space.

The first related decision we made after that was to join the church we had enjoyed for so long. We had looked for a good church and found one in First Baptist, Orlando, but we put off joining until we knew we'd be around a while.

Many people find a good church and know they're going to be living in the area for several years, but they are still hesitant to join. If they have convictions against church membership, based on their interpretation of Scripture, that's one thing. To dodge membership to elude accountability is quite another.

Many churches rightly limit their key workers to members. That way they know that board members and teachers agree with them on the fundamentals. When a member makes a financial commitment, there is a bond the leadership can trust and on which it can budget.

Don't avoid church membership. The body needs you to "serve the *Lord* with gladness" as much as you need to "enter into His gates with thanksgiving."

SEPTEMBER 16

READ: Hebrews 10:19–36
KEY VERSE: Hebrews 10:25

Christians who love the Lord love to be with God's people. Unfortunately, some Christians don't love God, or at least they don't appear to.

Writer Charles Allen reports that a recent survey of church members shows that

10 percent cannot be found . . . anywhere.

20 percent never attend a service.

25 percent admit they never pray.

35 percent admit they never read their Bibles.

40 percent never contribute to the church.

60 percent never study any Christian material.

75 percent never assume any responsibility in their church.

80 percent never invite anyone else to church.

95 percent never won another person to Christ.

100 percent expect to go to heaven.

Take your own spiritual temperature. Do you love to be with God's people? Love to go to His house? Love to talk with Him? Love to study His Word? Love to give to His work? Love to read Christian books? Love to get involved in ministry? Love to invite people to church or tell them about Christ?

We all know we can't earn our way into heaven. But what about our commitment to the One who has provided the way?

SEPTEMBER 17

READ: John 3:30–36
KEY VERSE: John 3:30

Having sung before many audiences and having talked with other musicians, Jill has discovered that very few people are responsive to music—very few smile, nod their heads, or even express their appreciation after a concert. One day these words came to her and have ministered to her many times since then.

Not For the Applause

Not for the applause,
Father remind me I sing for You.
Your gift is my song.
I am Your servant in all I do.
My life is in Your hands,
You lead me where You want.
And on Your Word I stand.
Reveal Yourself through me.
I just want to be available
To share with many or few
Make me willing and pliable
To be used Lord of You.
Times I don't feel like singing,
No one seems to care.

There's no response, no smiling.
I wonder, is anyone there?
   But then You gently whisper,
"My child, who makes you sing?"
And once again I remember
That to You all praise I bring.

(chorus)
   I am Your servant in all I do.
I am Your servant in all I do.

Copyright 1986 by Jill M. P. Williams

SEPTEMBER 18

READ: Proverbs 1:8–9
KEY VERSE: Proverbs 1:8

What's a parent to do? You read the scare stories in *Sports Illustrated* and other respected magazines, and you decide you'll never let your kids suit up for tackle football.

Yet Pat played football in high school, was a standout, and was never injured seriously, and participation in the sport proved to be a positive growth experience. In Florida, we're in the football belt, and the peer pressure will soon become almost unbearable for our kids. They love to play touch football in the yard and go out for Dad's passes. We watch pro and college games on television, and we can see the desire to imitate fairly bursting from the boys.

Many parents allow and encourage their kids to get involved in local football programs, and we're not here to say they're wrong. But we feel more comfortable channeling our kids into soccer and basketball and baseball and gymnastics.

We know kids can be seriously hurt in any of those sports, but the odds are more in their favor. True, if you make a mistake in any sport and land the wrong way, you can be injured for life. But in football, the players are getting bigger, stronger, and faster all the time, and the protective equipment, we fear, hasn't kept pace. For now, we're going to try to discourage their interest in tackle football and just enjoy it vicariously.

SEPTEMBER 19

READ: 2 Corinthians 6:14–18
KEY VERSE: 2 Corinthians 6:14

Sadly, approximately 500,000 children are sexually abused each year. Nine of ten abusers are men and turn out to be someone the child knows and trusts.

What can we as parents do? Child psychologists, law enforcement officials, and pediatricians offer these suggestions to reduce the risks:

1. Teach children about sex at their level of understanding. Use real names for body parts, and explain the difference between signs of affection and inappropriate fondling. Teach them to firmly object to any adult who tries the latter and to yell and tell.

2. Believe a child who claims to be sexually abused. Children almost never lie about something so alien to their experience.

3. Make sure that even your youngest children (as soon as they can speak) can state their full name and address and phone number.

4. Never leave your children in an unattended car.

5. Teach your children that if they get separated from you in a shopping mall or other public place, they should go to the nearest employee for help, not to the parking lot.

6. Know your child's friends and pay attention if the child no longer wants to play at a particular house. Find out why.

SEPTEMBER 20

READ: 1 Corinthians 5:9–13
KEY VERSE: 1 Corinthians 5:11

Pat admires Anthony Munoz of the Cincinnati Bengals, although he doesn't know the all-pro lineman personally. Munoz is considered one of the best offensive tackles in the game, and he was honored—of sorts—to be chosen by *Playboy* magazine to be interviewed about key matchups between offensive and defensive linemen.

Playboy is known among sportswriters for having an ambitious sports department, and apparently, they really do their homework for an annual Pigskin Preview. Munoz was to fly to their offices for photos and a major interview.

After prayer and consultation with his pastor at the Faith Evangelical Free Church in Milford, Ohio, Munoz declined the invitation, citing his Christian stand and his moral beliefs. *Playboy* doesn't realize how fortunate it is that he didn't accede to the request for an interview. It would have been the height of hypocrisy for the magazine to feature an active member of Citizens Concerned for Community Values who has helped raise money for antipornography groups.

Munoz reportedly said that he just couldn't see himself doing it. And because of that, no one else will see it either.

SEPTEMBER 21

READ: Isaiah 43:1–2
KEY VERSE: Isaiah 43:1

We haven't been able to find anything in the Bible about nicknames, but we're sold on them anyway. If the names called are positive and intended to build up, to "redeem," the receiver, as in these Scripture verses, they can reap tremendous benefits. Of course, it's never acceptable to use a nickname that pokes fun at someone or to use one that a person doesn't like.

Pat used to call Jill Jillo. It was okay for a while. Then the kids started calling her Mo, short for Mom. Lately, he has taken to trying to convince her she's unique. He asks her, "Who else does what you do? Singing, playing the violin, speaking, mothering eight, raising birds, and writing books?" Her new nickname, then, is Nique, short for unique.

We asked Jim some time ago what his favorite nickname would be. He chose Skip. We don't know why. We're not sure *he* does. But if that's what he wants to be called, that's what we'll call him. Of course, we're careful not to neglect his actual given name.

Bob is Bo. Karyn we call Special K. Sarah, whose middle name is Elizabeth, is our Lizzy. Andrea is Magic. Michael, no he's not the archangel. Around our place, he's Mickle the Pickle. And the twins are still getting used to their American names. Thomas has become T. J., and Stephen will probably be called Even Stephen.

SEPTEMBER 22

READ: Ephesians 6:10–17
KEY VERSE: Ephesians 6:17

Some people rarely crack a Bible anymore because they tried several times and didn't seem to get anything out of it. They didn't understand the language, so they gave up. If you find yourself in that category, try these five tips to help you get back into the Word:

1. Realize that God desires to speak to you through His Word. God cares so much for you that He has given you a Book, a road map that will guide you on the path of life. Think of the Bible as love letters from God to His much-adored child—you.

2. Find a version of the Bible that you like and can understand. There are dozens of choices.

3. Set aside a regular time each day to read and reflect on the Word. The benefits are tremendous. Consider your Bible reading a spiritual meal, as important to your spiritual health as eating dinner is to your physical well-being.

4. Begin your time of Bible reading and reflection with a simple prayer for insight.

5. Be a persistent digger. The Bible is a treasure trove of truth, and you can spend a lifetime uncovering its many riches. Near the end of his life, the great theologian Karl Barth said that the greatest truth he had learned was, "Jesus loves me, this I know, for the Bible tells me so."

SEPTEMBER 23

READ: Psalm 119:41–48
KEY VERSES: Psalm 119:44–45

People are starting to see the light on this issue of making too many commitments and taking time away from spouses and families. The secret is simple but not easy; it requires making and keeping priorities, standing up for what we know is right. There are no short cuts. We can talk all we want about putting our families first, but unless we prove it with in-the-flesh time, our loved ones know it's nothing but platitudes.

Michael Cooper, the outstanding sixth man for the Los Angeles Lakers, says that a lot of the ills of his fellow NBAers would be solved if their lives were centered on their families rather than themselves. The ones with the broken marriages or no marriage at all are often the ones who get in trouble with money or drugs.

Pat knows that the real strength in Michael Cooper's life is his wife, Wanda. They have two children, Michael, Jr., and Simone, and Wanda keeps all the outside commitments from threatening Michael's time at home. He calls her his buffer against the outside world.

It's a role she relishes. She says somebody in the family has to put a foot down, so she's the family heavy. "Somebody has to tell these people no sometimes," When the demands become too ponderous, she says, "Read my lips: 'NO!'"

SEPTEMBER 24

READ: Luke 10:38–42
KEY VERSE: Luke 10:42

We've mentioned before that we are avid readers. After reading a good book by Gigi Graham Tchividjian, Jill wrote these words.

MARTHA

She was fussing and grumbling, rushing around;
Guests for dinner and Mary couldn't be found.
Why? she thought, *do I always have to work alone?*
I'm not the only one who lives in this home!
She kept on complaining, then she heard His voice:
"Martha, your sister has made the right choice.
　"You need to take a 'Jesus break.'
Come, spend some time with Me, your work can wait.
Don't let the urgent things drag you down,
Don't be so busy hurrying around.
I'll show you what's important, what *I* want you to do—
But most of all it's love that I want from you!"
　How many times have I started my day
With hurrying and worrying, forgetting to pray?
For family and friends, giving of myself
Until He gently puts me on the shelf.
He says, "Stop your struggling, don't you see?
It's time to rest a while and remember Me.
　"Abide in Me and I will give you rest.
Only then will you be happy and blessed."

God doesn't want us to be like Martha—busy, busy, busy. He wants each of us to be a Mary—loving. He will not accept our labor in place of our love.

SEPTEMBER 25

READ: Psalm 78:1–8
KEY VERSE: Psalm 78:4

Is Christian school for every Christian family? Of course not, but if you can afford it, we recommend it. You'd be surprised how many Christian schools have tuition assistance programs for qualified parents. In our minds, it's worth whatever sacrifice is necessary, whether that means cutting back on entertainment or leisure, getting a second job, or whatever.

The problem with public schools is that even those that are good and not anti-God are generally neutral. Even if your child happens to have a Christian teacher, there are limits on what he or she can say during the class day.

At Christian schools, the teachers are not just teaching about God and relating God to every subject. They are; like their secular counterparts, teaching as much by how they model their lives as by anything they say. And our kids are catching it.

We don't want our children to think that the things of God and Christ are simply something we talk about at home and at church on Sunday. A child can easily think that God is not involved or interested in everyday life. If God is not mentioned at all during a whole day of school, what does that tell a child?

Forget the scary stories of religious persecution in public schools. The understated, subtle influences are worse.

SEPTEMBER 26

READ: Proverbs 24:3–4
KEY VERSES: Proverbs 24:3–4

Some Christian parents fear that if they send their kids to a Christian school, they will isolate them from the real world, will put them in a hothouse environment, and will leave them unprepared for dealing with society someday.

We don't want to downgrade that very real fear. We believe it's misplaced, but it's widespread enough to appear to have some basis. First, what is and what isn't the real world? If we believe God created everything and that Jesus Christ is the central Person in the history of humankind, Christianity is the real world. All else is counterfeit.

And lest anyone think that a child will be protected unrealistically from evil or bad language or dirty jokes or bullies, let us reassure you. The kids may be Christians, but they're not angels. Ours included.

What's wrong with a hothouse anyway? Aren't plants in hothouses the healthiest? Don't they transfer best to the soil outside? Don't they bear the biggest fruit and the loveliest flowers?

We like the idea of our kids studying in classrooms small enough that they get the individual attention they need from the teacher. There's no substitute for getting the modeling and the natural, unforced Christian perspective on every subject.

SEPTEMBER 27

READ: Proverbs 20:11
KEY VERSE: Proverbs 20:11

Pat was being taken to the airport after a speaking engagement and started talking kids and sports with the driver. His son was an eight-year-old soccer star, the best player on his team. But he had had a subpar game the day before.

The father was upset. It wasn't that he expected his son to excel every time he took the field, and he had never knowingly put undue pressure on the boy to succeed. It was just that there was a clear reason for the performance, and it was the man's pet peeve.

It's ours, too. It's when one of our children stays at a friend's house overnight. Now, no one is going to deprive a kid of that kind of activity, but there have to be some limits. At first, we think of this as a night off for the parents. One less kid to worry about.

But what about the next day? He comes home, he hasn't slept, and he's cranky. And if he has a ball game, forget it.

We've had to institute a few rules. No school nights. We tell our kids that if it's obvious they haven't slept, they can't go back to the same friend's house until we've talked with the parents.

And when kids stay at our place, we let them whisper for a half-hour or so, but then we separate them if they can't end the conversation and get some sleep. Works every time!

SEPTEMBER 28

READ: Job 5:17; Psalm 111:10; Proverbs 16:20; Psalm 36:7; and 1 Peter 4:14
KEY VERSE: Proverbs 16:20

There aren't enough happy people around anymore, and that goes for Christians, too. Too many people are not attracted to the faith because of the miserable samples they've seen.

Yet *happy* is God's Word. He wants us to enjoy our salvation. How can we? Here are four ways:

1. Don't chafe under chastening. God is fashioning an instrument He can use (see Job 5:17).

2. Dwell in the safety of the Lord. In these times of great danger, we can be anything but happy if we think we are alone (see Ps. 36:7).

3. Dare to fear God and walk His way (see Ps. 111:10).

4. Determine to roll with the punches. We can never get into as much trouble for Christ as He got into for us (see 1 Pet. 4:14).

SEPTEMBER 29

READ: Proverbs 28:21
KEY VERSE: Proverbs 28:21

How sad it was to read the story of Grace Kelly in James Spada's biographical exposé. She was a woman people referred to as the ice queen, the virginal beauty, and the pristine sweetheart. If she had nothing else, everyone assumed she had class. She gave the appearance of living up to the quality associated with her name.

The story is replete with her sexual encounters with dozens of men in Hollywood and all over the world. Sadly, the picture comes clearer as to why she had such a hunger. Grace Kelly apparently came from a strong, stern, dictatorial home. Some say she had a constant need to be reassured that she existed. When she won the Oscar for her performance in *The Country Girl*, her father is reputed to have said that it was the type of success he would have expected more from his older daughter, Margaret.

Are there others who are starved for affection because of their families? We don't want our children to grow up with such hunger and need. To be afflicted with such a great sense of emptiness and terrible loneliness has to be the worst feeling imaginable.

If there is anything positive in our lifestyles, we want that to shine through. We don't want to withhold from our children the affection and approval that Grace Kelly so deeply desired all her life.

SEPTEMBER 30

READ: Ecclesiastes 4:9–11
KEY VERSE: Ecclesiastes 4:9

The Williams family loves animals. If Jill really had her wish, she'd probably have at least one of everything in the back yard. But we do have some good neighbors, and we'd like to keep it that way. So we just have our birds, which are relatively easy to feed and care for, and we enjoy the many different kinds of animals by going to the zoo and collecting books about them. God's enormous creative capacity fascinates and thrills us as we read about His creatures.

One day we learned about wolves, who are believed to mate for life. Studies have shown that the male wolf seems to love his mate. Together, the wolf pair establish a den and work and sacrifice to care for their pups. A male and his mate are separated only by death.

Lewis Timberlake stated in his monthly newsletter that, fortunately for many marriages, there are men who, like the male wolf, commit themselves to helping and sacrificing for their wives for a lifetime. "In the Chinese language, there is a character meaning 'man' and a character meaning 'woman.' However, when these two characters are brought together, they mean 'good.' They mean exactly what God said when He brought man and woman together for the first time—'very good.'"

It's a couple that makes all the difference. God has shown us that marriage is the second most important thing to Him after creation. We must work together to keep it the beautiful and wonderful gift it is.

OCTOBER 1

READ: Proverbs 10:4–5
KEY VERSES: Proverbs 10:4–5

A survey held that a mother who is being pulled several different directions at once actually feels less overburdened than a mother with a more focused schedule. At first that sounds crazy, but as Jill thought about it, she agreed.

Even with eight children, Jill likes to read several books at a time (up to four) and do needlepointing (sometimes three at a time). She accomplishes these things in between running to and from baseball, soccer, and gymnastics practice and raising several clutches of baby parakeets and finches.

Jill has a feeling of fulfillment in doing so much. Even when it seems there aren't enough hours in a week for what she wants to get done in a day, she feels she's getting a lot out of mothering because she's trying to do so much for the family.

It's been a long time since she's sat around with little to do. And even though it will be ages before she has the problem of idleness again, she doesn't look forward to it. "It's when you really don't have things to do that you go batty," she says. "Something tells me that I'll never have to invent things to do, but I would if I had to."

This has been proved true in the work place, too. Employees are most frustrated when they are not kept busy. Is there a message here for teenagers?

OCTOBER 2

READ: James 2:14–18
KEY VERSES: James 2:15–16

We're inspired by people like Jodie Darragh. She's a housewife in Marietta, Georgia, who wanted to do something meaningful to help people. And she made it happen.

When she became aware of the need to fly Korean and other international orphans to adoptive families in the United States, she began in her kitchen a volunteer agency called Americans for International Aid (AIA). Using off-duty airline personnel, she sees that orphans are escorted to their adoptive parents in the United States. Agencies such as Holt International Children's Services, through which we adopted our two sets of orphans, would be unable to exist without the service AIA provides.

Holt is responsible for the details of the adoption, but getting the children overseas is the responsibility of the new parents. That's where Jodie Darragh's agency comes in. We've dealt with her enough to know that she knows her stuff and that she's persistent.

Jodie had a dream and she pursued it. Hers is no small effort. The complexities of licenses, passports, permissions, scheduling, foreign dollars, and all the other logistical details often take months to work out.

We've spoken on the phone, but we've never personally met Jodie. However, through her efforts, our four adopted children arrived without any trouble. We owe much love and gratitude to Jodie.

OCTOBER 3

READ: Luke 10:25–37
KEY VERSE: Luke 10:27

Never has the question asked in the Scripture passage for today been more important. Just who is your neighbor?

We have felt burdened about this question for years. It led Pat to ask a friend, a man who heads a huge international mission organization, for the latest statistics. The following information helped spur us to adopt four Korean children. Let it work in your heart, too.

More than twenty-five million Hispanics live in the United States, and their number is growing.

Ethnic groups form 36 percent of America's population.

No city in the world except Havana has as many Cubans as Miami. Only San Juan has more Puerto Ricans than New York City. Only Warsaw has more Poles than Chicago. No Central American *country* has as many Hispanics as Los Angeles.

Three million U.S. residents are Muslims. Another 2.4 million are Hindu.

Of the more than four billion people on earth, one-third have adequately heard the gospel. One-third have heard it inadequately. One-third have not heard it at all. Who is your neighbor?

OCTOBER 4

READ: 2 Timothy 6:3–5
KEY VERSE: 2 Timothy 6:5

When we were growing up, adoption was a hush-hush affair. It fell into the category of mental illnesses or epilepsy. We know now, of course, that these diseases are common, that they are not evidences of demon activity or any other such phenomena, and that they—more critically—are not to be somehow blamed on the victim.

We don't know why adoption was such a deep, dark secret. Jill remembers dating a young man who was adopted, and when one of her relatives discovered it, he was horrified. "Jill, be careful! You don't know anything of his real history." As if homicidal tendencies or illegitimate births are hereditary or contagious.

Maybe that was the rub. People assumed that all adopted children were illegitimate. Or maybe adoption exposed the "shame" of a couple unable to give birth to their own children, again, as if it was their fault.

We praise God that people have become somehow less superstitious over the years. To some people, adoption may remain taboo. But for those who have adopted a child, it's an indescribable joy. All we can do is recommend it. (We think adoption is every bit as miraculous as natural birth.) If you've thought about it, pursue it. Don't risk looking back in twenty years, wishing you had acted when you had the chance.

OCTOBER 5

READ: Proverbs 19:14
KEY VERSE: Proverbs 19:14

Since our marriage was rekindled in 1983, one of the things Pat has done is to let the world know he loves Jill. He does this in little ways.

For instance, he never forgets to introduce her in public, and when he introduces her, he doesn't just say, "This is my wife." She is a person. She has a name. He uses it. She also has several roles in life. She is a mother, a homemaker, a singer, a speaker, a violinist, a songwriter, a gardener, and a zoologist (okay, but she does raise birds!).

When she sings before Pat speaks, she chooses songs that fit the message, and he doesn't take that for granted. He refers to the songs, to the lyrics, and to the singer when he speaks. He ties the whole package together, but just as importantly he makes Jill feel appreciated. And when she feels appreciated by her husband, she feels special. And when special, loved.

We once heard John MacArthur say on the radio that if a man wants a wife "who adores you, relishes you, who's secure in you, then let that wife have the confidence that the whole world knows you love her. If *she* knows that the *world* knows that you love her, she has tremendous security. Women need to know they are loved, and they'll know they are loved not just when you tell them they're loved, but when you also tell everyone else."

OCTOBER 6

READ: Ecclesiastes 7:1
KEY VERSE: Ecclesiastes 7:1a

Many are offended when people who don't know them address them informally by using only a first name. Telephone solicitors seem to be particularly guilty of this. When one interrupts a meal, calls us by name, and then asks if we own our home, we've been tempted to say that we did own it until the bank foreclosed and Pa went to jail.

The offended parties may be right in those cases. But as a rule, people like to be called by their names. Your name is the only thing you really own, unconditionally and irrevocably. When someone asks you a question without preceding it by your name, do you sometimes miss it and not even answer?

Dale Carnegie was known for encouraging people to use others' names in order to win them as friends and to influence them. Pat tries to use someone's name several times during the first few minutes after being introduced so that the name sticks in his memory and is easily associated with the face.

It's amazing how people light up when their name is used in an appropriate manner. Do you use your spouse's and your children's names frequently and lovingly? You may be surprised at the atmosphere it brings to your home.

OCTOBER 7

READ: Jeremiah 18:1–11
KEY VERSE: Jeremiah 18:4

Pat enjoys the legends that surround sports. Not just the ones from eras gone by, but also those told by his friends and acquaintances in the business. One such story is told by O. J. Simpson, one of the greatest running backs in history. It seems that when O. J. was about fourteen in the early 1960s, he started running with a gang in the slums of San Francisco. He was already a star athlete and hoped that sports would be his ticket out, but he was very active in the gang, too.

One night he got caught shoplifting and was locked up with his accomplices over the weekend. When he got home, he knew what would happen. His mother would send him to his room and call her estranged husband, who would come over and give it to O. J. with his tongue and his belt.

Sure enough, O. J. was sent to his room and later called downstairs. But his father wasn't there. A famous visitor was there. Willie Mays. *The* Willie Mays, every kid's idol, especially every kid in San Francisco. Speechless, O. J. got to hang around with Willie for a day, running errands with him and chatting. No lecture, no big deal.

O. J. says that whoever set it up knew what he was doing. He got a view of a superstar as a normal, everyday human being. He knew his dream was possible, set his sights on it, and never turned back.

OCTOBER 8

READ: Hebrews 13:1–5
KEY VERSE: Hebrews 13:4

In a sexually saturated society, writes Tim Stafford, can we help teenagers abstain?

In his column in *Campus Life* magazine, he says a number of solutions probably won't accomplish much. He considers the following ones to be suspect:

1. "Just say no" should help kids who want to stick to their convictions despite the crowd; but peer pressure doesn't seem to be the major problem. Kids believe it's right because they love each other, not because "everybody is doing it."

2. Sex education programs, more-available contraceptives, or less-available contraceptives are unlikely to make a large difference. The schools can't effectively teach what the society doesn't believe.

3. Organizing parents to tell their kids what they think about premarital sex seems to have little effect. The kids simply do not believe their parents have a right to make such decisions for them.

Several factors *do* make a difference, however. Family togetherness is one. Kids from divorced families are about twice as likely to engage in premarital sex. A child from a family that displays a loving monogamy will have a strong reason to want to enter marriage a virgin. A Christian teen whose church articulates the same thing will have equally strong reasons.

OCTOBER 9

READ: Psalm 112
KEY VERSE: Psalm 112:4

When we were informed that Orlando had been awarded an NBA franchise, we learned a couple of lessons that could fall under the Blessing category in Dr. Ed Wheat's B-E-S-T program.

Jill was attending Karyn's soccer game when she overheard a man say to his daughter, in front of his wife, "Be nice. Don't be like your mother." He said it as if in jest, and a few people giggled. But it was clear to Jill that the mother was not amused. It was also apparent that the family had become accustomed to that type of talk.

Jill and I prefer the greetings of a telegram we received from the parents of one of Bob's friends. It read, in part: "Congratulations! We share in your joy! We thank God for answering our prayer to keep Bob and his family here. This community needs you. . . .

"Congratulations on *everything*. Your new sons/brothers are so blessed to be coming to your family. We'll pray for their safe trip to you and for their rapid adjustment. We look forward to meeting them."

That was probably the most expressive note we've ever received, and it was a tremendous encouragement to us. It's unlikely to have cost more than a dollar and a half, yet the value was immeasurable. Blessing, "dispersed abroad," is so easy, and so meaningful.

OCTOBER 10

READ: Colossians 3:1–11
KEY VERSE: Colossians 3:9

Novelist Sloan Wilson says one reason many young people are messed up with drugs and discouraged to the point of suicide is that they are fed four big lies that rob them of hope.

Lie No. 1. Youth should be the best time of life. If unhappy kids believe that, they have nothing to look forward to. Face it, youth is when everybody tells you what to do and you have to do it. Besides, young people are almost always broke.

Lie No. 2. Only people who are thin and in all ways physically beautiful have any real chance for love and happiness. Since most people in the world are rather plain looking, this lie creates a lot of unhappiness. It should be obvious to anyone that the really big prizes in adult life go to people with the best minds, spirits, and characters.

Lie No. 3. You have to get rich, famous, or both to enjoy much love or happiness. The woman in the advertisement very seldom comes with the new car or pool. Lonely guys and girls should try treating each other kindly instead of buying things.

Lie No. 4. Young people should save for old age. Children should spend time, energy, and money freely for the health, education, and cheer of their own children.

OCTOBER 11

READ: Proverbs 11:14
KEY VERSE: Proverbs 11:14

Over the years, Pat has worked for all kinds of bosses and owners of teams. Several have been dictatorial, letting him cruise along doing his job for a while, but then stepping in and telling him what to do next.

He knows how it has made him feel when he is told to do a certain promotion a certain way or to trade a player either against his better judgment or without his input. "When they cram decisions down your throat, your spirit is broken, your balloon is deflated, it crushes your joy in the job. When a decision that I've been paid to make has been made by someone else, I feel left out of it. It's a ghastly feeling."

These very feelings helped Pat learn to be less dictatorial in his relationship with Jill and the children. There are times when as head of the home and spiritual authority, he must make an unpopular decision, but there is no call, he feels, for arbitrarily and coldly announcing it, especially without consulting Jill or the ones it affects.

Besides, he feels he has a lot to learn from Jill. She has the capacity, and the right, to change his mind at times. "She's more often right than I am in sizing up a person, for instance. If I'm the president of this corporation, she's the vice president, and I would never make a major decision without her."

OCTOBER 12

READ: Proverbs 15:23
KEY VERSE: Proverbs 15:23

Sometimes it's fun to reminisce about the cute things your kids have said. Do yourself a favor, though, and write them down. As cute and unique as they sound the first few times you tell them, they do have a way of slipping from memory over the years.

Someone who saw our picture in the paper with all eight kids said, in front of the kids, "I don't know how you do it. I have two kids, and I don't know if I'll survive."

Bob was nine at the time, and with his customary twinkle, he said, "Yeah, a lot of people who have only one or two kids say that. We have eight, and we're surviving perfectly."

Coming out of church one Sunday, then five-year-old Andrea noticed it was raining. "We can't go to the car without an umbrella," she said. "It's dribbling out."

A friend of ours says that his toddler said the wise men brought the baby Jesus gold, frankincense, and fur.

Karyn wrote a phone message for Pat. "Mr. _____ called and left this number: erya code . . ."

We know of a family whose four-year-old boy was playing with his food. His mother said, "You're gonna sit there until you finish those beans."

He looked at the pile of beans and said, "Mom, by that time, I'll be five!"

OCTOBER 13

READ: Proverbs 25:11–12; 29:1
KEY VERSE: Proverbs 29:1

Have you ever made ridiculous threats to your children? We know of a woman who asked her cranky preschoolers if they wanted her to lock them in the car. It was midnight. Young as they were, they knew as well as she did that she wasn't about to go through with it.

We overheard a man trying—rightfully, of course—to keep his toddler away from an electrical socket. "Do that again, and I'll bite off your hand!" The force of the words was lost in the giggling of the child. He'd have liked to have seen that!

Bill Gothard says that parents should concentrate on promising only those realistic punishments that we are willing and determined to carry out. By warning children of real dangers and realistic consequences, we give ourselves more room to be calm.

It's so much better to simply say, "Johnny, if you do that, Mommy is going to have to _____." That threat will be tested only a few times, and when Johnny learns that Mommy means it, it will be an effective deterrent in the future. No yelling, no ridiculous threats, just a verbal contract. Johnny will eventually learn that he gets what he's asking for. "Like . . . fine gold is a wise man's rebuke."

OCTOBER 14

READ: 1 Timothy 6:1–10
KEY VERSE: 1 Timothy 6:10

We recently heard on the radio that the way a couple handles money can make or break their marriage. A ten-year study of over three hundred couples by researchers at the School of Business at the State University of New York revealed that in happy marriages, wives had more say over funds than did wives who later were divorced. Happily married couples generally shared the financial load; in unhappy marriages, wives had less influence.

Happy wives, so the study said, were more likely to be in charge of bill paying and to be responsible for balancing the budget and the checkbook. That's not to say they ran the show, even if they made the major food purchases. Husbands were dominant in the area of big purchases.

That was gratifying to know because Jill is still the money person in the family. She works with the banks, the accountants, and the tax man, provides Pat cash, and handles all the details. He's a broad brush guy; she's more buttoned down. He brings in the checks; she deposits them.

He says candidly that she's better at it than he is, though not necessarily more frugal. It isn't that she's one of these women with a black belt in shopping whose credit cards have racing stripes. But he's basically conservative—well, tight. She's the business manager. For the Williamses, it works.

OCTOBER 15

READ: 2 Corinthians 3:1–3
KEY VERSE: 2 Corinthians 3:3

David C. McCasland offers these Ten Commandments for Spouses:

1. Thou shalt not wrap thy husband's sandwiches in magazine articles about a man's responsibilities to love his wife.

2. Thou shalt not leave Scripture verses about submission taped to thy wife's hair dryer.

3. If thou teachest Sunday school, thou shalt not use thy spouse's shortcomings for lesson illustrations.

4. Compare not thy spouse with the spouse of another, lest thou be likewise compared and found wanting.

5. Thou shalt help with tasks thou thinkest are not thine, lest they become thine alone.

6. Thou shalt not use the excuse, "This is just the way I am," to keep from becoming what thou couldest and shouldest be.

7. Thou shalt not say, "You always . . ." or "You never . . . ," when thou speakest with thy spouse.

8. Thou shalt impress upon thy children the strengths, and not the weaknesses, of thy spouse.

9. Thou shalt spend thy money buying memories, not things.

10. Thou shalt pray together each day so that thou shalt stay together until thy hair grayeth upon thine heads.

From *Living Today*, June/July/August 1984. Copyright 1984. Reprinted with permission from SP Publications, Inc.

OCTOBER 16

READ: Song of Solomon 3:1–5
KEY VERSE: Song of Solomon 3:4

In Pat's opinion, Larry King of radio, television, and newspaper fame is the best interviewer in the country. He's widely read and a great sports fan, a former die-hard Dodger supporter. Pat met Larry in Miami in the early sixties when Pat was moving from the field to the front office in the Phillies organization.

King feels that the art of interviewing has been generally lost. He has a list of the ingredients of a good interview, and Pat noted how many of them can be applied to good marriage relationships.

King says a good interviewer listens to his subject. Instead of thinking of the next questions, he hears the answer to the first question and hitchhikes the next question off that.

He also looks at the interviewee. He doesn't fumble with notes or books or microphones. Further, he's thoroughly briefed about the person and his area of expertise. Here is one area in which any spouse can improve. What higher compliment can be paid to loved ones than to *really* know them?

King recommends that a good interviewer ask questions rather than make statements to get a reaction. And keep them short, he says. Don't use big lead-ins and find out if the person agrees.

See how all these techniques apply to communicating with spouses, too?

OCTOBER 17

READ: Psalm 133
KEY VERSE: Psalm 133:1

For whatever advantages there are to our lifestyle, there are drawbacks for Jill to be a visible woman married to a visible man. The problem is a lack of close friends.

Make no mistake, Jill has good friends, including some she feels close to. But she struggles with the way many women react to her.

They say they want to call, but they tell her later that they assumed she was too busy. "I wish people wouldn't assume anything," she says. "I can get a sitter, and frequently, most of the kids are in school. I need breaks. I need a friend who just wants to go to lunch or go shopping or come over and talk." In truth, after talking with her precious little people all day, she can think of nothing more appealing than a session of adult talk.

Sometimes people say to her, "Let's get together sometime." Jill avoids saying that at all costs, because she has learned if it is put off, it won't happen. Instead of *insisting* that you have to get together, do it or get out your date books and set a time. Otherwise, quit pretending that you really want to.

Equally vague is the phrase "If there's anything I can do, let me know." Jill believes in offering specific ways you'd like to help. When Jill was involved in a Bible study in the Philly area with Turquoise Erving, she found that Turq had the same problem. "Everybody assumed I had a million things going," Turq says. "Basically, I was lonely a lot of the time."

OCTOBER 18

READ: John 14:1–14
KEY VERSE: John 14:6

Dennis J. DeHaan of the Radio Bible Class says that no one would be foolish enough to believe someone who had a reputation for being a liar. Yet regarding salvation, many well-meaning people are being deceived by someone Jesus said is a liar—Satan himself (see John 8:44).

Let's look at three common untruths that keep thousands of people out of heaven. They sound believable, but when examined in the light of Scripture, they are quickly seen for the lies they are.

1. "I am good enough to get to heaven."

The truth is: "There is none righteous, no, not one" (Rom. 3:10; see also 3:23).

2. "I am too great a sinner to get to heaven."

The truth is: "Christ Jesus came into the world to save sinners, of whom I am chief" (1 Tim. 1:15).

3. "A loving God will not condemn anyone to hell."

The truth is: "He who believes in Him is not condemned; but he who does not believe is condemned already, because he has not believed in the name of the only begotten Son of God" (John 3:18).

Jesus said, "I am the way, the truth, and the life. No one comes to the Father except through Me" (John 14:6).

OCTOBER 19

READ: Proverbs 27:8
KEY VERSE: Proverbs 27:8

It's never been easy for Pat to leave Jill and the kids for his many trips throughout the year, but somehow, now that the family has swelled to eight children, he finds it tougher than ever.

Maybe it's the guilt of leaving Jill with all the responsibility. Maybe it's just the tug of all those heart strings at once. The kids are all at tender, impressionable ages, and they don't want to see Dad leave.

Recently, on his way to a speaking engagement in another state, Pat had the worst wrestling match ever in trying to leave the house. "I literally was hoping that I would get delayed, miss the plane, and have to head back home."

Two of the boys had ball games, which he hates to miss and hardly ever does. He just flat didn't want to be away. On the plane, he read a story about Rob Wilfong, a utility infielder who had been away from the major leagues for more than a year when he was signed on by the San Francisco Giants. He had been with the club only a couple of weeks again when he went to manager Roger Craig to tell him how upset he was. Apparently, during his hiatus from baseball, Wilfong had gotten used to being with his family most of the time. He was having a terrible struggle being away from them. Because of the timing, Pat was in total sympathy.

OCTOBER 20

READ: 2 Timothy 4:6–8
KEY VERSE: 2 Timothy 4:7

While lunching in Nashville on a business trip, Pat noticed the music playing in the background. It was the theme from *Brian's Song*, a movie about the life of former football star Brian Piccolo. What a flood of memories it brought back!

Piccolo had been a running back at Wake Forest University when Pat was a student there, and in 1969 (when Pat was general manager of the Chicago Bulls), Brian was in Chicago as a member of the Bears.

Piccolo roomed with Gale Sayers, the first white and black roomies the club had ever had. They became fast friends, a bond that was tested and found strong when Piccolo contracted cancer while in his midtwenties.

The unabashed fondness between Sayers and Piccolo was an inspiration to sports fans everywhere, and then to the public at large when Billy Dee Williams played Gale and James Caan played Brian in the motion picture.

Pat remembers that Brian Piccolo had a card printed, which he passed out to any new acquaintance. It read simply, "You can't quit; it's a league rule."

What a legacy, an example to us and to our children. Piccolo (like the apostle Paul) never gave up until he died in June of 1970 at the age of twenty-seven.

OCTOBER 21

READ: Proverbs 14:1
KEY VERSE: Proverbs 14:1

On this date in 1972, Pat and Jill were married. Since then, we have created a lot of memories. One of our favorites involves an athletes' Bible study we were privileged to help start in Philadelphia. Several professionals joined us weekly. Bob Boone, Mike Schmidt, and Garry Maddox of the Phillies might come, along with 76ers Bobby Jones and Julius Erving, as well as some Eagles and Flyers.

Dr. Wendell Kempton taught the study, but one night we had as special guests a missionary couple named the Davises. The wife, Gail, shared a challenging story.

She said that when she first went to the mission field with her husband and their five small boys, she was frustrated. Her husband was trekking hither and yon through jungles and up and down rivers, preaching the gospel to the lost. "I felt I should be going with him, joining him on these missions for God."

But she was simply raising children much like she would have in the States, except that she was in the bush. She agonized for quite some time, deciding it was unfair and she was not doing what she had been called to do. But then, she said, she received a message from God in prayer.

"It was as if He said to me, 'Gail, the most important thing you can do is to raise those sons so they can serve Me.' I became a contented wife and mother, and all five of our sons are grown and are serving the Lord full-time. That made it all worthwhile."

OCTOBER 22

READ: Romans 8:31–39
KEY VERSES: Romans 8:38–39

Now that we've had two experiences in international adoption, we've been impressed by what happens to these little people once they have been with us for a while.

When they first arrive, Jill reflected recently, it's almost as if they have no life in their bodies. They are soft, and there's no muscle tone, spark, or zip. There's little life or twinkle in the eyes. They're like dead weights.

They've been in orphanages where they have been fed and clothed and sheltered adequately. Conditions could have been better, but their basic physical needs have not been neglected. They come to us hungry not for food necessarily, but for love.

They have been beaten and battered by life, abandoned and then taken in, not knowing why they are where they are nor where they are going. Does anyone really love them? Does anyone really care? And then, just when they have decided that they are victimized pawns in the game of life and have resigned themselves to simply surviving, they are flown halfway around the world and deposited into our laps.

No doubt they feel victimized again, until we convince them that they have been truly adopted into their forever family, that we love them and want them. Then come the life, the spark, the muscle tone, and the twinkle. How like our own spiritual journeys!

OCTOBER 23

READ: 1 Peter 5:1–9
KEY VERSES: 1 Peter 5:2–3

From Walk Through the Bible Ministries' *Family Walk* come five hints on raising a child who freely shares his or her feelings. If you have children, you know the joy of parenting such a child.

Practice these tips for effective listening:

1. Look at your child. Eye contact says, "I'm involved."
2. Make listening acknowledgments verbally or through nodding or facial expressions to let your child know you're hearing him. Cut out the distractions. Give your child the same kind of attention you want

from others. Listen to your child the way you want him or her to listen to you.

3. Give your child time. If you aren't free when he or she wants to talk, arrange a time to talk later and make it inviolate.

4. Be sensitive. Sometimes your child needs you to listen *now*. At other times he or she may simply want attention. Learn to discern his emotional needs.

5. Accept your child's feelings and help identify his emotions. Your child may say, "I hate her; she made fun of me." Instead of starting a sermon against hatred, identify by summarizing, "You are upset because she embarrassed you, aren't you?" That mirrors the child's feelings and helps give perspective on the situation.

Parents are shepherds over the lambs God has entrusted to us. When He appears, we will truly receive the "crown of glory" for representing Him to His children.

OCTOBER 24

READ: Ephesians 6:4
KEY VERSE: Ephesians 6:4

Most every dad thinks his kid is big-league material in whatever sport he chooses. You'd think a dad like Pat, one who is an executive in professional sports and must live with the statistics every day, would be more realistic about his own children.

In fact, Pat is the worst. Every move with the boys is geared to making them ballplayers. Fortunately, they love it. He had the Korean boys in the yard one hour after we brought them home, hitting them ground balls, pitching to them so they could hit, and having them run sprints.

A major problem is that many high-school and college athletes concentrate so much on their sports, in full expectation of striking it rich in pro sports, that they let their studies slide and wind up out of sports *and* out of work. From the mid-1970s to the mid-1980s, as an example, the number of New York high-school students involved in athletics grew from approximately 280,000 to nearly 440,000. Only 2.5 percent of major college football players ever make it to the National Football League, and only 1.1 percent of major college basketball players make it to the National Basketball Association. It forces parents to walk the fine line between encouraging a child and telling him the true odds against him.

OCTOBER 25

READ: Deuteronomy 14:2–21
KEY VERSE: Deuteronomy 14:3

Our former across-the-street neighbors from Moorestown, New Jersey, Paul and Connie Beals, vacationed in Florida and took us to dinner recently. Dr. Beals is one of very few physicians who is versed in and committed to nutrition. He told us that as a nation, "We're digging our graves with our teeth."

We were surprised to learn that in the last ten years, the number of women who smoke is up 10 percent, and lung cancer has caught up with breast cancer in frequency among women.

Dr. Beals said that smoking among men is down 20 percent, and the incidence of heart disease has also been reduced over the last five years. He feels this is due to improved diets, lower in fat, sugar, salt, and red meat. That's good news, he says, for the chicken and fish industries.

We have found that on this issue of nutrition, most people are either committed to it or not. There's no halfway. If you stay off salt and sugar and red meat one day, then gorge on sweets the next, you eventually lose your taste for the healthy foods, and your resolve is gone.

We try to maintain balance. We don't say that we'll never let the kids have a sugary dessert or a fast-food meal. But as a rule, we snack on fruit and grains and nuts. Our diet is low in cholesterol and fat, and we've never felt better.

OCTOBER 26

READ: Proverbs 3:1–12
KEY VERSE: Proverbs 3:11

One of our favorite authors is Dr. John F. MacArthur, Jr., pastor-teacher of the Grace Community Church of the Valley, Panorama City, California. He lists seven ways to develop self-discipline:

1. Start small. Train yourself to put things where they belong. Then extend that discipline to your entire home.

2. Be on time. Develop the ability to discipline your schedule so that you can arrive places when you're supposed to.

3. Do the hardest job first. That will prevent it from being left un-done.

4. Organize your life. Use a calendar and make daily lists of things you need to accomplish. If *you* don't control your time, everything and everyone else will.

5. Accept correction. It helps make you more disciplined because it shows you what you need to avoid. Accept it gladly.

6. Practice self-denial. Learn to say no to your feelings. Occasionally deny yourself things that are all right, just for the purpose of mastering yourself. Discipline in the physical realm carries over into the spiritual life.

7. Welcome responsibility. When something needs to be done, volunteer for it if you have talent in that area. It forces you to organize yourself.

OCTOBER 27

READ: Titus 2:1–8
KEY VERSE: Titus 2:8

It had been a perfect Mother's Day until an ill-spoken comment ruined it for everyone.

Pat had had to be away the day before, but he took a 5:30 A.M. flight to get back for the festivities.

Bob prepared breakfast in bed for Jill, and all the kids gathered around to watch her enjoy it.

The news media had kept up on the adoption of the twins, so a family photo appeared on the front page of the *Orlando Sentinel.*

Jill had been invited to sing at a church downtown, so both Karyn and Bob joined her and sang with her.

Then the whole family went to a nice cafeteria. It was perfect. Until one of the kids said, "When a certain person in this family is absent, there's no fighting, but I'm not going to say who."

It may have been intended as an innocent comment. And whoever the speaker had in mind may indeed be the usual catalyst for bickering and arguing. But a pall had been cast on the lunch, even on the day as a whole.

The offender was instructed to apologize for the comment, but it couldn't be taken back. Each of the others wondered who had been singled out. We all learned a hard lesson on the reining in of the tongue.

OCTOBER 28

READ: Proverbs 26:27
KEY VERSE: Proverbs 26:27

We had occasion to visit another church several Sundays ago, and we heard a competent, but not spectacular, preacher who sent us away with some meat, despite his laid-back approach. Too often we have decided early in a sermon that a minister is dry or too academic, and we tend to tune him out and start making mental, or real, lists of the week's duties.

He said that having a good, happy, Christian family really comes down to simply making the commitment. It almost sounded too basic at first, but that's what he intended. "That's what's missing," he said, "in the American home."

He told the sad story of a family who had not made that commitment until well after it was too late. A woman who had divorced her husband was intrigued by his treatment of the visitation rights he had been awarded. Apparently, he realized that he had lost his family, so he never missed a scheduled visit. He was there each and every day he was allowed, and he spent hours with his son, talking with him, teaching him things, and going places with him.

The former wife could only shake her head in disbelief. "If only he'd spent the time with his son when we were married that he does now, we never would have had this problem."

Commitment from the beginning saves a lot of grief.

OCTOBER 29

READ: Jeremiah 29:10–14
KEY VERSE: Jeremiah 29:11

We like today's verse. When people lose their dreams, their hopes and aspirations for what God can do through their lives, they run the risk of losing their reason for living.

Ken Hutcheson wrote in *Worldwide Challenge* magazine that there are several ways to kill God's dream for you, even after you have discovered what it is. The first, he says, is timidity of belief. You haven't really bought into the reality that God has a plan for you.

The second is closely related. It's a sense of inadequacy, the feeling that you're insufficient for what is required. The best way out of that dilemma is to realize that you're right. God is sufficient, and that's all you need.

The third way to kill God's dream for you is through fear of failure and of disappointing others and yourself. If God is encouraging you to take a step, that step is a success even if the result appears a failure.

The fourth dream killer is avoiding risk. Results are always worth the cost when you move in the will of God.

The last way to kill a dream is by pursuing your own dream instead of His. There's always a vast difference between the two.

OCTOBER 30

READ: Proverbs 23:24–25
KEY VERSE: Proverbs 23:24

One of the differences we've learned to live with in our marriage is one we've mentioned before: Pat is a broad brush kind of a guy while Jill is a detail person.

This is never so obvious as when it's Pat's turn to put the kids to bed. First, he sends them to their rooms with a fast list of instructions that they should basically know by now. Then he sneaks in a few pages of his latest book on the Civil War, all the while assuming they're doing just what he told them to.

After about twenty minutes, he returns to read and pray with each child. He doesn't seem to see the stuff scattered all over the floor or sticking out from under the bed.

Jill, on the other hand, goes with the kids to their rooms and supervises them as they take off clothes, turn them right side out again, put them in the hamper, straighten socks, put shoes together, and lay out clothes for the next day. She also watches the tooth-brushing operations and makes sure the top is put back on the toothpaste tube.

To be a parent can be tiresome and time-consuming, sometimes more so for the moms. It's critical that the dads help as much as possible. There are no days off.

OCTOBER 31

READ: Acts 4:36–37; 11:22–25
KEY VERSE: Acts 11:23

With Jill's love for children and her background as a teacher, she enjoys few assignments more than ministering in a Sunday school or Christian school setting.

Frequently, she sings and plays the violin, then either tells a story or just speaks from her heart. The kids bring out the best in her, and because she has a big smile and is eager to maintain eye contact, the children seem to enjoy her, too.

The tough thing to know with kids is what to say to them. Are they from broken homes? Are they lonely? Are they latch-key kids? Are they born again? Are they shy? Do they have a handicap, or are they teased because of some physical oddity, such as skinniness or obesity?

She believes that children need at least one adult who is crazy about them. In her own family, she knows each kid has at least two adults who feel that way.

For a crowd of children, she simply decides that for that day, for that brief period, she will be that person in each of the lives she touches. She recently asked a junior-high principal if there was a theme he wanted her to follow when she sang and spoke. He said, "Give 'em the gospel and call 'em to repentance."

She did it, but it was accomplished in love, just the way she knew he intended.

NOVEMBER 1

READ: Philippians 4:14–19
KEY VERSE: Philippians 4:17

As a history buff, Pat specializes in the Civil War and likes to visit famous battle sites when he travels. While in Nashville, he visited nearby Franklin, Tennessee, site of the Battle of Franklin, November 30, 1864.

Even more intriguing, though it was outside the era of the Civil War, was to be in the vicinity where Andrew Jackson is most revered. His home is just outside Nashville, and Pat saw statues of him all over town.

As a Tennessee citizen, Andrew Jackson is truly a favorite son. The reason Tennessee calls itself the Volunteer State and the University of Tennessee sports teams call themselves the Volunteers is due to the following:

During the War of 1812, Andrew Jackson led the Tennessee militia against a rebellion of the Creek Indians. In 1815, as a major general in the United States Army, he won a major battle against the British in what has become known as the Battle of New Orleans.

At one point he pledged that he would find 10,000 volunteers from Tennessee alone. When the dust cleared, more than 60,000 had stepped forward. Somehow, this performance is not reminiscent of what happens in our churches; too often we ask for five volunteers and are lucky to get one.

NOVEMBER 2

READ: Exodus 15:1–18
KEY VERSE: Exodus 15:1

We have several buzzwords around our home. We assume you do, too. These are words or phrases that mean something only to the family or the parents.

When Jill says, "Mother Bear," Pat's ears perk up. That means she has reason to come to the defense of one of her cubs. Someone is messing with the den.

At home the children are used to strict, daily discipline, but when someone outside the home gets involved, the Mother Bear in Jill comes out, and there could be trouble. That doesn't mean she always takes the side of the child. Often other adults are right and proper in wanting to exert some control over the children. But let that appear to happen unjustly, and Jill's claws extend. She's ready to take on the adversary, the threat.

It's important for her to get all the facts and not just blindly defend the children. But once that is done, it's totally right and proper for her to be their protector. It's in her job description.

We'd like to think that's how God feels about His role as our protector, too. He may allow certain dangers to intrude for our chastisement or correction. But if we are attacked unjustly by forces of evil, we are confident we can pray to the everlasting Father, for whom no one is a match.

NOVEMBER 3

READ: Romans 12:9–21
KEY VERSE: Romans 12:12

Little is so widely written and talked about, yet so infrequently practiced, as prayer.

J. C. Ryle, the nineteenth-century bishop of Liverpool, wrote, "I have read the lives of many eminent Christians who have been on earth since the Bible days. Some of them I see were rich, some were poor. Some were learned, some were unlearned. Some of them were Episcopalians, and some Christians of other denominations. Some were Calvinists, and some Armenians. Some have loved to use a liturgy, and some chose to use none. But one thing I see they all had in common. They were men of prayer."

Another nineteenth-century giant, founder of the Moody Bible Institute and namesake of the Moody Memorial Church of Chicago, D. L. Moody, said, "I work like everything depends on me; I pray like everything depends on God."

Remember these five fundamentals of prayer:

1. We can pray anywhere and anytime.
2. We can pray in any manner.
3. We can pray about anything, so be specific.
4. We must pray according to His will (see 1 John 4:14–15).
5. We must pray in faith, believing, and expect results.

Samuel Chadwick said, "Satan laughs at our toil, mocks our wisdom, but trembles when we pray."

NOVEMBER 4

READ: Proverbs 10:19–22
KEY VERSE: Proverbs 10:19

Pat travels quite a bit in his job, and coming home to a wife and eight kids is an experience and a half. When he was gone to New York recently, everyone was eager for him to return.

As soon as he got in the door, he was practically knocked down by the kids, wanting to tell him every detail of everything that happened to them since he left.

Jill wasn't much different. After talking with only little people for several days, getting a chance to talk to your husband at last is like discovering someone in a foreign country who understands your language.

Not long after welcoming him, Jill started in with the litany of events that were coming up. Karyn had gymnastics, Bob had baseball practice, and Jim had a soccer game.

Pat took it all in stride, but the rest of the family learned something. He needed time to realize he was home. It's difficult for him to switch gears, to quit thinking about flights, cab rides, meetings, conferences, negotiations, and assignments and start thinking about daily at-home duties and events. Jill said, "*We* know he's home, but *he* doesn't know it yet."

Now everyone tries to give him some room, some time just after he arrives. He should be able to unpack, sit and relax, and get used to his home environment. He should get a chance to greet each one and spend some time with each, before having to assume all his previous roles.

NOVEMBER 5

READ: Romans 8:9–11
KEY VERSE: Romans 8:11

When Michael was two, he hit a stretch where he wouldn't let anyone do anything for him. He had to do everything himself. He had to spread his own butter, put on his own shoes, pour his own milk, and open his own door. And shame on anyone who forgot!

He would cause such a scene that we had to take his shoes off, pour the milk back in the bottle, or even scrape the butter off his toast so he could start over and do it himself.

In the case of a toddler, in spite of the aggravation, you look for such signs of independence. They're natural, and they signal that the kid is growing up. You're not going to have to do everything for him for the rest of his life.

When he's an adolescent, Michael will probably think we're from another planet. We'll look and sound stupid to him, and he'll show even more clear signs of wanting to be on his own, and well he should.

But what about when we as Christians start showing our natural inclination to be independent of God? Then it's not so encouraging. It may be predictable, but it's not healthy.

When a child wants the milk put back in the bottle so he can pour it himself, even though it results in a slower process and sometimes a mess, it's part of growing. When we yank our lives from God's hands, we make messes we can never clean up.

NOVEMBER 6

READ: Philippians 2:9–11
KEY VERSE: Philippians 2:9

We look for ways to build our children's self-confidence. We recognize from our lives, from the people we meet, and from what we read that everyone, not just orphans, not just plain-looking children, and not just handicapped kids, needs boosting. Even beauty queens and sports stars do.

One way we do this is to buy or make plaques or other types of wall hangings that show the name of the child and a biblical meaning of the name. We hang these on the door of each of the kids' rooms, giving them a sense of identity and ownership, as well as letting them know that we think they're special. Each plaque carries an encouraging Bible verse, too. You can buy these in Christian bookstores, or you can needlepoint them or write them on three-by-five cards. Your hope, as ours, is that the child will know the meaning of the name and will try, with God's help, to live up to it.

Ours are as follows: Pat—"noble one," Jill—"young at heart," James—"successor," Robert—"illustrious one," Karyn—"pure one," Sarah—"princess," Andrea—"womanly," Stephen—"crowned one," Thomas—"one of equality," and Michael—"like unto the Lord."

Most kids have to grow into these definitions, of course.

NOVEMBER 7

READ: 1 Thessalonians 3:6–13
KEY VERSE: 1 Thessalonians 3:12

The world and especially the people around you need encouragement today more than ever. Barnabas, the Scripture is clear, was a mentor of the apostle Paul. His very name means "son of encouragement."

Phil Sell of the Parkview Evangelical Free Church of Iowa City, Iowa, suggests ways to become an encourager:

1. Be willing to give of yourself to help others.
2. Be willing to see the best in people.

3. Have an inclusive spirit. Strive not to exclude people from bless-ing or feeling a part of an activity or situation. This is particularly difficult for most people, even though they may not realize it. Do you want to add to your game a person who apparently is not as talented as the other players? Which team will get stuck with him? How about that new couple at church who don't dress as nicely as you and your crowd? Are they invited out for coffee later?

4. Be willing to forgive. Give people a second chance.

5. Have a spirit of humility. Barnabas had the humility to step aside and see that the one he trained became greater than he was. An en-courager is willing to see the one he is encouraging succeed and even surpass him.

NOVEMBER 8

READ: Psalm 119:113–115
KEY VERSE: Psalm 119:113

Shortly after Harvey Schiller became commissioner of the South-eastern Conference, he was rushing through the Atlanta airport on his way to a plane. He grabbed a discarded newspaper, hoping to read a preview of the football game he was about to attend. When he got settled on the plane and opened the paper, he had everything but the sports page. There was another paper on an empty seat near him. To his disgust, it had no sports section either.

Pat has had this experience more times than he can count. He has to agree with Commissioner Schiller that while busy air travelers may not have time for world affairs, they take the time to keep up with their favorite sports.

This insatiable hunger for sports was one of the contributing factors to the near disaster in our marriage. Admittedly, keeping up on pro basketball had to be Pat's full-time job, but with the advent of cable television came the potential to watch sports twenty-four hours a day.

If Pat wasn't working or speaking or running or studying his Bible, he was watching television till all hours of the morning, justifying it by scouting top college prospects. Even as a professional sports ex-ecutive, he had to bring this hunger into line to help save the mar-riage.

NOVEMBER 9

READ: Luke 10:25–28
KEY VERSE: Luke 10:27

One of our good friends is Tanya Crevier, a diminutive, young lady who has devoted her life to being the best basketball handler in the world. She can dribble several balls at the same time and can spin nine at a time by strapping pegs to various parts of her body. Christian music plays in the background.

She does things with a basketball that Pistol Pete Maravich, Marques Haynes, and Curly Neal never dreamed of. Her halftime show has been a hit all over the National Basketball Association. We used her in Philadelphia and will use her in Orlando, too.

Tanya is an outspoken Christian and is often sponsored by the Fellowship of Christian Athletes. Before a Christian group, she gets the kids chanting with her while she dribbles and spins. She coaches them on what to say, then leads them through a series of questions and answers.

She'll call out, "Who do we love?"

They answer, "Jesus!"

She says, "What do we have?"

They say, "Enthusiasm!"

"How do we feel?"

"Fantastic!"

"What are we?"

"Winners!"

Vince Lombardi once said, "Winning is not a sometime thing; it's an all-time thing. You don't win once in a while; you don't do things right once in a while; you do them right all the time."

NOVEMBER 10

READ: Galatians 6:1–5
KEY VERSE: Galatians 6:2

Pat admits that he was never much of a student. He didn't have any trouble learning, but he didn't apply himself beyond the point of making the grades he needed to stay eligible for sports. It's interesting that now as he approaches fifty, he's a voracious reader and a Civil War buff.

As a result of his less-than-enthusiastic role as a student, however, he mispronounces an occasional word or places the emphasis on the wrong syllable. Very few people notice, because few do much better, but Jill's background was education, with special emphasis on English and grammar.

So when Pat is speaking and Jill is in the audience, she makes a mental note of the little mistakes and tells him later. He has always appreciated this and tells her so. And he works at not repeating a mistake.

However, recently he told her that he has always wished there could be more of a gap between the performance and the critique. Pat is extremely funny and articulate, and he is in great demand. Response to his speeches is always good. And then comes the gentle, loving critique.

"I do the best job I know how, feel that the people have enjoyed it, and hear them say so. I'd like to bask in that a while. I still want the critique, but when I'm in more of a mood to accept it and learn from it."

NOVEMBER 11

READ: Joel 2:28–29
KEY VERSE: Joel 2:28

Jack Wyrtzen has always been an inspiration to us. He still has the same energy at seventy-four that he had as a young man when he was saved as a hustling insurance salesman and trombonist in a jazz band.

When the NBA granted Orlando an expansion franchise, Jack was in China, thinking of us and praying for us. When Pat tried to call him later, Jack had returned but was in the middle of taping fifteen radio programs so he could leave the next week for Portugal!

After his wife of many years, Marge, died some time ago, he remarried, and his new wife, Joan, had added zest to his life that he thought he'd lost when he was widowed. He has such enthusiasm, which he likes to remind people means "God in us," that just being around him makes everyone feel as young as he acts.

Fifty years ago, he founded Word of Life Camp at Schroon Lake, New York, where thousands camp every summer at the trailer park, the island, the ranch, and the inn. Our family spends at least a week there every summer, each of the kids heading for the appropriate age group and Pat and Jill enjoying the adult conference.

No matter when we go or how long we're there, no one can keep up with Jack himself. He even rides horseback, setting an example for everyone of every age.

More challenging than Jack's physical stamina, however, is his vision for the Lord. After more than fifty years of walking closely to the Lord, Jack's excitement for winning lost souls around the world is greater than ever.

NOVEMBER 12

READ: 1 Timothy 6:20–21
KEY VERSE: 1 Timothy 6:20

The great Dallas Cowboy wide receiver Drew Pearson spoke at an Orlando Chamber of Commerce breakfast, and Pat got a chance to chat with him. Pearson is now in the athletic cap business and appears every bit as committed to excellence now as he was when he was a standout on the Cowboys' Super Bowl championship teams.

The Cowboys have been down and struggling in recent years, and Pat was curious about the effect that was having on their legendary coach, Tom Landry.

Landry has seen it all. He's been there from the beginning, when they were a winless expansion team and the public and press were calling for his head on a block. He went through the building years, seeing the team grow into a power that was synonymous with a sophisticated approach to the game.

They've been to the Super Bowl several times. Surely, the old coach doesn't need this hassle, the ignominy of going out with a losing season or two when the whole thing falls apart. Isn't he going to get out while the gettin's good?

On the contrary, Pearson told Pat. "He's more enthusiastic now than ever. This is the kind of challenge he loves. He's deeply committed to excellence, and when the resources are few, savvy is required. That puts the responsibility on the shoulders of the coach, and that's right where he wants it."

NOVEMBER 13

READ: Philippians 1:20–21
KEY VERSE: Philippians 1:20

Jill constantly fights a battle with her identity as Pat Williams's wife. It's not that she doesn't love him or her roles as his wife and the mother of the children; it's just that she sometimes feels her only identity is as someone's wife or someone else's mother.

If that's all she is, pleasant and challenging as that is, who is she? Is she anyone in herself? Sometimes she feels guilty for having these thoughts, but they are very real, and she assumes many women feel the same.

Make no mistake, she's not a feminist. Though Betty Friedan's *Feminine Mystique* hit on this very subject years ago and struck a chord with tens of thousands of women, Jill believes that a mother's place is indeed in the home.

The problem is in being recognized for who she is as an individual. She wonders sometimes if people invite her to speak or play or sing because she's Jill Williams or because she's Mrs. Pat Williams.

The real fear revealed by these feelings, of course, is that if she were not married to Pat, she would have no identity of her own. She realizes that she must be spiritually motivated to be selfless and to be used of God not for attention or applause, but simply in His service.

NOVEMBER 14

READ: Psalm 71:9–16
KEY VERSE: Psalm 71:15

When Jill's ninety-three-year-old grandmother visited us in Orlando, we planned to take her to Epcot Center. Secretly, Jill checked with Mom to see if Nana was up to all the walking. Mom checked with Nana. "Of course!" was her response.

She was not only up to it, she kept up with the family for six solid hours. That evening, Pat stuck out his hand. "Congratulations. You did it! I'm impressed." He was stunned by the strength of her grip. "How do you do it?"

Here's her "secret": for sixty-five years, she has done her exercises faithfully every morning in her apartment on the lower level of Jill's parents' home. She walks several miles a day, rain or shine. She doesn't go to aerobics classes or wear the latest in designer sweat togs, but she can outlast a large percentage of the younger set.

She's a convicting example to us. We try. We eat the right foods, we exercise, we jog, and we talk about it, emphasize it, and preach it. But here's a woman who long ago could have retired to a wheelchair to laze away her final years, yet she has refused.

Her body, old but not so frail, is the temple of the Holy Spirit of God, and for as long as she is able, her plan is to keep it in shape. And she does!

NOVEMBER 15

READ: Isaiah 43:5–7
KEY VERSE: Isaiah 43:5

We have tremendous respect for the late Harry Holt, originator of what is now known as Holt International Children's Services, Inc. His widow, "Grandma" Bertha Holt, is known as the grandmother of tens of thousands of orphans from all over the world, but primarily from Korea.

After the Korean War, Mr. Holt felt the Lord leading him to that country to serve Him. Holt had no idea what God had in mind, but he went on what he thought was just a fact-finding tour.

The closer he got to Korea, the more deeply he felt the moving of God in his heart. What was he to do? What was his mission? How could he best serve? By evangelizing? By praying? By working with the homeless, the destitute, or the children? And what could he do with them? There was little chance of his being of much help to homeless children in their own nation.

God put it in his heart to adopt Korean children and take them back to the States with him. But how could he know for sure? He wasn't even in Korea yet. He was in a hotel room in Tokyo.

The Lord led him to his Bible and to today's key verse. He went on to Korea to see the need. He was so moved that he arranged to bring back eight infant orphans and adopt them. He and his wife raised them as their own and generated so much interest from around the country that now some fifty thousand have been adopted, four of them into the Williams's family!

NOVEMBER 16

READ: 2 Corinthians 3:5–6
KEY VERSE: 2 Corinthians 3:6

This case history gives pause to even the most militant pro-lifer. The father is syphilitic. The mother is tuberculous. Their first child is born blind, the second dies at birth, the third is deaf and mute, and the fourth is tuberculous. The woman is pregnant again. What now?

Upon hearing this scenario, many well-meaning people, medical students and doctors alike, would elect to terminate the pregnancy, which is a pristine euphemism for abortion, a euphemism for killing the fetus, a euphemism for baby, life, human being.

No matter how people camouflage it with new terminology, if the fetus is human life, terminating it or ending it requires killing it. Perhaps it's unfair to call it murder since the procedure is temporarily legal, but it's still the taking, the killing, of life.

But what of the poor family? Surely no thinking person would expect them to bring another child into that situation. No doubt they're poor, living in cramped quarters. And for the man to be syphilitic means that he has been immoral and the woman could easily and will most likely contract syphilis, too.

What if it were transmitted to the baby in the birth canal, which is likely? Would you decide on abortion in this case? If so, you would have deprived the world of Ludwig van Beethoven.

NOVEMBER 17

READ: Proverbs 28:23, 26
KEY VERSE: Proverbs 28:26

As did most of the nation, we read with horror in 1987 of the devouring of a boy by a polar bear in a New York City zoo. Three boys had scaled the fence and swum in the bear's pond before two were scared off by the mauling of the third.

The story eventually emerged that the boys had pulled the stunt on a dare. This gave us an occasion to have a serious powwow with our kids. How often have they been, or will they be, dared to cross a busy highway, try alcohol, smoke, or do dope?

We told them that all their lives they will run into so-called friends who will dare them to try all manner of illegal, crazy, or irresponsible things. Our advice? Be prepared to be mature. Be prepared to walk away. Be prepared to say no. Your life could depend upon it.

Jerry Kramer, the former Green Bay Packer guard, said that what made the Vince Lombardi-coached teams so great was his obsession with fundamentals and repetition. "He paid meticulous attention to detail, running us through the same plays over and over and over, a hundred times, two hundred times. He worked to make everyone perform perfectly, teaching technique, technique, technique. That's how we won."

That's the kind of parents we want to be, drilling into our kids the courage to say no to dares.

NOVEMBER 18

READ: Proverbs 22:5–6
KEY VERSE: Proverbs 22:6

We happen to be among those who believe that parents have as much to do with the success or failure of a child in school as the teacher, the school system, and the child do. Even though we have half the battle licked by having our kids enrolled in Christian schools, we don't leave it all up to the fine people there. We get involved and stay involved.

Among the most important things we do to help our kids do better in school are talking to them and reading to them. Those may sound too simple, but from our perspective, not enough parents do either one. Reading to young children gives them an appreciation for books and builds a foundation that says good things come from books.

They can learn, too, from daily conversation, if it is enhanced with easy, unforced teaching. For instance, we have a lot of birds. Any conversation with the children about the birds can include their habits, their appetites, their coloring, anything.

We listen to our kids, too, which we hope makes them know we respect them and want to learn from them. We've always said we learn more when we are teaching a class, so it follows that if the children are trying to teach us something they learned at school, they will solidify their learning by our studying under them.

NOVEMBER 19

READ: Matthew 15:18–20
KEY VERSE: Matthew 15:19

Something scares us about what Christian leaders are saying about all the immorality we see today. Many people get married and divorced several times, leaving in their wake broken homes, shattered lives, and needy children.

Even secular psychologists say that promiscuous men and women were generally children who never felt accepted and loved enough. They didn't get the hugging and kissing and cuddling they craved as children, and now no amount can satisfy them.

Such an individual might start with a marriage to someone who is sexually attractive, but as soon as that person gains weight or gets pregnant or ages a bit, it's time to move on.

The problem then becomes a vicious cycle. Because daddy or mommy has left the home, the children produced by that marriage wonder about their significance. Did they cause the breakup? Can the remaining parent give them enough love and attention alone?

They grow up, rebellious, wounded, full of guilt, and craving the physical closeness they've never known. And there we go again.

People think they've really arrived when they wind up in an executive office, sheltered from the real world, working sixteen hours a day, but neglecting their families. The very families they claim to be achieving for are left wanting and will produce more of the same.

NOVEMBER 20

READ: 1 Corinthians 15:57–58
KEY VERSE: 1 Corinthians 15:58

Pat has had his share of rough setbacks on the job in several of the cities he's worked. In Spartanburg, South Carolina, the year he turned the Phillies around and saw record attendance, creative promotions, and a championship season, he was devastated not to win the coveted Front Office Executive of the Year award from *The Sporting News*. (He won it the following year, 1967.)

In Chicago, as the youngest general manager in the history of pro sports, he was victimized by a coup that saw him stripped of the power to spend more than ten thousand dollars without the permission of the owners. That took from his hands the bargaining for big-money ballplayers and in effect reduced his job to that of a business manager or an errand boy.

In Atlanta, he found the basketball team was just one of several enterprises owned by the people who owned the stadium, and getting what was needed to run a quality program was next to impossible. In Philadelphia, he worked for a succession of owners that cost him a lot of sleep.

His strategy was to hang on and hang in. Always give it another day; put off leaving until tomorrow. It was during times like those that his faith was the most precious and the most real. He resisted the temptation to doubt God's goodness or to do something rash.

We've heard that God cannot use a man greatly until He has hurt him deeply. We've been through the fire, "but He knows the way that I take. When He has tested me I shall come forth as gold" (Job 23:10).

NOVEMBER 21

READ: Acts 20:32
KEY VERSE: Acts 20:32

One of the things that first impressed Jill about Pat years ago was his ability to make people feel special. In his office, at the stadium, or in whatever environment he has worked, he has made it a point to learn people's names and use them often.

After Bulls' games, he would station himself at one of the gates and thank everyone he could for coming. He became the most well-known and recognized general manager in town because he had personal contact with the people. He greeted many of the regular fans by name, and he spoke to the ushers, custodians, and cheerleaders by name.

In the office, he tries to make people feel good about themselves and the organization, too. He remembered hearing stories in college about how Harry S. Truman, as president, had fostered loyalty in his subordinates with heartfelt, not cosmetic, actions such as the following:

Walking to a subordinate's office rather than calling him on the phone or having the secretary buzz him.

Greeting workers at the door when they came to meet with him rather than letting them approach with him sitting at his desk.

Passing credit on. He allowed his cabinet members to make important announcements. He was simply applying the golden rule.

NOVEMBER 22

READ: Proverbs 4:20–27
KEY VERSE: Proverbs 4:24

A hallmark of Christian character is integrity. "His word is his bond" is a first-rate compliment about anyone. Proverbs 11:3 indicates that honesty builds while dishonesty destroys: "The integrity of the upright will guide them, / But the perversity of the unfaithful will destroy them."

Before giving exams at Vanderbilt University, mathematics professor Dr. Madison Sarratt charged his students: "I am giving two examinations, one in trigonometry and one in honesty. I hope you will pass both. If you must fail one, fail trigonometry. Many good people in the world can't pass trigonometry, but no good people can fail the examination of honesty."

Herbert Hoover epitomized honest character. As food administrator for the Allies in World War II, Hoover was sent $12 million a month that was processed through his personal bank account, guarded by nothing but his integrity.

Hoover handled the gigantic sums without question. The hundreds of millions he dealt with over the years were considered as sound as a government bond by all the leaders of Europe, simply because they trusted one man implicitly.

All interpersonal relationships are built on trust. Spouses must be able to trust each other to tell the truth. Integrity makes up for a host of other shortcomings.

NOVEMBER 23

READ: Proverbs 31:29–31
KEY VERSE: Proverbs 31:30

With all the talk on avoiding divorce and building solid marriages, we are thinking about our kids getting close to the dating age. It's a scary time, and we are beginning to formulate some guidelines. The toughest aspect of all this is that no one knows when a child is really ready to be paired off, even in a first-date situation.

From our perspective, young kids in early adolescence need many activities that mix boys and girls in a big group, like a large date, without pairing them off. This allows the kids to get to know one another as whole beings, not as that frightening person they are alone with for the first time.

We hear so much about good marriages being built on mutual respect, trust, and knowledge of the whole being. Why then do we want to see children thrust into adult situations before they are ready? Younger and younger kids wear make-up, have their hair done, and try to look glamorous (and the boys are just as bad!).

We wind up with kids dating younger and younger, spending more time together, and feeling forced to evaluate one another on the basis of sex appeal and looks. If we don't put the brakes on and counsel them, we're going to wind up with another generation with a high divorce rate and messed-up kids to boot.

NOVEMBER 24

READ: Matthew 19:13–15
KEY VERSE: Matthew 19:14

We believe in child evangelism, not just the organization, but also the evangelization process itself. Pat was not converted until adulthood, but Jill became a Christian as a five-year-old.

Her family attended an evangelistic crusade led by chalk artist-preacher George Sweeting, who would go on to become pastor of the historic Moody Memorial Church in Chicago (and would be Pat's pastor before he even met Jill), the president of the Moody Bible Institute, and finally chancellor of Moody.

That night he drew a beautiful picture of Christ walking on the water. The message of trusting Christ got through to Jill. When Sweeting gave the invitation to receive Christ, she went forward and trusted Him.

Some people believe that children do not think symbolically enough to understand all that it means to put faith and trust in Christ. But Scripture doesn't indicate a requirement to understand everything. The crucible is belief, and children can certainly have that.

We agree with those who say that no child should be coerced or forced in any way to make a profession of faith just because a parent or other authority figure desires it. But when a child is ready, the discerning parent knows and should be a faithful guide.

NOVEMBER 25

READ: Colossians 1:3–5
KEY VERSE: Colossians 1:5

Thanksgiving Day was extraspecial the first year our Korean twin boys were with us. Of course, they remind us as much of their new Korean sisters as of anyone, and we are thankful for what these four mean to our family.

When Andrea and Sarah graduated from kindergarten, we beamed as they received awards for having read the most books. All we could think of was how limp and bewildered and lost they had been less than four years before when they arrived.

That was before we realized how much life a dose of love and security could pump into a body. They blossomed into articulate, extroverted, and studious little girls.

A second cousin of Jill's read in the *Miami Herald* of our adopting the boys and wrote the following to Pat: "I have seen the pure love you give your kids; I enjoy especially the rapport you have with Jim and Bob.

"Now you have two more little boys to whom you can teach baseball and basketball. They will be blessed by having you as their daddy, not only because they are part of a wonderful earthly family, but because they also have the opportunity to accept Jesus as Savior and one day to have eternal life."

Our friend Norm Sonju wrote, "Isn't it wonderful that these two boys will wind up in heaven because of this?"

NOVEMBER 26

READ: Psalm 103:11–14
KEY VERSE: Psalm 103:13

Have you ever wondered if God has a sense of humor? Does the same God who pities us and knows we are nothing but dust also laugh with us or even at us in His love and enjoyment of us? We know we sometimes disappoint Him, break His heart, cause Him grief. But surely we must amuse Him and even delight Him at times.

A friend of a friend tells of his stressful days at Bible college after getting out of the armed forces. He went to class all day, was involved in a ministry all evening, and studied until well after midnight.

After a shower he knelt by his bed in a T-shirt and boxer shorts full of holes, but several minutes later, he woke up, draped over the edge of the bed. He didn't even have the strength to stand. He just crawled atop the bed and under the covers, and to this day, he believes he heard God's chuckle. It was as if he could see the Lord smiling and shaking His head at this ridiculous creature.

Jill once discovered two-year-old Michael after he had spent quite a while alone in the garden, imitating Mom, doing his "shubbeling." He came out from the underbrush, "shubbel" in hand, with only his eyes not covered with dirt. She laughed at the very enjoyment of her racoonlike son and somehow knew that her Heavenly Father must sometimes do the same with her.

NOVEMBER 27

READ: James 5:7–11
KEY VERSE: James 5:11

During this special time of the year, Pat is thankful for two lessons he learned as a young man from two very important people in his life. Sometimes he wonders what he might have made of himself or what might have become of him if he had not been put on track by these two mentors.

The first was his grandmother. She was riding with Pat and his mother to Pat's first-ever organized baseball game. It was the summer after his eighth-grade year, and Pat had finally found a league where he could play regularly on a team. None of the teams had uniforms, but at least the league was organized and the teams had a place to play.

Pat was nervous. He had been to a few practices and enjoyed them, but now it was time for the first game: live pitching, umpires, competition, the whole bit. It worried him. Finally, he said, "Well, if it doesn't work out, I can always quit."

With that his grandmother spun around in the front seat and shook a finger in his face. "You don't quit anything! You start it, you see it through!"

Eight years later, as a catcher in the Phillies minor-league system, Pat played under manager Andy Seminick, a former big-league catcher. From Seminick Pat learned that he must bear down on every pitch, every detail of every out of every inning of every game. He has tried to apply that truth to the rest of his life.

NOVEMBER 28

READ: Ephesians 6:1–4
KEY VERSE: Ephesians 6:4

Pat ran across an old quote the other day from late Supreme Court Justice Oliver Wendell Holmes: "I find the most important thing in this world is not so much where we stand as in what direction we are moving."

It reminded us of a continual theme of psychologist and author, Dr. James Dobson. He says that fathers and husbands are the ones who must be responsible for directing families in the way they're going to go.

Many men who are totally hands-on in their businesses let their families dissolve by letting them go any direction they want. Dr. Dobson's great challenge to American males is to wake up, get in the game, and get started. Each man controls the future of his family.

Some men are too stubborn, the way the great Boston slugger Ted Williams was in the 1940s when Lou Boudreau, then manager of the Cleveland Indians, shifted his entire defense to the right side, daring Williams to hit to the left. Boudreau shared his strategy with Pat when they broadcast a Cubs–Houston game together in 1987.

All Ted would have had to do was hit line drives into left field, which he could have done in his sleep, but he had too much pride for that. He hit into the strength of the shift, and because other managers copied Boudreau's idea, he faced the "Williams shift" in every city he played for during the next thirteen years.

NOVEMBER 29

READ: Ecclesiastes 7:8–10
KEY VERSE: Ecclesiastes 7:8

Frank Lucchesi is one of Pat's old friends from his days in the Phillies organization. At a Cubs game in Houston, Pat ran into him. Frank is now a coach and scout for the Cubs. They reminisced about old times.

Lucchesi remembers bringing Larry Bowa to the big leagues as a rookie shortstop. Bowa would go on to play more games at short than any player in history and will be remembered as one of the best, because in spite of the number of games, he had the highest fielding percentage of anyone.

But when Bowa came up, he was totally overmatched, especially at the plate. He simply couldn't hit. Never known for an easygoing attitude, Bowa struggled, frustrated with himself. He worried about going back down to the minors, and his hitting slump affected his defensive game, too.

Lucchesi, then manager of the Phillies, remembers calling Bowa into his office and telling him in no uncertain terms: "You're my shortstop. I don't care if you never get another hit in the major leagues."

That settled him down, and he became a great hitter. When Bowa became a manager himself years later, Lucchesi advised him, "The one lesson you need to learn is patience." As parents that's the greatest lesson we must learn.

NOVEMBER 30

READ: Matthew 25:44–46
KEY VERSE: Matthew 25:45

In our opinion, Dr. Tony Evans, pastor from Dallas, Texas, is *the* outstanding black preacher in America. We met him on our China trip several years ago, and ever since then, Pat has been recommending him as a speaker to churches, camps, and conferences all over the country.

No doubt he turns down more invitations than he could ever accept. When Pat was chairman of the Orlando Prayer Breakfast, the theme was the family, and more than fifteen hundred were expected to attend. Pat asked Tony to speak.

We got a real look that day into what it's like for the typical black family in America. Dozens of invited mayors and their wives heard Tony speak of the continuing deterioration of black families.

He let the statistics speak for themselves. More than 50 percent of the black children are born to unwed teenagers. Approximately 60 percent of the children grow up without a father in the home, and 85 percent are born to unwed parents. The black community makes up 12 percent of the American population, but 47 percent of the prison population.

Most black males who die between the ages of fifteen and twenty-four will have been victims of black-on-black crime. The divorce rate is twice as high as among whites, and 12 percent of black children live with neither parent. And we are still troubled about the situation in South Africa!

DECEMBER 1

READ: Proverbs 23:15–16
KEY VERSE: Proverbs 23:15

Pat was asked to speak to a group of elementary-school children, which—for one who usually speaks to adult audiences—is a tough crowd. The sense of humor is different, the interests a world apart, and the attention span short.

Pat asked our kids what he should say, and they came up with twenty suggestions, some predictable, others surprising. Which would you have used in the same situation?

1. Obey your mother and father. 2. Keep your room neat. 3. Be kind to everyone. 4. Don't slurp your cereal. 5. Eat healthy foods (no gum, candy, or sodas). 6. Go to bed at the right time. 7. If you're going to do something, don't quit in the middle of it. 8. Keep the TV off. 9. Keep in good physical shape. 10. Work as hard as you can. 11. Stay away from the wrong friends. 12. Don't waste your time. 13. Set clear goals. 14. Always tell the truth. 15. You're responsible to live with every decision you make. 16. Help around the house without being asked. 17. Don't talk to strangers. 18. Always tell your parents where you're going (they don't trust the rest of the world). 19. Don't follow the world.

20. If your dad asks you what to say to kids your age, be careful what you tell him; he may tell you the same things, and since they were your idea in the first place . . . .

DECEMBER 2

READ: Proverbs 22:15
KEY VERSE: Proverbs 22:15

One of our older kids had a friend over the other night to sleep with him out in the tent. This caused jealousy on the part of one of the younger siblings, of course, and he wanted to do everything the big boys were doing. He wanted to go where they went, do what they did, and sleep where they slept. But they didn't want him around. Eventually, Jill had to step in and tell the younger boy the bad news.

That resulted in an unusual display of shouting, crying, and pouting, yet the decision had to stand. It would have been easier to give in and force the older boys to let the younger one play with them. But it wouldn't have been right. One reason we encourage our kids to have

225

friends over is so they can have a break from one another and can learn about people outside our family.

We're strict about not giving in to temper tantrums. Even if the child convinces us that we have been wrong and he is right, we will not cater to outbursts. We may admit he was right in principle, but we tell him that such outbursts will keep us from changing our minds for the moment.

As painful as these experiences are, we feel they are a necessary part of growing up. As adults, we don't have everything going our way, either, but we can't pout, shout, or cry without paying for it.

DECEMBER 3

READ: Psalm 11:1–3
KEY VERSE: Psalm 11:3

Needless to say, it was impossible to find a house in Florida for a family of eight when we weren't even sure if Orlando would be awarded a franchise in the NBA. The day it was announced, however, Jill was on the phone to contractors, ready to take bids on additions that would make our large but still cramped home all that it needed to be for such a family.

A few weeks later, she was chatting with one of the bidders, who said he was finally about to get away with his wife for a vacation. He hadn't taken one for a couple of years and he really needed it. He had been putting it off, he said, until he and his crew had finished laying the foundation for a major project they would finish when he returned. "I wanted to go before, but we just had to get to that foundation. Once you get the foundation right, the rest goes up easily."

He smiled sheepishly at Jill as he realized how profound his statement had been. "I guess it's just like life," he added.

The story made Pat think of the site of the Orlando sports arena, which is a multi-acre plot with four huge concrete pillars sunk two hundred feet in the ground and rising to a hundred feet above the ground. The entire facility will rest on those four foundational posts. Scripture is replete with similar illustrations. We've learned this lesson in our own lives and in the lives of our children.

DECEMBER 4

READ: Acts 10:34,35
KEY VERSE: Acts 10:34

One of the major transitions in Pat's life has been that as an adult, he was thrust into working relationships with blacks. He hadn't been prejudiced before; rather, he had gone to a private high school because his father coached there, and he had attended Wake Forest University before it was integrated.

As a minor-league ballplayer in Miami in 1962, Pat got to know several black teammates and discovered that one, Fred Mason, was from his hometown. Early in the season, they casually agreed that Fred would ride home with Pat at the end of the season.

Late the first night, they stopped at a gas station in Jacksonville, Florida. Pat went in to pay the bill while Fred went looking for the restroom. As Pat got back in the car, here came Fred, eyes wide, face in terror, racing for the back door. On his heels was the station attendant, swinging a huge crescent wrench and screaming obscenities.

Pat and Fred dove in the car and raced off, badly shaken. The offense? Fred was black. That was all. He hadn't done or said anything, but a black man was not welcome at that gas station. In fact, for daring to set foot on the property, according to the attendant with blood in his eye, Fred deserved to die. Pat remembers that night twenty-five years ago as if it were yesterday. Blatant racism at its worst.

DECEMBER 5

READ: Romans 6:1–14
KEY VERSE: Romans 6:12

It breaks Pat's heart to see athletes ruin their lives with drugs. It's as hard for him as for anyone else to understand why young men in the prime of their lives, in top physical condition, making millions of dollars, would throw it all away.

More confusing is why they need the highs in the first place. What could be more satisfying, from a strictly secular point of view, than being admired by crowds, being asked for autographs, having stories written about you, being somebody?

Yet the problem continues. And for the few who kill themselves, dozens go into rehabilitation centers. And for every one of those, dozens more have hidden their problems to the detriment of their games, the disillusionment of their loved ones, and the loss of their own self-respect.

Psychologists are at a loss to explain it, too. Some say that fear of intimacy is the most common reason for substance abuse. Everyone, they say, has a craving to be intimate with others, yet some people are afraid of rejection or loss of independence or identity. So they retreat into their own worlds with drugs.

Some think they are being intimate with others by doing drugs with them, but their highs are private. We know the only answer to the deepest cravings for intimacy is found in Jesus Christ, and we never want to hesitate to present Him to people.

DECEMBER 6

READ: Romans 15:1–9
KEY VERSE: Romans 15:2

The great novelist Pearl S. Buck wrote in one of her earliest novels about a Chinese family custom of assigning each child to be in charge of the happiness of a sibling. People we have known who have put this into effect have been thrilled with the results.

Some siblings help the others do homework or chores. Others are particularly helpful when the other is ill. Except in a family of just two children, each can be put "in charge" of another's happiness. It's difficult for those who are not inclined toward this, but because they get treated so well, they can't ignore their partner in need.

The most gratifying result we've heard of is from families whose children are grown. The sibling in charge of the other's happiness is the first to come to his aid when something goes wrong.

The greatest benefit from this Oriental custom is that it's contagious. Parents should want to do it just because it's right and a parental act. Soon everyone is in on it, and the family is committed to a lifetime of mutual support.

DECEMBER 7

READ: Philippians 3:12–14
KEY VERSE: Philippians 3:14

One of the great loves of Pat's life is what God is doing through the sports chapel programs. The effort to bring Christ to the locker rooms and front offices of professional football was pioneered by the former Cleveland and Detroit star Bill Glass.

In baseball, the catalyst was a *Detroit Free Press* sportswriter, Watson (Waddy) Spoelstra, who went to then-commissioner Bowie Kuhn with the idea and has now seen Baseball Chapel reach both major leagues, the minor leagues, and even the winter leagues.

In pro basketball, chapel programs started slowly, possibly because of the heavy Muslim element, but the message of Christ is gaining a foothold in many cities now. The NBA effort has equaled if not passed up the other major sports already in acceptance of the program.

The format is simple and similar in all sports. Both teams are invited, coaches included, and guest speakers from pastors to lay leaders give a brief challenge from Scripture, sometimes evangelistic, sometimes not.

Players are being saved. Christian athletes are growing in their faith. In many cities, midweek Bible studies for the wives have seen greater attendance than the locker room meetings. When their husbands are on the road, the wives need such support.

DECEMBER 8

READ: 2 Timothy 2:20–23
KEY VERSE: 2 Timothy 2:22

We fear that a major cause of all the infidelity we hear about these days is people making their decisions too hastily. They make their wedding vows, which apparently sound like nice, medievel sentiments, then they forget them. Though they have sworn before God and man, they go on to break the vows with dispatch whenever they can justify it.

We wonder why people don't think about their vows and decide in advance that they are going to mean them, abide by them, and uphold them, regardless of the situation or the crisis. Malachi 2:14 is the best definition of marriage ever given—that is, it is essentially a contract between a man and a woman that they'll live together and maintain the husband/wife relationship for the rest of their lives. Even when marriages fall on bad times, as ours did, partners should never feel the freedom to break their vows.

In fact, though she felt she had been stripped of all emotion and had lost any spark of love for Pat, Jill was never tempted to look for someone else or leave him, because she had promised she wouldn't.

For Pat, leaving Jill was out of the question. Although he had a miserable wife at home, and he was unable to please her, unable to reach her, despite trying everything he knew, one thing that never crossed his mind was seeking another woman. He made the vow to keep.

When temptation comes, whether it's on the road or on the job, the decision to remain pure should have already been made.

DECEMBER 9

READ: Colossians 4:2–6
KEY VERSE: Colossians 4:5

The empty nest is something with which we are totally unfamiliar, but we have to admit that occasionally we look ahead and anticipate it with great joy. Not that we don't love our children, because our children and—we hope—grandchildren will play a major role in our empty nest.

We look forward to having time to go back to school, maybe taking a night class in some esoteric subject, or maybe substitute teaching in a Christian school or elsewhere.

We look forward to a little more spontaneity in our lives, the ability to come and go as we please, for Jill to go with Pat on trips without worrying about who will take care of the kids or get them from here to there.

We look forward to having a little more spending money. We are comfortable, but we can't have anything we want without planning for it. And as our crew reaches college age, we're going to go through some budget crunches.

We look forward to moving into a smaller place, still big enough for the kids and their big families to come back and visit but not so big that we rattle around and echo or die trying to keep it up.

We're cultivating our relationship with each other now so we won't have to get to know each other when we're suddenly alone.

DECEMBER 10

READ: Proverbs 22:6
KEY VERSE: Proverbs 22:6

Is there any way to avoid parental guilt if kids fall away from the faith or go off the deep end? We try everything we know to train them in the way they should go so that when they are old, they will not depart from it, but what if they do? We've seen this happen to countless parents. Although we can't be behind closed doors and see how they're raising their kids, they certainly appear to be model parents.

One thing heartbroken and disappointed parents need to realize is that they may have done nothing wrong except not to protect their children from outside influences. Peer group pressure is nearly unbearable these days. It's crucial that we know who their friends are, who they run with, and where they go.

Provide activities in your home that will attract young people to come there rather than spur your children to go elsewhere. We find it especially satisfying when, after our family activities, one or more of our kids says, "I really had fun today."

We try to protect our children as much as possible from the mass media. There is so much garbage on TV now that we regulate it as if it has a lock and key. No one watches TV in our house without our permission—and that is rarely given.

Also, watch out for other adults. Sometimes, in an attempt to be "in," other adults present conflicting views to what you have taught your kids. Keep the lines of communication open.

DECEMBER 11

READ: 1 Timothy 4:11–15
KEY VERSE: 1 Timothy 4:12

A music student from nearby Rollins College had been giving Jimmy guitar lessons for several months when it came time for her to head home at the end of her term. As she departed she said to Jill, "Thank you for the opportunity to do this. Very few people will give a college student a chance."

We hadn't thought we were giving her a chance. She was a gifted teacher, and we felt privileged to have her. But she made us think. How often do we despise someone because of his or her youth? How many times have we looked for someone with more experience, possibly passing up the most qualified, the most motivated, the hungriest candidate?

Dr. Anthony Evans tells the story of his having been an underachiever in undergraduate school, yet Dr. John Walvoord, then president of Dallas Theological Seminary, took a chance on him. Dr. Walvoord recognized the potential in Evans and guessed that, given the right opportunity and motivation, Evans could make something of his abilities to serve the Lord.

Evans took advantage of the chance, became a stellar student, a sold-out servant of Christ, graduated with honors, and exercised his scholarly pulpit gifts whenever he got the chance. He earned his doctorate and is emerging as a leading preacher in America.

DECEMBER 12

READ: Hebrews 4:11–13
KEY VERSE: Hebrews 4:12

Ever since Pat became a Christian, he's heard the old saw about the Bible being a difficult book to believe. Either it's supposed to be full of errors, or "surely you don't buy into all that fundamentalist stuff about Adam and Eve, Noah and the ark, Jonah and the whale, and all those miracles?"

Yeah, 'fraid so. If God can speak the universe into being, become Man to reach man, die for the sin of everyone, and then rise again, why can't He put a man in a fish's belly and bring him out alive three days later?

According to *The Second W. H. Allen Alternative Book of Records*, there has indeed been a modern-day Jonah to lend credence to the biblical record. On February 7, 1891, two crew members of the American whaler *Star of the East* fell overboard off a small boat while trying to harpoon a thrashing sperm whale. The whale was eventually harpooned and killed and hoisted to the deck of the *Star of the East*.Sixteen hours later, the whale's stomach was slit to reveal its contents.

Inside, unconscious but alive and with his hair and skin bleached white by the whale's digestive juices, was seaman James Barley.

DECEMBER 13

READ: James 1:2–4
KEY VERSE: James 1:2

Many Christians can't understand why things always seem to go wrong. They haven't learned that adversity causes growth. This was the lesson Pat had to learn the hard way after having been a Christian for five years.

We know we're supposed to be like Jesus, to be conformed to His image, yet we forget that He was, of all men, oppressed unto death. Perhaps we should make this clearer when we share our faith with someone. Rather than emphasize the warm fuzzies, we need to be honest about the cold pricklies. It's not going to be all sweetness and light until we get to heaven.

When we see hundreds streaming forward to receive Christ, we should make sure that everyone has counted the cost, that the high cost of discipleship has been outlined.

We heard Charles Swindoll on the radio, warning of what he calls the Four Spiritual Flaws:

1. Because you are a Christian, all your problems are solved.
2. All the problems you will ever have are addressed in the Bible.
3. If you are having problems, you are unspiritual.
4. Being exposed to sound Bible teaching automatically solves problems.

DECEMBER 14

READ: Matthew 5:27–32
KEY VERSES: 1 Corinthians 7:3–5

Our hearts are grieved each time we hear about another Christian brother or sister who has engaged in an immoral relationship. Of course many factors lead to the final act itself, but we cannot condone adultery for any reason or under any circumstance.

We understand that it takes two people to make a marriage work. The husband's responsibility is to love his wife as Christ loved the church—that is, to give up his life for her (Eph. 5:25). That may mean his giving up an occasional golf game, night out with the "guys," or TV basketball. Men must display affection for their wives with plenty of hugs and kisses and nonsexual touching, kind words and common courtesies. That is important for wives to feel secure in the relationship.

First Corinthians 7:3–5 commands husbands *and* wives to render to each other the affection due. We find that none of us has authority over his or her own body, but our spouse does. After the hundreds of phone calls and letters Pat and Jill have received, they believe that a couple's entering joyfully and *often* into the act of intercourse with each other is a good start to cement their marriage.

We cannot risk sending our mate into the marketplace with his or her sexual needs unsatisfied. It doesn't matter how strong we are spiritually, we are vulnerable to Satan's attacks.

DECEMBER 15

READ: Luke 11:9–13
KEY VERSE: Luke 11:11

Jill was down at the dock and Pat had come inside to check on the napping Michael, when the two Korean boys came running in, fear on their faces, calling out to Pat in Korean.

He raced out to the pool where Karyn lay draped over the railing, a pool of blood beneath her. Pat turned her around and saw the gash in her forehead. He yelled for Jill, who came running in terror. The amateur gymnast had tried a stunt on the railing by the pool, slipped, and cut her head open. The wound was appalling.

An hour later, Karyn was back from the emergency room with three layers of stitches—eleven in all. She would be all right. The same couldn't be said of Jill, though. In her fear and helplessness, she needed to get it off her chest. The only daughter born to her, her future Miss America, her flawless one had been scarred, she feared, for life. She lashed out at Pat.

He should have been watching more closely. He let it happen. It was his fault. But her fear and frustration were talking. He wasn't trying to be Mr. Perfect, but he reminded her, gently, of the times when the other kids had been injured and he wasn't around, yet he had never laid a guilt trip on her.

She saw it immediately and apologized, assuring him he would not hear of it again.

We live and we learn.

DECEMBER 16

READ: Galatians 5:22–26
KEY VERSE: Galatians 5:23

People are in such a hurry to become winners and achieve inner peace that they don't even realize they are their own worst enemies in the pursuit. Success doesn't bring the peace they believed it would; in fact, it changes them. Maybe only in little, hardly noticeable ways at first.

With Pat, it was his temper. One of his most embarrassing memories as a minor-league baseball executive in his midtwenties is of the time he smashed the glass of his desk top with a baseball bat because some little detail didn't appear to be going his way. He shocked Claire Johns, the club secretary, a wonderful woman who scolded him and, in effect, told him to grow up.

What was wrong with him, he wondered, a grown man, a success, acting like a spoiled child? It wasn't working. The great American dream with its attendant foolproof plan was proving foolish.

It wasn't until he became a Christian that he realized he had been merely spinning his wheels in his feverish race for success. "I was such a persuasive salesman in those days that I even had myself convinced that there was no basis for my emptiness. I didn't want to wake up one day staring at full-fledged suicidal depression. Thank God, I accepted Jesus Christ before that ever came about."

DECEMBER 17

READ: Proverbs 6:20–23
KEY VERSE: Proverbs 6:20

With our kids of so many differing ages, we read everything we can find, listen to anything we can hear, and attend any meeting or conference where we think we can get help in raising them.

Recently we heard a prominent Christian leader at a seminar. He said, "Discipline is the deliberate creation of stress in a relationship with your children, in order to help them learn. Punishment is what happens when discipline fails."

He made the point that biblical discipline is goal-oriented and that the goal is maturity.

That's good counsel for parents, especially in this day in this society when kids tease that "Raising parents is a tough job, but somebody has to do it." This is a day in which parents, seventy percent of them—according to research—would not have children if they had it to do again.

A Lord of Wales was quoted, "Nowhere in my travels have I seen parents obey their children as well as in America."

That's the opposite of our goals with our kids. We don't want to tyrannize them; but we will parent them, not they us. We've developed some very basic rules as our first becomes a teen and the others will soon follow: 1) If it's right, enjoy it. 2) If it's wrong, you know what to do. 3) If you don't know, it's probably wrong. 4) Always call if you're going to be late.

DECEMBER 18

READ: Acts 5:23–31
KEY VERSE: Acts 5:29

In May of 1967, an unusual man made an impact on Pat. Paul Anderson, Olympic gold medal winner for weightlifting in 1956, gave a demonstration at a Spartanburg Phillies game. He drove a nail through a board with his bare hand and lifted eight of the heaviest players on a table on his back.

Anderson is listed in the *Guinness Book of World Records* for lifting the most weight of any human being, more than six thousand pounds. He didn't have to say anything at the ballpark that night; he could have let his feats speak for him.

That's why it shocked Pat so when Paul told the crowd that he, the strongest man in the world, couldn't get through one day without Jesus Christ. He said Christ was the most important thing in his life.

Pat was stunned. It was one thing to be religious, to go to church, and to be a Christian athlete and all that. But to bare your soul like that, to talk about something so personal in front of all those people . . . Pat didn't know what to make of it.

It wasn't until after he became a Christian that Pat fully understood what Paul Anderson had been talking about that day. And since then, he and Paul have become friends and coworkers in the kingdom.

DECEMBER 19

READ: Matthew 6:33
KEY VERSE: Ezra 7:10

Everyone needs security, food, and shelter. Jesus refers to our basic needs and wants and wraps up His whole package of life in one simple statement in Matthew 6:33.

How do we go about seeking the kingdom of God and His righteousness? The answer, oddly enough, can be found in the Old Testament book of Ezra. In today's key verse, a threefold plan is revealed.

First, Ezra pursued the truth, to learn it. The truth, of course, is found only in God's Word, and Pat is ashamed to admit that it was many years after his decision to trust Christ before he embraced the Word as he should. Now he's trying to make up for lost time.

Second, Ezra practiced what he learned. He *did* it. The New Testament writer James warns us to be not merely *hearers* of the Word, who delude themselves, but *doers* of the Word (see James 1:22).

Third, Ezra taught what he had learned and done. So, he pursued it, he practiced it, and he preached it. That's how we seek the kingdom of God and His righteousness.

That's the Christian ideal. As the immortal G. K. Chesterton said, "The Christian ideal has not been tried and found wanting; it has been found difficult and left untried."

DECEMBER 20

READ: Acts 20:17–38
KEY VERSE: Acts 20:24

Despite what the Bible indicates, it's shocking to think that by running from the things we've always coveted, we'll gain them. But even if we believe that, accomplishing it totally on our own is a ridiculous idea. The biggest thing in the way is our own ego.

And what about motives? Will God honor us with prosperity if we give to the needy, even if we give only because we want to get? It's not all cut and dried. It's not easy. The negatives, the paradoxes, and the reversals of commonly held truth are keys to true happiness. But they are not easy.

To attempt the rough road of others-oriented living without Christ in our lives is to court disaster. We are not following the teachings of a man; we are in union with God Himself. Giving, dying, weakening, caring, loving, and deferring, even with the prospect of receiving, living, strengthening, being cared for, being loved, and being exalted, go totally against the grain of materialistic Americans.

That's why there's good news for every self-respecting, card-carrying egotist who ever lived. Christianity, Christ's way, is a turnkey operation. Mary Crowley hit it right on the head with her statement that "Christianity is not a way of doing certain things, but a certain way of doing everything."

DECEMBER 21

READ: Ephesians 3:14–21
KEY VERSES: Ephesians 3:17–19

Pat believes that one of the great puzzles of the Christian life is why we resist Christ's invitation for so long. It's as if we expect Him to make sourpusses of us or send us to Africa or take all the joy from our lives. He does just the opposite, but we don't know that until we quit fighting, quit resisting, quit running, and surrender to His love.

Pat heard sportscaster Gary Bender, speaking in New Orleans at a Fellowship of Christian Athletes basketball coaches' breakfast in 1982, suggest five things Jesus Christ would say to a person if He appeared today:

1. "I love you."
2. "I know you."
3. "I understand you."
4. "I forgive you."
5. "Do you know Me?"

Who wouldn't want to know someone who could make those first four statements? Can a parent make them? A spouse? Some very unusual parents and spouses can, and there may be a good friend somewhere who could. But really? They love you even though they truly know you and understand you, including the secrets of your mind and heart?

And who has the power to forgive everything? Only Christ.

DECEMBER 22

READ: James 4:1–10
KEY VERSE: James 4:10

Easily as puzzling as the paradoxes of God is the strange dichotomy within the Christian's life between humility (due to the realization of personal unworthiness) and a sense of well-being (due to the recognition of being special enough to God that He would send Christ as Savior).

It's extremely important to separate these two attitudes, because if either slips over to the wrong side of your being, problems arise. Remember that humilty is one of the paradoxical keys to being exalted of God. But if you are so weighed down by the fact of your unworthiness that you become blind to your special spiritual place in Christ, you'll miss out on the joy.

We once heard a man pray, "Lord, thrill us with who we are, and remind us gently who we're not."

The humility born of spiritual unworthiness versus the thrill of being chosen of God is something that many Christians wrestle with their whole lives. When Pat became a Christian, God needed him humbled. A power-and-money-and-fame-grabbing young man did not square with a God who deserves all honor.

Pat had to learn, and quickly, that humility does not mean thinking less of one's self; it means not exalting one's self at all.

DECEMBER 23

READ: James 1:17–18
KEY VERSE: James 1:17

God called us to be humble servants so that we might draw men unto Him. The enemy of humility is pride, of course, and the antidote to pride is gratitude. Gratitude is the result of looking upon everything we have in this world as an absolute gift of God.

That may not be our first thought, but isn't it so? God could snuff out our lives anytime He wants. Everything we have, from our next breath to our next meal, is in His hands. When we look at it that way, we can't help being grateful.

Nothing comes to us apart from the graciousness of God Himself, and if that doesn't develop a humble attitude in us, nothing will. Are you thrilled with your spouse? Your children? Your parents? Your job? Your home? Your church? Your freedom? Give the gratitude to God and watch pride slide away. And when pride is gone, true humility will replace it.

We don't mean to make it sound like a vicious cycle, but when pride has given way to gratitude and humility, we have to be on guard against self-pity and fear. Sometimes we get so wrapped up in the fact that we are nothing without God that we forget He chooses to use our personalities and our traits, the gifts He gave us in the first place, to do great things for Him.

Not for us. For *Him.*

DECEMBER 24

READ: Luke 2:1–20
KEY VERSE: Luke 2:11

Christmas is one of the favorite times of the year around our house. Imagine our first Christmas with the Korean twin boys, the newest additions, still trying to understand the language.

What must Stephen and Thomas think of the tree, the lights, the presents, the wrapping, the secrets, the stockings, and the unusual way everyone treats everyone else? There won't be snow in Orlando, but the movies and specials on television will be all about white Christmases and miracles. Oh, to be inside each little boy's head!

There is indeed magic at this time of the year, and we play it to the hilt. We want the kids to go to bed knowing that when they wake up on Christmas morning, we will be loving one another and trading presents, singing, smiling, and rejoicing because God gave us the greatest love gift of all in His Son, Jesus.

We know that our kids will be just as impatient as anyone else's to dispense with the reading of the Christmas story and get on with the gifts. We also know that there will be jealousy and quibbling over which present belongs to whom and who gets to play with what first. But we'll still read the story and remind the kids of what it's all about. And they'll do the same with their own children someday.

DECEMBER 25

READ: Matthew 2:1–12
KEY VERSE: Matthew 2:6

This is the one day of the year that may start the earliest and, except for New Year's Eve, end the latest. It will start the happiest, get on your nerves eventually, and end with the most fatigue.

But what fun! And what memories will come of this!

Is it the first Christmas that one of your children will really understand or remember? Or is it the first one without that college-age son or daughter? Or will your kids come home in the crush of holiday traffic, maybe unexpectedly?

This is the day, above all days, when sometimes painful hatchets are buried. People make peace with one another. They look each other in the eye. They touch. They embrace. Old wounds are healed.

What will happen in your home today? Will Christ be honored not just by reading and thinking and praying, but by some act of contrition, reconciliation, or worship?

Make memories today, memories that will glorify Christ. Make this the Christmas your kids will talk about for years, the one they will tell their children and grandchildren about. Do something silly, something spontaneous, something out of character, just because it's Christmas. Make it one *you'll* always remember, too.

DECEMBER 26

READ: Acts 27:13–36
KEY VERSE: Acts 27:22

In Pat's circles, the difference between a mediocre athlete and a class one is often the difference between one who gives up and one who doesn't. You can see how that analogy carries over into all of life. Are you a quitter or a survivor?

Being called a survivor is one of the highest compliments a person can be paid today. But that sounds so mundane. Just a survivor? Someone who didn't die? Yet think of it. In this day, when everyone and everything seems to be going belly up, it takes a champion to be a survivor.

Anyway, mundane, lowest-common-denominator compliments are in vogue. It's as if we're so tired of the superlatives the sports commentators send washing over us that we go to the other extreme to really compliment someone.

For a pitcher like Mike Scott or Roger Clemens, other players simply say, "He can throw" or "He can bring in." For a superstar basketball scoring machine like Michael Jordan, they exult, "He's a player."

So, being called a survivor is no small honor. A survivor is one who won't quit. He's the one with the right attitude, the coachable, teachable spirit. Pat has always said that there are two kinds of people in the world: those who think they can and those who think they can't. And they're both right.

DECEMBER 27

READ: Romans 8:18–28
KEY VERSE: Romans 8:28

As you look forward to the new year with hope and determination, you may benefit from a classic story of someone who took his eye off the goal, whose perseverance flagged for only an instant but at the worst possible moment.

John Landy was a great Australian miler in the late 1940s and early 1950s, a contemporary of Briton Roger Bannister, who was the first to run the mile in less than four minutes. Not long after Bannister's world record performance in May of 1954, Landy broke the record, and the stage was set for a dream match between the only two men to have accomplished such a feat.

The race was held in Vancouver, British Columbia, that same year, and Landy led most of the way. It became a grueling, gut-wrenching charge that took everything from both men, but on the final straightaway, Landy took his eyes off the finish line and glanced over his shoulder for Bannister. It was all the Englishman needed. He shot past to win, and that brief lapse cost Landy the victory.

Many people quit after they have failed. The only thing to keep in mind at such a time is that it was not you who failed; it was your plan. So you were wrong. So you miscalculated. You aren't a failure. Don't quit. You aren't the only person God has tested and strengthened through adversity. Impatience with such testing can hamper true victory.

DECEMBER 28

READ: Psalm 63
KEY VERSE: Psalm 63:1

We want to develop in ourselves and in our children a desire for perfection, a hunger to win. Not at all costs, but with the goal of giving each endeavor all we've got to give. If we do less than our best, we have done nothing.

Hal Greer, the former 76er guard, will probably be remembered as one of the greatest middle-distance jump shooters to ever play the game. He could wake up in the middle of the night during the off-season and sink twenty in a row from fifteen feet.

A gift? A natural shooter? Sure, but few NBA players *aren't* naturals. What made the difference for him? From the time he was old enough to pick up a basketball to the day he retired at age thirty-seven, he shot a couple of hundred times a day, the year around, even on game days.

He became a great shooter and stayed a great shooter by going to the Philadelphia Athletic Club and honing his shot to perfection. Dick Motta, coach of the Dallas Mavericks and former coach of the world-champion Washington Bullets and the Chicago Bulls, used to say that the difference between a good shooter and a great shooter was five hundred extra shots a day the year around.

We should be so obsessive in our pursuits for God.

DECEMBER 29

READ: Matthew 13:45–46
KEY VERSES: Matthew 13:45–46

Do you want to be a person of character in this upcoming new year? We do. And we realize that there will be obstacles. But obstacles are often opportunities in disguise. What do we do with the irritations that come into our lives? Do we have the character to react to them and make of them something beautiful and valuable? Or do we run from them, pass them off onto someone else, make excuses, wonder *why me?* and let them depress us?

The person of character, the person who seeks first the kingdom of God, will turn misfortune into victory. Mistakes should be stepping stones, not tombstones.

The person of character will recognize that God knows about everything that comes into life, good or bad. He may not have sent it—God is not the author of adversity—but certainly He allowed it. So passing off problems as accidents or bad luck is not acceptable.

The source of irritation can be wrapped, not with a physical substance like mother-of-pearl, but in prayer. The person of character is to keep praying and be joyful, but that doesn't mean laughing at troubles or pretending they don't exist.

Joy refers to the deep peace that remains, even through adversity. Not giddiness, not frivolity, not hilarity, but the abiding comfort from knowing that God is still in control.

DECEMBER 30

READ: Revelation 2:8–11
KEY VERSE: Revelation 2:10

The year 1981 was the fifth straight that the Philadelphia 76ers were expected to win the NBA championship. All they had to do was beat the Boston Celtics, in Boston, for the right to play Houston for the title. It was a best-of-7 series, which the Sixers had led 3–1, but now it was tied at 3–3. The final game was being played in the Boston Garden.

Pat can't sit still during a regular season game, let alone a play-off or a championship contest. He's a walker, a stander, and a pacer. As he watched from the runway ramp in the balcony high above the court, he saw the Sixers lose the lead in the waning moments, finally calling a time-out with seconds to go, trailing by one point.

Knowing the time-out would be lengthy because of television commercials, Pat headed for the first door he could find and wound up in a broom closet. He burst into tears. Building for a championship had been the goal of his professional life since he had come to the Sixers in 1974. He wanted it so badly that he sobbed out a prayer. "Lord, please let us win. I'll do whatever You want me to, but please let us win!"

Suddenly, it was as if God were saying, "Calm down. Get hold of yourself. I'll take care of the wins and losses. You just be available for Me." Pat felt peace. But the Sixers' final play failed, and they lost.

DECEMBER 31

READ: Revelation 5:7–13
KEY VERSE: Revelation 5:12

Exactly a year later, the Sixers ran up a 3–1 lead against the Celtics, only to see it dwindle to a tie and force the final game, again in Boston. It was a nationally televised game on Sunday afternoon.

The Sixers played well and took control of the game in the fourth quarter. During a time-out with a couple of minutes to go, when victory was irrevocably in hand, Pat went back to the closet he had visited the year before.

Again, he was emotional, but he was also thrilled and full of joy. And the joy stemmed from more than the upcoming victory on the court. "Lord," he prayed, "all I can do is say thank You. You promised that if I would be faithful, You would take care of the wins and the losses. My job is to be available to serve You."

The Sixers won and went on to be blown away by the mighty Los Angeles Lakers for the world championship. But God was faithful. He was in control. The Sixers' turn came the following year in 1983, when they beat the Lakers for the NBA title.

Our prayer is that we will remain committed to staying available. And that you will, too, as you continue to seek to serve the One who is able to keep you from falling and to present you faultless before the presence of His glory.